Leaving Home

By JAY HALEY

(as author, coauthor, editor)

Strategies of Psychotherapy
Family Therapy and Research: A Bibliography
*Advanced Techniques of Hypnosis and Therapy: Selected Papers of
  Milton H. Erickson, M.D.*
Techniques of Family Therapy
Changing Families: A Family Therapy Reader
The Power Tactics of Jesus Christ and Other Essays
*Uncommon Therapy: The Psychiatric Techniques of Milton H. Erickson,
  M.D.*
Problem-Solving Therapy

LEAVING HOME

The Therapy of
Disturbed Young People

Jay Haley

McGRAW-HILL BOOK COMPANY

New York / St. Louis / San Francisco
Auckland / Bogotá / Hamburg / Johannesburg / London
Madrid / Mexico / Montreal / New Delhi / Panama / Paris
São Paulo / Singapore / Sydney / Tokyo / Toronto

LIBRARY OF CONGRESS CATALOGING IN PUBLICATION DATA

Haley, Jay.
  Leaving home.

  Includes bibliographical references and index.
  1. Adolescent psychotherapy. 2. Family
psychotherapy. I. Title. [DNLM: 1. Family therapy.
2. Psychotherapy—In adolescence. 3. Runaway reaction.
WS463 H168L]
RJ503.H25   616.8'914   79-21865
ISBN 0-07-025570-9

123456789 DODO 89876543210

The editors of this book were Lawrence B. Apple and Suzette H. Annin. The designer was
Christopher Simon, and the production supervisor was Teresa F. Leaden. It was set in
Electra by University Graphics, Inc.

It was printed and bound by R. R. Donnelley & Sons Co.

To Ingrid and Magali

Contents

Introduction

This book presents a way of doing therapy with families at the stage when children are leaving home. It does not present a therapeutic approach with a scientific outcome study to support it, although a discussion of outcome is presented later in this introduction. It is about a time in the life of a family, but it does not offer research data about this stage of family life. Nor is this a self-help book for families who face a crisis of the kind discussed here. It is a work which defines a problem area, describes the social forces involved, and offers a therapy approach which causes positive change and has a low risk of doing harm. It is a book designed to improve the strategy and skill of therapists.

This work includes a special classification of young people with problems; it groups them all together despite the varieties of behavior they exhibit. Psychiatry and psychology have been especially concerned with making distinctions between different types of individuals. Whether a person should be classed as a schizophrenic, a delinquent, a psychosomatic case, or a depressive has been the cause of innumerable hours of testing and research, and has occupied many hours of case conferences. If one's goal is to achieve correct diagnosis or to collect research findings, such differences are important. For the clinician, the differences are largely irrelevant, unless the diagnosis determines a special way of doing therapy (which certainly has not been so in the past).

Some clinicians might find it confusing to class in one group a young person diagnosed as schizophrenic, a heroin addict, a lost young vagrant, an anorectic, a delinquent, a retarded person, and a case of habitual vio-

1

lence. What is relevant, however, is whether the same therapeutic strategy applies to all of them. It is argued here that when the concern is therapy, the particular life-stage of a family is more important than the symptom category of the young person. Even though a general strategy applies, obviously the specific tactics will vary not only with the individual case, but with the class of behavior. While involved in a particular way of disengaging parents and young person, a therapist will still deal in different ways with the families of a violent young person, a retarded one, and a self-starvation problem.

OUTCOME

The outcome of this therapy approach has not been properly investigated. It is based on twenty years of experience practicing and teaching therapy and watching successes and failures. There is also some suggestive evidence to support the approach, which will be described here. A plan to do therapy with a sizable sample and to follow a matched control group was aborted when funds could not be obtained to support such an endeavor. As a result, the outcome data have been collected only in passing rather than as part of serious research.

A few years ago, I began to supervise volunteer student therapists on the side, not as part of a regular training program, to do therapy with young people diagnosed as schizophrenic and their families. This "Schizophrenia Project" had certain criteria: a problem young person was included in the sample only if there was an offical diagnosis of schizophrenia by someone outside the project, it was a first hospitalization, and two parents were available. A total of fourteen families were treated by twelve therapists over a period of four years. The therapists consisted of nine psychiatric residents, two psychology interns, and a social worker (Charles Billings, M.D., Charles Fishman, M.D., Paul Gross, M.D., David Heard, Ph.D., David D. Hunt, M.D., Gary Lande, M.D., Lawrence Miller, M.D., David Mowatt, Ph.D., Lee Petty, M.D., Alberto Rish, M.D., and Fran Ziegler, M.S.W.). A follow-up ranging from two to four years, depending on the date therapy terminated, can be summarized here and in Table 1 (see below).

The primary goals of the therapy were to have no future hospitalizations and for the young person not be a failure. Although the assessment of failure is sometimes difficult, hospitalization is a clear act (even though the motive may be complex, as when a young person arranges hospitalization to obtain disability funds). To put the matter another way, success may be difficult to define, but failure is usually evident. Out of the fourteen families reported here, there were four clear failures, a 29 percent failure rate. One of these was a tragic suicide which occurred as therapy was ending;

the other three were rehospitalizations without self-support, or with only intermittent self-support, afterwards. In two cases there were rehospitalizations during therapy, but successful functioning afterwards. In the remaining eight cases there were no rehospitalizations in the two- to four-year follow-up.

There are many problems in estimating the validity of this outcome if one wishes to judge it in terms of any rigorous methodology. There was no untreated control group; the follow-up was done by the therapists rather than by a researcher; and the reliability and length of time since therapy are such that it can only be considered suggestive. Both success and failure with these problems can be influenced by so many factors inside and outside the therapy that one needs a large sample to be able to say which changes took place because of the therapy and which were due to other factors. In many cases, the therapist is dependent not only on the cooperation of the police and the medical community but also on the family's economic situation. Some of the families in this group are low-income and black; finding work to achieve one of the goals, self-support, can be a problem.

There are two other outcome samples which support this therapy approach, but they are even less scientific in their methodology and so are only suggestive. In the training programs at both the Department of Psychiatry at the University of Maryland and at the Family Therapy Institute in Washington, D.C., the therapists are asked to report on their outcomes. Their cases are varied but include some institutionalized patients. At the end of therapy the therapist is asked to fill out an outcome form reporting his success or failure. Such a procedure is a training, rather than a research, endeavor. In this way, the supervisors can keep track of successes or deficits in training therapists to deal with particular problems, and therapists become oriented toward outcome. There is no routine long-term follow-up of these cases, but those which were easily located were inquired about for this summary. The outcome in the Psychiatry Department sample, as shown in Table 1, was two out of nine rehospitalized after therapy, or a failure rate of 22 percent. The Institute outcome was four out of nineteen, or 19 percent rehospitalized. The combined result of the forty-two cases in all three samples was a failure rate of 24 percent. The average number of interviews was eleven. The time since therapy terminated is given in the "follow-up time" column in the table. It varies from a period of three to six months, which means some inquiries during the year the training therapy was done, to two years afterwards in those cases where the families (and the therapists) have only recently been located.

The sample from the Psychiatry Department and the Family Institute is more diverse than the Schizophrenia Project's. The selection included several different diagnoses, not merely schizophrenia (in the table, a diagnosis

Table 1   Outcome

	Family	Presenting Problem	Number Interv.	Previous Hospit.	Hospitalization during Therapy	Hospitalization since Therapy	Follow-up Time
Schizophrenia	1	Diag. Schiz.	16	1	0	0	2 year
Project	2	Diag. Schiz.	2	1	0	0	2 year
	3	Diag. Schiz.	4	1	0	0	2 year
	4	Diag. Schiz.	20	1	1	0	2 year
	5	Diag. Schiz.	12	1	1	0	2 year
	6	Diag. Schiz.	20	1	0	0	3 year
	7	Diag. Schiz.	30	1	0	0	3 year
	8	Diag. Schiz.	21	1	0	1	3 year
	9	Diag. Schiz.	6	1	0	1	3 year
	10	Diag. Schiz.	6	1	0	Suicide	3 year
	11	Diag. Schiz.	7	1	0	0	4 year
	12	Diag. Schiz.	1	1	0	0	4 year
	13	Diag. Schiz.	27	1	0	0	4 year
	14	Diag. Schiz.	20	1	0	2	4 year
		Average	14			4	
Psychiatry	1	Violent	10	1	0	0	3–6 mo
Department	2	Depr. Suicide	7	1	0	0	3–6 mo
	3	Drugs, Runaway	2	1	0	0	3–6 mo
	4	Alcoholic	13	1	0	3	1½ year
	5	Drug Psychosis	12	1	0	0	1½ year
	6	Psychotic	4	1	0	0	1½ year
	7	Psychot. Alcoh.	15	4	0	1	1½ year
	8	Psychot. Viol.	15	3	0	0	1½ year
	9	Suicide, Alcoh.	9	8	1	0	1½ year
		Average	10			2	
Family	1	Psychotic	3	5	0	0	6 mo
Therapy	2	Suicidal	20	1	0	0	6 mo
Institute	3	Suicidal	1	1	0	0	6 mo
	4	Psychotic	16	1	0	0	6 mo
	5	Psychotic	15	1	0	1	6 mo
	6	Anorectic	15	0*	0	0	1 year
	7	Anorectic	12	0*	0	0	1 year
	8	Anorectic		0*	0	0	1 year
	9	Psychotic, Violent	7	1	0	1	1½ year
	10	Psychosomatic	7	3	0	0	1½ year
	11	Suicidal	9	1	0	0	1½ year
	12	Psychotic	12	2	0	1	1½ year
	13	Psychotic	7	1	0	0	1½ year
	14	Suicide, Psychotic	5	3	0	0	2½ year
	15	Phob. Compulsive	11	3	0	0	2½ year
	16	Violent	4	1	0	0	2½ year
	17	Drug Addict	7	1	0	1	2½ year
	18	Depr. Suicide	7	2	0	0	2½ year
	19	Exhibitionism	16	1	0	0	2½ year
		Average	10			4	
		Total Average	11				

*The anorectics, who were all eighteen years or older, had received medical treatment but had not been hospitalized in a psychiatric hospital. None of them has been in any kind of hospital since therapy.

of "psychotic" usually means "schizophrenic"). In all cases the young person had been hospitalized (except for the anorectics as noted in the table); some were chronic and had been hospitalized several times. Some also had only one parent or other relative available for therapy. The age group is the same, since the sample reported here includes only an age range of late teens and twenties, the age of leaving home.

The therapists in the Psychiatry Department involved in this particular sample were Barbara Cephas, M.S.W., Kay Donahoe, M.S.W., Gerald Hunt, Ph.D., James Hill, M.D., Sheldon Starr, M.D., and Stanley Weinstein, Ph.D. The Institute group participants were Geroge Brown, M.D., Lila Caffery, M.A., Jean Driggers, M.S.W., Phillip Hill, M.D., Joan Hoffman, M.S.W., Judy Lansing, M.S.W., Betsy Lawrence, Ph.D., Marcha Ortiz, R.N., Kathy Reuter, PhD., Ralph Scoville, M.D., Jane Terry, M.D., Stuart Tiegel, M.S.W., Jerry Waletzky, M.D., Gene Waterman, M.D. and Melvin Williams, M.D.

Therapists with different levels of experience from different professions used this therapy approach successfully; there were also two different supervisors for the Psychiatry Department and Family Therapy Institute groups. The other supervisor was my wife, Cloe Madanes. We have supervised together not only at the University of Maryland and the Family Institute, but also at the Department of Psychiatry of Howard University, where we worked with particularly difficult lower-class families, each with a hospitalized member.

Cloe Madanes contributed many ideas to this book and to this general approach to therapy over the years we collaborated together.[1] She has a rare skill in teaching therapists how to do therapy with the families of mad young people.[2]

There is support for this approach in two other projects where the therapeutic operations were similar in many ways. One was a research project on the outcome of family therapy with hard-core heroin addicts. This was a carefully controlled study of twenty-four families with a long-term follow-up planned. The success rate, with success defined as staying off heroin, was 80 percent.[3] I was involved as a supervisor and in planning the therapy

---

[1] C. Madanes and J. Haley, "Dimensions of Family Therapy," *J. Nerv. Ment. Dis.*, 165:88–98, 1977.

[2] C. Madanes, "The Prevention of Rehospitalization of Adolescents and Young Adults," to be published.

[3] This was a research project supported by the National Institute of Drug Abuse, directed by M. D. Stanton with T. C. Todd, consultant and clinical supervisor. They are the authors of a report on the program called "Structural Family Therapy with Drug Addicts," published in E. Kaufman and P. Kaufmann (eds.), *The Family Therapy of Drug and Alcohol Abusers*, Halsted, New York, 1979.

strategy in that program, and the approach was essentially similar to the one presented here. Some of the therapists were in both projects, and one of the cases from this heroin project is discussed in Chapter 9.

Another research project with a similar therapy approach and a success rate of 86 percent was initiated by Salvador Minuchin, M.D.[4] Although he was working with a population that differed from ours in both its problems and its stage of family life, the focus on the family organization was much the same. The similarity was in the emphasis on hierarchy, with the parents in charge and taking responsibility for changing their problem offspring. There was also, in the anorexia nervosa cases, a sharp focus on the presenting problem, since it was a life-threatening situation. In both therapies the therapist intervenes to draw a generation line between parents and children, making the parents work together to resolve the problem of the child.

It is not surprising that there are similarities between the work of Dr. Minuchin and the therapy approach in this work, since we labored together in the same place for ten years. With Braulio Montalvo we struggled to clarify the issues of therapy and ways of training therapists.[5] Minuchin and Montalvo had developed a structural approach while working with chaotic families of the poor,[6] and Dr. Minuchin with his colleagues applied that approach to psychosomatic families as well as others. My own work came out of Gregory Bateson's research project where, particularly with Don Jackson, we developed a structural approach out of the work with chaotic families of schizophrenics. In the decade that Montalvo, Minuchin, and I worked together, we shared many problems and worked out many innovations. Despite some differences, there are obvious similarities between requiring parents to force a starving child to eat and requiring parents to force a disturbed young adult to stop being delusional and get to work.

While acknowledging influences on this work, I would like to mention John N. Rosen, M.D.[7] In 1954 the Bateson project studied Rosen, and his work became part of our thinking about the nature of therapy. At that time he was one of half a dozen therapists who specialized in the therapy of schizophrenics and who influenced all of us who work with the "mad." These men included Murray Bowen, Don Jackson, Thomas Malone, Ed Taylor, John Warkentin, and Carl Whitaker. One of Dr. Rosen's services

[4] S. Minuchin, B. L. Rosman, and L. Baker, *Psychosomatic Families: Anorexia Nervosa in Context*, Harvard University Press, Cambridge, 1978.

[5] B. Montalvo, "Aspects of Live Supervision," *Fam. Proc.*, 12:343–359, 1973.

[6] S. Minuchin, B. Montalvo, B. Guerney, B. L. Rosman, and F. Schumer, *Families of the Slums*, Basic Books, New York, 1967.

[7] J. N. Rosen, *Direct Analysis*, Grune & Stratton, New York, 1951.

was to go from state hospital to state hospital and interview patients in the presence of the staff. He would show that people called schizophrenic were human and responsive to a human conversation. That was a revolutionary idea at that time. I think the possibility, if not the necessity, of doing therapy with schizophrenics outside a hospital setting was established by Rosen.

Another major influence on this approach to therapy was Milton H. Erickson.[8] He had a special skill with young people and a family orientation at a time when few therapists did. Implicit in his work with out-of-control young people was a concern with hierarchy in the family. As early as 1958 he was explaining a distinction to me which was difficult to appreciate at the time. The Bateson project had shown that trying simply to detach a young schizophrenic from his family didn't work. We were essentially doing the opposite by attempting to bring about family togetherness. We interpreted, clarified communication, and explored the origins of behavior in the past. Erickson pointed out that at this stage of family life the developmental task was not to bring about togetherness but to achieve disengagement. Although we did not accept this idea immediately, in time our goal was to bring a young person and his parents together to help them get apart.

A major influence on me, as well as on everyone with a family approach, was Harry Stack Sullivan.[9] I was most influenced by him through Don D. Jackson, my first supervisor in my work with schizophrenics; he had been personally supervised by Sullivan. In the 1950s, the members of the Bateson project worked with individual schizophrenics, supervised by Jackson, and later we began to do therapy with families. Jackson was the most innovative among us in dealing with these families of mad young people and, despite a proper medical education, he had somehow achieved an awareness that there was nothing wrong with a schizophrenic except his social situation.

I am indebted to many others in this field who were associated with me over the twenty years of investigation into the mysteries of therapy for madness. For the decade of the Bateson project,[10] John Weakland was my col-

---

[8] Cf. J. Haley (ed.), *Advanced Techniques of Hypnosis and Therapy: Selected Papers of Milton H. Erickson, M.D.*, Grune and Stratton, New York, 1967, and J. Haley, *Uncommon Therapy: The Psychiatric Techniques of Milton H. Erickson*, Norton, New York, 1973.

[9] At one time I considered placing in the appendix of this work a reprint of a statement of admiration for Sullivan which I had written as a comment on a review of a book in 1967. It was published as "The Doctor as Part of the Schizophrenic Interchange," *Internat. J. Psychiat.*, 4:531–542, 1967.

[10] For a history of the ideas of the Bateson project see J. Haley, "Development of a Theory: A History of a Research Project," in C. E. Sluzki and D. C. Ransom (eds.), *Double Bind*, Grune & Stratton, New York, 1976.

league and friend in the adventure with schizophrenia. He also wrote, with Don D. Jackson, one of the earliest reports on outcome with the family of the schizophrenic.[11]

I am indebted to Braulio Montalvo for many ideas in the approach I have to therapy. We spent innumerable hours together discussing therapy issues over the years. I am particularly indebted to him for taking the time to read this manuscript and for offering many helpful suggestions for revision.

Many other colleagues and students contributed ideas to this approach. Only a few are mentioned in the text, when I quote their interviews. Many families, by succeeding or failing, also contributed to our learning what should be done with this problem. The families remain anonymous, and all those mentioned in this work have had names and circumstances changed to protect their identities.

The family interviews presented in these pages are verbatim except for editorial corrections to eliminate redundancies.

Important Note

There is a point that must be made clear to avoid any misunderstanding. With some therapy approaches it is assumed that the philosophy of the therapist, and how he behaves in relation to a client are directly relevant to normal living. That is not assumed in this approach. What is done in therapy and how one normally lives are not directly related. The therapy presented here is designed to increase the power and authority of the parents in relation to the problem young person. That does not mean that it is assumed that "normal" families should be authoritarian or that parents should have extreme power and authority when raising children. As I have said elsewhere, the fact that one puts a plaster cast on a broken leg to heal it does not mean that children should be raised with casts on their legs. This book is not about how to raise children correctly; rather, it is about how to do something for them when they have gone mad.

[11] D. D. Jackson and J. Weakland, "Conjoint Family Therapy: Some Considerations on Theory, Technique and Results," *Psychiatry*, 24:30–45, 1961.

Chapter 1

Ideas That Have Handicapped Therapists

Therapy techniques for problem young people have been improving over the years. Many ideas that caused consistent failure have been discarded, and new strategies have led to more success. Discarding ideas and theories that one has learned in training from respected teachers is never easy. It would seem that only when the social milieu of a therapist changes is it possible for him or her to change ideology and behavior.[1] The illusion that the individual freely chooses his ideas and theories, no matter what his social network, is in itself a difficult idea to abandon. A review will be offered here of the ideas that handicapped therapists of young people, particularly those defined as schizophrenic, and which have been abandoned over the last twenty years, at least by therapists who learn from experience.

Whether an idea is useful for a theory of therapy can be determined on the basis of certain criteria. The most obvious criteria are the following:

1. The ideas should be relevant to a theory which leads to successful outcome. Not only should the theory lead to better results than some other theory, and to results superior to no therapy at all, but it should not lead a therapist to acts which cause people harm.

This chapter, in a somewhat different form, was originally a paper given at the 1977 conference called "Beyond the Double Bind." It was published as part of the proceedings of that meeting in M. M. Berger (ed.), *Beyond the Double Bind*, Brunner/Mazel, New York, 1978.

[1] It is not appropriate to use only the pronoun *he* in referring to a therapist or a client, since they come in both sexes. The author uses *he* routinely for reasons of convenience and acknowledges the inequity of the traditional use of the masculine pronoun.

2. The theory should be simple enough for the average therapist to understand. When important issues are clearly understood, the therapist is not distracted by clients who are experts in complexity and obfuscation.

3. The theory should be reasonably comprehensive. It need not explain all possible eventualities, but it should prepare a therapist for most of them.

4. The theory should guide a therapist to *action* rather than to reflection. It should suggest what to do.

5. The theory should generate hope in the therapist, client, and family, so that everyone anticipates recovery and normality.

6. The theory should define failure and explain why a failure occurred when it did.

Given these criteria as the most obvious ones for a theory of therapy, their opposites are what a sensible therapist should avoid. A therapist should not accept a theory that prevents a definition of a goal, leads to poor therapy outcome, or does harm. He or she should avoid any theory so complex it is incapacitating, one that attempts to explain everything, one that leads to philosophical speculation rather than action, one that does not generate hope, or one that causes everyone to be uncertain about whether they have succeeded or failed.

UNFORTUNATE IDEAS

A few of the ideas which most handicap therapists who work with problem young people can be summarized.

Organic Theory

There is a tradition from nineteenth-century European psychiatry that there is something organically or genetically wrong with deviant young people, particularly those who have been diagnosed as schizophrenic. Although there are those in psychiatry, especially among clinicians doing therapy, who do not take this idea seriously, still it remains a major assumption in the field. The impression given in the literature and in the teaching of psychiatric residents is that there is solid evidence for a genetic or physiological cause of psychosis. That is simply not true. In fact, the literature contains statements that there are "indications," "leads," "expectable trends," "possible pathways for research," and "hopeful possibilities" in that direction. There is no physical test that shows that a person diagnosed as schizophrenic is different from any normal person, nor is there any solid genetic finding. The clinician who doubts this should ask that his patient by physically examined to determine whether he or she is schizophrenic or not. The response will be a discussion of vague hopes for the future.

Millions of dollars went down the drains of research laboratories to find evidence of organicity, and that research was necessary and important. Unfortunately, the public-relations job to raise money for the effort persuaded many professionals and the lay public that something must be physically wrong with people diagnosed as psychotic. Probably no class of people was ever so stigmatized on so little evidence. Monthly announcements continue to appear, saying that the breakthrough promised for a hundred years is about to occur; the biological and biochemical discussions have become more complex and mystifying; and the results remain negligible. (There is more evidence that being a psychiatrist, or certainly being a doctor, is genetic than there is that being a schizophrenic is genetic.)

Today the argument between the organic and social views is not a minor one. The consequences for adopting the idea that there is a physiological cause for madness have been significant.

1. The assumption of a physical cause for psychosis has determined the custody settings for many problem young people. They were called "sick" and placed in hospitals under the care of doctors and nurses, even though nothing was found to be physically wrong with them.

2. Because of a supposed physical problem, massive doses of medications have been used in ways which civil libertarians would not have allowed with any other deviant population, such as criminals. These medications have proved to be not only incapacitating in many ways, because of their side effects, but actually dangerous. Irreversible neurological damage, such as tardive dyskinesia, is being caused in thousands of people by both the irresponsible and responsible use of these drugs. Many medical people continue to drug people even when they would rather not because the focus on medication in their training has left them not knowing anything else to do. Nonmedical people are unable to prevent the use of these drugs because of the power of medical people in the field and because of their own doubts about whether the organic theory is a myth.

3. The organic theory required a family-oriented therapist to believe that a schizophrenic behaved in strange ways because of a mysterious disease and also in response to his family. That is, the disease theory held that the patient was responding inappropriately and maladaptively because he suffered from an internal defect. The family view held that the strange behavior was adaptive and appropriate to the person's social situation. Attempting to combine these views led to a therapy of mystification and confusion, not only for the therapist but for the clientele. While taught that psychotics had an underlying biological defect which was incurable, the therapist was also taught that he should do therapy to cure them. This meant the client faced someone who was trying to cure him with a theory that he was incur-

able, which was a rather classic double bind and provoked strange and bizarre behavior.

4. The therapist with an organic theory would think of the schizophrenic as a defective person who was limited in intelligence or ability. Since such young people were typically failures, the organic theory seemed reasonable to young professionals, who thought there must be something wrong with someone who was not striving to succeed. If, however, one recognizes that the social function of young psychotics is to fail, in spite of having nothing wrong with them to give them the excuse to fail, their abilities deserve more respect. Such young people are more skillful interpersonally than the average therapist, and so they are able to fail more successfully than the therapist can cause them to succeed. A theory that they were defective caused the therapist to underestimate their interpersonal skill and so to lose in the struggle with them. To assume a crazy young person is defective, and then try to win in a contest with him or her, is like entering a chess championship match with the idea that your opponents are retarded.

These objections to findings that remain mythical does not in any way imply that a mad young person should not have a careful physical examination. There should also be the most sophisticated neurological investigations whenever they are indicated. One of the objections to psychiatry departments today is that they are so quick to assume a chemical imbalance as a causal factor that they do not carry out the obvious neurological investigations.

A final argument is that the medical theories and the medications that have followed from them have not solved the problem, and hundreds of thousands of young people continue to fail in life and behave in strange and bizarre ways. The wisest strategy for a therapist is to assume that there is no organic basis for mad behavior and to proceed as if the problem is a social one. His success will increase.

According to the criteria of a theory of therapy, the organic theory was obviously a disaster and has become a heavy burden to psychiatry. Since the approach confused social control and therapy, it did not lead to success and even prevented spontaneous remission in clients who would have changed if they could have gotten away from the professional. Treatment by custody, medication, and pessimism because of a supposed physical defect reinforced the need for custody, medication, and pessimism. The biological theories were not simple, and even medical researchers did not seem to understand them. No hope was encouraged in client or family, and the theory could not define success. If a person called schizophrenic became normal, he or she was said to be either temporarily in remission or to have been misdiagnosed.

Psychodynamic Theory

Another theory that proved unfortunate was an ideology which, like organic theory, was based on the notion that the individual had something wrong with him independent of his social situation. That was the psychodynamic theory of repression and the therapy that followed from it. Although it is difficult to describe that theory simply, without seeming to parody it, the relevant points for the therapy of young people can be mentioned. According to that theory, a person behaved as he did primarily because of past ideas and experiences that were repressed outside awareness. He was secondarily influenced by his current social situation, although the emphasis was largely on how he viewed that situation through the conceptions built into him by the past. The merit of the theory was that it offered researchers interesting explanations for different varieties of strange behavior. When the ideas were brought into the therapy situation, however, the theory was a handicap. With the theory of repression, it was difficult for a therapist to view the family members as interrelated in their responsive behavior. The unit was a single individual, not a dyad or triad. Each person was viewed as a repressed individual responding to projections and misperceptions. The symptoms of a person were not seen as responsive and appropriate to his social milieu, but as maladaptive, irrational, and a response to past experiences more than present circumstances. Therefore the present, which is all that can be changed, was not focused on as the area to be changed. How extreme this view can be is illustrated by therapists I knew who worked in hospitals and did therapy with individuals, and who were so focused on the past that they did not know if the patient was married.

It is difficult to take a positive approach in therapy with a psychodynamic theory, because the orientation is toward the negative side of people. It is the darker side that is repressed, including fear, hostility, hatred, incestuous passion, and all that. When the primary therapy technique available is to make interpretations to bring this repressed material into awareness, it forces a focus on hostile and unpleasant aspects of people. (I recall a family therapy team presenting a case with a schizophrenic. They reported proudly that after three years of therapy the mother finally admitted that she hated *her* mother. This seemed to me to be irrelevant to getting the son and family back to normal, but to them it was a triumph, because they operated from the theory of repression.)

Psychodynamic theory tends to encourage a therapist to be an exploring consultant to the family rather than someone involved in giving directives and getting changes to happen. The tendency of the therapist to explore the past leads to the parents being blamed, since the past was their responsibility. When past actions are the issue, the parents are implicitly accused of causing the young person's problem. The therapist with a theory of historical causes often sees himself as a savior of the patient from parents who were a noxious influence, and so his exploratory interpretations tend to antagonize parents and make it difficult to win their cooperation. When the therapist observes their lack of cooperation, it confirms his idea that the past behavior of difficult parents caused the problem, and he feels he must save the young person from them.

Another therapy procedure following logically from the theory of repression was the idea that people would change if they expressed their emotions. It was thought that if people expressed their bad feelings to each other and got their anger out, even by screaming, everyone would be cleared of their repressed feelings, and the schizophrenic would go off whistling down the street.

The free expression of feeling might have merit in some situations, like religious revival meetings, but in family therapy interviews it was a misfortune which could prevent changes in organization. The experiential therapist trained to bring out emotions in artificial groups had no theory of organization and so did not know how to reorganize a family. A family member could avoid an issue or disrupt an interview at any time by getting emotional, with the encouragement of the therapist. Everyone had a catharsis and did not have to follow a therapeutic plan or achieve any goal. The young person, whose job it was to prevent conflict developing between the parents, could become self-expressive and upset whenever necessary, and so prevent the resolution of any parental conflicts. Sessions based on making behavior conscious and bringing out feelings tended to be incoherent, disorganized, concerned with defense and proof of innocence, abrasive, and interminable. They also encouraged a "communication theory" of the families of schizophrenics, because such interviews generated peculiar communication.

The theory of repression did not lead to good outcome, was not simple, did not guide the therapist to action (but rather to reflection), and did not generate hope, because the causes were rooted in unchangeable childhood experience. It did not define failure or explain it when it occurred.

Systems Theory

The organic and psychodynamic theories were carried over from the past, while the social theories developed at mid-century. The idea of family systems was based upon cybernetic theory, which was developed in the late 1940s.[2] With this theory it was possible for the first time to conceive of

---

[2] See N. Wiener, *Cybernetics*, Wiley, New York, 1948. The systems idea was circulated from a variety of sources, one of the more important ones being the conferences supported by the Josiah Macy Jr. Foundation in the late 1940s and early 1950s.

human beings not as separate individuals but as an ongoing group responding to one another in homeostatic ways, and so behavior had *present* causes. The family system was said to be stabilized by self-corrective governing processes which were activated in response to an attempted change. The idea that a family, or any other ongoing group, was a system maintained by feedback processes brought a whole new dimension into the explanations of why human beings behave as they do. There was the awesome realization that people seemed to do what they did because of what other people did; the issue of free will came up in a new form. Family members were seen to be helplessly caught up in sequences which repeated and repeated, despite the wishes and attempts of the members to do differently. Therapists too were caught up in these repeating sequences, both in endless therapy and in endless conflicts with fellow staff members in agencies and hospitals.

The chief merit of a systems theory is that it makes certain happenings predictable. The chief demerit of the theory for therapeutic purposes is that it is not a theory of change but a theory of stability. Family therapy, the attempt to change families, developed within a theory of how a family remains the same. As interesting as this theory might be for explaining animal and human behavior, it was not a simple guide to what to do in therapy. It even handicapped the therapist by leading him to believe that an attempt to intervene activated resistance, because of governing processes to keep the family unchanged. This led to the kind of pessimism that ideas of resistance in psychodynamic theory had led to. This theory also suggested that if you caused a change in one part of a family, there was a response in another part. For some therapists, this activated the old myth about symptom substitution and caused them to hesitate to take action to bring about change.

Systems theory, as it was applied to families, tended to describe participants as equals, which made the theory difficult to use when planning the restructuring and reorganization of the family hierarchy. To consider the power of a grandmother, or to support parents as authorities over a child, was difficult within a theory which tended to equalize everyone as responsive units.

A primary problem for a therapist is the way systems theory takes away individual responsibility from the participants in a system. Each person is driven to do what he does because of what someone else does. Interesting as that theory may be for a philosopher concerned with free will, family therapists seem, in practice, to need to emphasize individual initiative. So within a theory that people cannot help doing what they are doing, the therapist is suggesting that family members act differently.

Family systems theory did not seem to lead to good outcome. It also was not a simple theory, as one found when attending theoretical discussions.

Often one did not understand what the speaker had said, though it sounded profound. The theory, because of the emphasis on high levels of abstraction, was even used to obscure the issue of whether anyone had really changed during therapy.

The Double Bind

Finally, there was the double-bind theory, published in 1956, which was not a theory of family therapy but became part of the enterprise. That theory included the idea of describing communication in terms of levels, with the possibility that those levels could conflict and generate a paradox, or bind, where no acceptable response was possible. The theory was an attempt to describe some of the processes in the learning situation of the schizophrenic. At first it was described as a bind imposed on a child by parents, and later as a reciprocal bind that people impose on each other. There was also a suggestion that a person could impose a "therapeutic bind" by so binding a person that he was forced to behave normally.[3]

As interesting as that theory was, and as valuable as the concept of levels was in describing behavior, I don't think the theory was helpful to therapists of families of schizophrenics. Not only was it a hypothesis about what happened, rather than a suggestion for how to change what was happening now, but it encouraged a description of a family in terms of a victim; helpful therapists found themselves siding with the victim against the parents. Since therapy is an art of coalitions, it is difficult to plan carefully how to be involved in factional family conflicts if one's theory biases one toward rescuing someone in the family. Just as the idea of a "scapegoat" was a misfortune for therapy, so was the idea of a "victim" of a double bind. From what we know today about the nature and importance of hierarchy, for an expert to side with a "victim" low in the hierarchy against someone higher can cause family distress rather than relieve it.[4]

---

[3] G. Bateson, D. D. Jackson, J. Haley, and J. H. Weakland, "Toward a Theory of Schizophrenia," *Behav. Sci.*, 1:251–264, 1956. For a history of the ideas of that project see J. Haley, "Development of a Theory: A History of a Research Project," in C. E. Sluzki and D. C. Ransom (eds.), *Double Bind*, Grune & Stratton, New York, 1976. The reader interested in the communication ideas of the Bateson project should read the writings of the project members, who were: Gregory Bateson, Jay Haley, John Weakland, and part-time consultants Don D. Jackson and William F. Fry. They published extensively from 1956, when they wrote the article on the double bind, to the end of the project in 1962. Their seventy papers and books are listed in "A Note on the Double Bind, 1962," in *Family Process*, 2:154–161, 1963. Bateson's basic ideas are presented in *Steps to an Ecology of the Mind*, Ballantine, New York, 1972, and *Mind and Nature*, Dutton, New York, 1979.

[4] For a description of hierarchy in these terms see J. Haley, *Problem Solving Therapy*, Jossey-Bass, San Francisco, 1976.

The view of the family implicit in a theory of victims was the negative view that people do bad things to each other. This orientation made it difficult for a therapist to organize his thinking in a positive way and gain the cooperation of the family to bring about change.

Whatever the problems of using the "double bind" in a family description, they were compounded when combined with the idea that change is caused by making interpretations to help people understand what they are doing. Family members were forced to listen to helpful therapists point out what dreadful double binds they imposed on each other. The response was defensive and angry behavior by the family members at being misunderstood. This was interpreted as resistance to the therapists, and so the therapists condemned the behavior they were evoking, which is rather like a double bind.

With the theory of the double bind and the concept of levels, the communication processes in the family became more interesting from a research viewpoint. Body movements, vocal intonations, and words with multiple meanings showed an astonishing intricacy. There were metaphors about metaphors about metaphors. A therapist who explored these meanings in interviews found himself unknowingly obscuring more basic issues. There were fascinating and endless discussions with a mother about how she wanted her child to do what she said spontaneously. It was pointed out to a father how he condemned his son for thinking as he himself did. The family seemed to prefer such discussions to taking any action toward change.

Researchers and Clinicians

I have summarized a few of the theoretical and research ideas of the past, but there was another assumption that seems strange today. It was taken for granted that a therapist and a researcher were of the same species (although the therapist had a more second-class status). It was even thought that research training was a way to train a therapist, and many young people spent years in graduate school doing research as a way of getting a degree to do therapy. Today, it seems more apparent that the research stance and the posture of the therapist are quite the opposite of each other. The researcher must keep distant from his data, be objective, and not intrude on or influence what he is studying. He must also explore and explain all the complex variables of every issue, since he is a seeker after truth. The therapist's stance is quite different. He must be personally involved and human, not distant and objective. He must intrude actively on the data to influence people, so that what has been going on will change. He must also use simple ideas that will accomplish his goals and not be distracted by explorations into interesting aspects of life and the human mind.

It seems evident that the creation of a researcher and the creation of a therapist are different enterprises. Yet in the past these enterprises were confused. When looking at an interview, one could not tell whether a person was doing research on a family or setting out to change them.

FAMILY THERAPY FROM THESE IDEOLOGIES

Given these theories, what therapy with the family of a schizophrenic logically followed? A family would be brought in, and the parents would expect to be blamed for driving their offspring crazy. Otherwise, the therapist would only have done therapy with the offspring. The parents would typically behave in distant and defensive ways because of the accusatory context. Sometimes they would ask, "Do you think it is our fault our son is crazy?" The therapist was likely to reply that the cause was complex. If the parents said, "We did not drive our child crazy," the therapist would say, "Oh?" with just enough of an inflection to let them know they were at fault. The scene was like a Kafka trial, where parents began to defend themselves against charges which had not been made. Since the approach was psychodynamic and nondirective, the therapist did not take charge and organize what was to happen. He did nothing and waited for the family to initiate action. The family did not know what they were supposed to do and so waited for the expert to do something. There were long, significant silences. Sometimes the therapist would say, "Isn't it interesting what a silent family this is?" or, "How does it feel to be so silent?" To fill the silences without revealing signs of guilt, a father would try to talk about other things, like the cold in Antarctica. The therapist would point out to him that he was being tangential and avoiding the real issues. If the father asked the expert, "What are the real issues?" the therapist would reply, "What do you feel they are?" When the family began to be upset or angry, the therapist would ask, "Have you noticed that you are upset and angry?" This would make the family angrier, which pleased the therapist, since he had the idea that being emotional would help them unrepress their emotions. If the parents got too upset, the schizophrenic child would do his job by being rude or acting delusional, to make it clear that he was the problem, not the parents. With relief, parents and therapist would talk about the patient's irrational ideas. Sometimes, if the therapist could not think of anything else to do, he would interpret the family members' body movement to them and point out its real significance. Soon the family members did not know how to sit to avoid the therapist's making comments about their underlying negative impulses.

The task of the therapist was to keep the family coming to the interviews and getting them to talk, in the hope that something would change. The task of the family was to find out what they were supposed to say and do in the interviews and why they were there. The therapist could not tell the family to do anything because that would be manipulative, which was against the rules of therapy in the 1950s. He could not ask the parents to take charge of the child and make him or her behave, thereby structuring a hierarchy, because the therapist operated from a theory that the parents were a noxious influence; they had harmed the child in the past and should not be in charge in the present. Another reason the therapist could not put anyone in charge was that he could not take charge himself. He could only respond as a consultant to the family, with the idea that they somehow should help themselves; his task was only to make them aware and hope for the best. His only therapy technique was an interpretation; a comment on the meaning of something, no matter how trivial. If the family gave up trying to find out what to do and merely sat, the therapist helped them understand how resistant they were to facing their resistance to dealing with their family system.

Typically, the therapist communicated an underlying apathy, despite a forced cheerfulness, because his theory said that the patient was really a biological and genetic problem, or fragile from infantile traumas caused by the parents, from which he would never recover.

If the patient turned normal and the family began to reorganize, the therapist was often surprised by a colleague stoning the patient with medication or hospitalizing him because he had become troublesome. Then the therapist had to start over, waiting for the family to initiate something so he could respond with an interpretation, and hoping that somehow everyone would get "better," whatever that was.

NEW DEVELOPMENTS

How did therapists recover from these theories? One could not merely put aside past theories and adopt a new one, because there was not a new one that was satisfactory. Every therapist faced the difficult task of choosing which ideas to discard and which to retain.

I have experienced a transition in my own thinking which parallels the change apparent in the work of many therapists. Dealing with mad young people over the decades, it has become more evident that madness is an expression of a malfunctioning organization. What became clearer to me was that all learning animals organize and cannot avoid doing so. The organizations are hierarchical in form, some members having more authority and status than others. This obvious fact was slow to be appreciated in the family field. Families were described as groups of individuals, as a coalition system, or as a communication system, but only slowly was it acknowledged that they were organizations with a hierarchy deserving of respect. A therapist who ignored a powerful grandmother or joined a child against parents was simply naïve. His theory did not include the fact that levels of power in an organization must be recognized by an outsider entering the organization. Sometimes therapists were quite concerned about status and power in their clinics and hospitals but ignored such issues when dealing with patients and their family organizations. In an interview, a child would be encouraged to bring out his hostility by attacking his parents, without concern for the effect on an organization when an expert called in by parents encourages a problem child to attack them.

Over the years, as more families were observed, it became increasingly evident that, both in the hospital and at home, a mad young person was responding to a particular kind of organization. The hierarchy was not the usual one of parents in charge, with executive authority over their children, and with the grandparents advising the parents. Cross-generational coalitions were occurring, in that one parent sided with a child against the other parent, or a grandmother was joining a child against parents, or the expert joined one faction of a family against another. There was confusion in these families and also in mental hospitals, where it was not clear whether the doctor had authority over the whole ward, or the nurse, or an aide. Similarly, the powers of a hospital social worker or psychologist over other staff members or a patient remained undefined.

When it became clearer that psychopathology was the result of a malfunctioning organization, it became self-evident that the task of a therapist was to change the organization. It was also evident that some past theories made that task difficult if not impossible. For example, to encourage free association in an interview among all family members was a way of introducing randomness rather than a way of restructuring an organization.

The steps in my own thinking and in the thinking of many other therapists were as follows: In the 1940s it was believed that a mad individual suffered from confused thought processes which *caused* him to communicate strangely and to establish deviant relationships. The therapy task was to correct the person's disordered thoughts and misperceptions of reality on the assumption that, as his thoughts were corrected, he would communicate differently and organize different relationships. In the 1950s the families of mad young people were observed, and it was noticed that the intimate relatives communicated in deviant ways. It began to be assumed that a young person had deviant and disordered thoughts because he lived in a communication system where such thoughts were appropriate. If a mother communicated to a child that he should spontaneously obey her, that multilevel paradoxical communication was thought to be causal in the child's disordered thinking. The therapy task was to focus on changing the communication system by educative and other interventions, and then the young person's mad thoughts would change.

Finally, in the 1960s, came the realization that people communicated in deviant ways if they were organized in a way that required such communication. The disordered thought process was therefore a product of disordered communication produced by a malfunctioning organization. For example, if a mother communicated to a child that he should spontaneously obey her, the mother was in an organization where she did not have sufficient executive authority over the child to *require* him to obey her. Some other adult at her level, such as the father, was joining the child against her and giving the child more power than she had. Or an authority at another level, such as a grandmother or an expert professional, was in coalition with the child against her. Therefore the mother did not take charge of the offspring because the organization was of such a nature that the child had more power than she did, and there would be organizational consequences if she exerted authority. When an organization was thus confused, the therapeutic task was to reorganize its structure so that the adults, particularly the mother and father jointly, had executive authority in the family. When the family was reorganized, the communication system would change, and so would the thought processes of the mad offspring.

As this way of thinking spread, it became evident that other theories made the therapeutic task difficult and would certainly fail to change the mad young person. For example, if the therapist viewed the offspring as a victim of parents who had been a noxious influence, the therapist would attempt to save this "scapegoat." That approach would mean joining the child against the parents, increasing the malfunctioning nature of the organization and thus further confusing the hierarchy rather than restructuring it.

From this view, past theories can be examined in terms of how they handicap the therapist.

Organic Theory

The trouble with the biological or genetic theory of schizophrenia is not only that there is no evidence to support it but that the mad young person's problem is defined as being in the medical rather than the parental domain, and so the therapist has no leverage to restructure the family hierarchy. He can only commiserate with the parents for having an incurable child. The problems became so severe that I largely discarded the term "schizophrenia." A therapist becomes incapacitated by that term and cannot approach the problem with hope, particularly if he or she is a psychiatric resident. I was reluctant to give up the term, but it proved impossible to keep the focus on therapy when "schizophrenia" was used. The focus could never be shifted from diagnostic issues, and from endless discussions about which medication to use, to therapy technique. If the Food and Drug Administration bans psychiatric medications because they have dangerous side effects and cause irreversible neurological damage, this generation of psychiatrists is likely to be mute in case discussions.

The main reason I dropped the term "schizophrenia" was that it so handicapped the teaching of therapy. I found it almost impossible to persuade psychiatric residents—or social workers, since they follow the lead of psychiatrists—to expect a "schizophrenic" to become normal. They would hesitate when they should have pushed for normal behavior, and the family would hesitate because the expert did so. Soon everyone was treating the "patient" like a defective person, and therapy failed.

I have never understood why some therapists escaped from the biological view and others could not. I was greatly influenced by Don D. Jackson in my therapy with these families. He believed that there was nothing wrong with a person diagnosed as schizophrenic. It was inspiring to watch him work with a family with a mad offspring who was an expert at failing. I recall one who would not speak. She would sit pulling at her hair like an idiot. Yet Jackson treated her as if she were perfectly capable of normality, given a change in her family and treatment situation. The family was forced to accept her normality, partly because of Jackson's certainty.

When teaching therapy, I tried different ways of dealing with this problem. With some students, I found it effective to say that the person was misdiagnosed as schizophrenic, despite the hallucinations and delusions. The therapist could then treat the person like a human being, because he was not really schizophrenic.

In desperation, I also created a new diagnostic category to solve the problem. I said the person was a "pseudoschizophrenic;" that is, a person who has all the symptons of schizophrenia but is not really schizophrenic. That effort was defeated too, and finally I simply dropped the category "schizophrenia." I tried to avoid calling anyone that and searched for other terms: "mad," "crazy," "eccentric," and "problem people."

Some psychiatrists can escape this problem by staying within the politics of medicine while using more of the advances of modern medicine. The idea that schizophrenia is genetic or irreversibly biological is nineteenth-century medical ideology. In this century, medicine is more flexible in diagnosis, more concerned with stages of an illness, more doubtful about the irreversibility of any ailment, and more innovative in the temporary use of drugs.

Psychodynamic Theory

Psychodynamic theory is based on the idea that the psyche of the individual is the problem, not the situation in which he lives. It is therefore difficult, if not impossible, to use that theory effectively to change an organization. The psychodynamic therapist focuses on the person's misperception of the organization. Essentially, that theory guides a therapist to encourage a mad young person to express himself and guides authorities to be permissive and allow that expression. From that posture, it is almost impossible for a therapist to require parents to assume executive authority and to expect respect from the offspring. To restructure an organization, conversation must be directed and organized by a therapist rather than being free-flowing and expressive. The permissive, passive therapist and the correction of hierarchy are not compatible.

Often clinicians with a psychodynamic view criticize more active therapy and object to the use of any force. This view is hypocritical in that such clinicians often avoid treating crazy people, and so they criticize without offering an alternative. More important, they tend to hire other people to use the force. I can recall permissive and benevolent therapists doing psychodynamic therapy in mental hospitals, particularly private ones. They would say the therapist should only be kind and encourage self-expression, and they would object to any therapist asking parents to restrain their offspring physically if he or she got violent. Yet these same therapists worked in a setting where hired employees handled the violence, while therapists pretended they did not. Muscular aides taught patients how to behave on the wards with force and violence, while the psychodynamic therapist chatted with the patient in his office and called the aide if there was trouble. The institution also used shock treatment, medications, tubs, packs, and isolation rooms, so that the psychodynamic therapist would have a compliant patient to be kind and permissive with. Ignoring the social situation and focusing on the psyche allowed a therapist to avoid thinking about the social system of which he was part.

A final important aspect of psychodynamic theory is its assumption that what people do is based on aggression, hostility, and self-defense. Such a view is the opposite of that offered in this work. It is best for a therapist to assume that what people do, no matter how seemingly destructive, is basically protective. It is the benevolence of people that poses problems. If a wife has a sudden onset of anxiety attacks that make great demands on her husband, it is best to assume that she is protecting him by that problem. Whether anxious or angry, a spouse should be assumed to be motivated by a benevolent concern for the other spouse. Similarly, it is best to assume that a mad young person is not defending himself or being hostile to his family by his troubled and violent behavior. The question is, what would happen to his family if he did not behave that way? For therapeutic purposes it should be assumed that mad young people are sacrificing themselves to stabilize their families. Stability in a system is the motivating force that drives the members. If he has that view, a therapist tends to be more positive in his approach to everyone involved in misfortune.

If one wishes to do effective therapy with mad people, it is best simply to abandon psychodynamic theory. The therapist who attempts to be broad-minded, trying to bring together psychodynamic theory and an approach based on restructuring a family, will be the most handicapped.

Systems Theory

Systems theory is a more difficult problem because it has many merits as well as demerits. I found it necessary to deemphasize the issues of homeostasis and stability and to focus more on the aspects of change. Thinking in terms of systems, one can plan a therapy in which a crisis is induced in a family, and the family must reorganize to deal with it. Alternatively, one can begin a small change and persistently amplify it until the system adapting to it must reorganize.[5]

The chief merit of systems theory is that it allows the therapist to recognize repeating sequences and so make predictions. He can then plan his therapy in anticipation of what will happen. There remain the problems of how to simplify the sequences so they become recognizable and useful, and how to use the concepts of hierarchy and sequences in a system. The past tendency to equalize the elements in a system makes all family members equally powerful, and conceptualizing differing statuses and powers in a hierarchy is correspondingly difficult.

The Double Bind

I largely discarded the term "double bind" and returned to Gregory Bateson's original term "paradox." I found I did not know what a double bind was anymore, because so many people used it in so many different ways. Paradox is a clearer and more precise term for describing conflicting levels of communication. The term "paradoxical intervention" also has a less negative connotation than "double binding" a client.

The communication ideas which came out of the Bateson project are a valuable way of describing human beings dealing with one another. The idea that a message at one level conflicts paradoxically with a message at

[5] M. Maruyama, "The Second Cybernetics: Deviation-Amplifying Mutual Causal Processes," in W. Buckley (ed.), *Modern Systems Research for the Behavioral Scientist*, Aldine, Chicago, 1968.

another can be carried into a description of organizations. After all, an organization is merely a system of repeating sequences of communication. As people communicate with each other in systematic ways, that communication becomes the organization. When one person tells another what to do, and the other does it, a hierarchy is being defined by that process. When one person tells another to "disobey me," the communication is paradoxical, and the organization is likely to be a malfunctioning one.

Out of the struggles with difficult young people and their families have come a number of ideas. Something valuable has been developed from systems and communication theories, while at the same time a new view of organizational power has been developing. Out of failure, as well as out of success, has come the view that youthful madness is best understood as a product of a family life-stage where reorganization is taking place, and that the youth's behavior is adaptive to that social context. Only with a change in the social context can normal behavior become appropriate. Changing a social organization to which they belong is the task of family therapists, and theories that guide them to induce that change are necessary for effective therapy.

Chapter 2

A Family Orientation

There is a group of young people who behave in unusual and bizarre ways, frightening the community by unpredictable and unsocial behavior. They talk to imaginary people, or behave in agitated and seemingly random ways, or wander the earth as vagrants, or waste their lives obtaining and taking drugs and alcohol, or commit such unreasonable criminal acts as stealing unneeded objects. These young people typically go to one of two extremes of behavior: they make trouble, or they are apathetic and helpless and will not do anything to support themselves. At either extreme they bring community agents of social control into the lives of their families. What is most characteristic of such young people is that they are failures: they do not support themselves; they do not train successfully for a career; they do not form intimate relationships with other young people and so do not develop a normal social base outside the family. Whether withdrawn and unresponsive, or outspoken and offensive, such young people have in common their failure to live normal lives.

It is usually clear who belongs to this class of failing young people and who does not. They do not merely deviate from some popular norm and march to the beat of some different, but legitimate, drum. Young people can be without money or community acceptance because they belong to an unpopular political sect, or are deviant artists, or are rebels in some other way, but they are still not failures. It is when young people behave incompetently in whatever they do, no matter how promising their potential, that they belong in this class. They are professional failures in living, and their families must remain involved with them, if only to continually reject them.

Choosing a name for this class of problem young people is important; the label can determine the way the problem is defined and action taken. In recent years, a medical or psychiatric term has been commonly used; if one tries to discard the medical framework and seeks a more socially oriented name, it is difficult to find an appropriate one.The term "social deviant" is too broad and mild to do justice to someone who would sacrifice his life on the back ward of a mental hospital. To call the person "disturbed," or a "problem person," also tends to minimize the extreme behavior they exhibit.

The term "mad" can be used for this class of young people, although it has an unfortunate history and some bad connotations. The chief demerit is that it can be considered demeaning to call someone "mad." In this work, a "mad" act is defined as a way of doing service to others, often at considerable personal sacrifice, and therefore the term is not meant as demeaning. Another term which might be used is "eccentric." Young people can certainly be eccentric in the ways they deviate from normal behavior. At times they are also savage. Even though "eccentric" sounds like too casual a term for a person who wastes his life in an insane asylum, still it does not demean people or categorize them in the ways that previously led to the loss of all hope about them.

Excluded People

This book is not about scientific research on young eccentrics, nor is it about their nature and history. The focus is narrowly on the practical matter of how to change them. The work is also not about *all* problem people. Excluded are problem children and problem old people. The age range emphasized here is from the late teens through the late twenties: that is the age of leaving home, and this work is about people at that stage of family life.

This work is about young people whose difficulties begin because of family instability. To avoid argument, it should be conceded at once that there are undoubtedly a certain number of eccentrics whose difficulties are not caused by the family. There are young people with undiagnosed brain tumors, and those who have suffered irreversible damage from illegal drugs or legal medications. There are others whose strange behavior is caused by some form of mental retardation or by undiagnosed physiological difficulties. There are also young people scarred by poverty, mistreatment, frequent abandonments, many hospitalizations, or foster homes. The therapeutic approach described here is only partially effective with such young people. This work is about the average "mad" young person—those who populate psychiatric wards, juvenile halls, and drug rehabilitation centers, and who cause trouble in the community because of their mad and eccentric ways.

A therapist facing a mad young person should first assume that he or she is responding adaptively to a mad social situation. The therapist should expect the young person to have the potential to become normal. Very occasionally he may be dealing with a unique case, such as an organic problem that has no remedy, but that is unusual enough to be a last hypothesis. Often, a therapist can be fooled into thinking that a problem young person is not expressing a family problem. Part of the skill of the eccentric young person is the ability to persuade experts that he is a physiologically handicapped person, if not a congenital idiot. One should also keep in mind that a goal of therapy is to maximize a person's possibilities; even the physiologically limited can benefit from this family-oriented therapy. It is common to see mentally retarded youths who are limited, but not to the point where parents must button their shirts for them and keep them in the house. Extremely handicapped behavior has a family function whether physiological problems exist or not.

Failure to Disengage from the Family

At one time, it was theorized that a young person behaved bizarrely at the moment of success because of his or her fragile nature and inability to tolerate responsibility. It was also postulated that there was an inner fear, perhaps carried over from childhood, that terrified the young person when confronted by self-sufficiency and autonomy. Failure was thought to be caused by inner anxiety. Such an explanation was the only one available, because causes were assumed to reside inside the person rather than in the social context, which was not observed. In the 1950s, when whole families were brought together and observed within a concept of systems, it was noticed that a young person who behaved in a bizarre way could be described as responding adaptively to peculiar communication within his family. For the first time, it was suggested that the thought processes and inner anxiety of a person were responses to the kind of communication system in which he was embedded. When people communicate in deviant ways, their thought processes are deviant.

As observation of families continued, it was noted that people communicate in deviant ways in response to an organizational structure of a deviant type. A special organization leads to special communication behavior, which leads to peculiar inner thought processes.

Today, when clinicians and researchers look at a young person behaving in a bizarre way, they tend to conceptualize the problem in different ways:

1. Some clinicians assume the issue is peculiar thought processes. These thoughts cause peculiar communicative behavior, and the person forms relationships which make a deviant organization. The therapy focuses on correcting disordered thinking and misperceptions.

2. Other clinicians assume that the disordered, deviant communicative behavior of the people intimate with the problem person causes the bizarre behavior and thought processes. Their therapeutic endeavor is therefore to clarify and change communication among intimates in the family.

3. Still other clinicians assume that the problem is a malfunctioning and deviant organization. That organization requires peculiar communicative behavior and therefore peculiar thought processes.

It is the argument of this work that the most effective therapeutic intervention is directed at the basic organizational structure. As that changes, so do other factors. In fact, if one thinks in organizational terms, a therapist cannot avoid being part of the family organization. As a therapist talks to a young person about his thought processes, he is an outsider dealing with a family member, and the organization has rules for dealing with outsiders. If he clarifies family communication, by that act he has become an authority in the family hierarchy. To overlook the organizational situation can lead to naïve interventions which prevent change or even make matters worse. In fact, families will make use of a naïve clinician to stabilize and avoid change.

The importance of the social situation has been overlooked in the clinical field for a number of reasons. For centuries, individual character and personality had been emphasized; the scientific task was to classify individuals, not social situations, into types. In addition, cultural institutions are based on the idea of the individual as the unit of responsibility. To allow the social situation to be causal would lead to the jailing or hospitalization of families and friends rather than individuals. Many facets of the culture depend on the fact, or myth, of the individual as a unit.

Until the concept of systems, there was no adequate theory of social situations. To describe behavior which keeps repeating, and so forms an organizational structure of habitual responses, is a new way of thinking about people. The concept of a self-correcting system of relationships is difficult for many people to grasp, much less to take for granted. It is easier to say a particular person caused a difficulty than it is to think of the difficulty as one step in a repeating cycle in which everyone participates.

Another problem in accepting the social situation as a unit is the simple idea that people live in social situations, and so they take them for granted. Ordinary situations, like stages of family life, seemed so obvious that they were not considered a subject of scientific concern. Everyone knew there was a family life-stage when young people leave home, but it was not thought important, so no one noticed the conjunction of malfunctioning people and that life-stage. It is now appearing that, in any organization, the time of greatest change occurs when someone is entering the organization or leaving it.

When a young person succeeds outside the home, it is not merely a matter of individual success. He is simultaneously disengaging from a family, which can lead to consequences for the whole organization. A young person's success or failure is inextricably part of the reorganization of a family, as new hierarchical arrangements are made and new communication pathways develop.

In the normal course of family living, young people graduate from school and begin to work and support themselves while still living at home. Sometimes they physically move out of the home when they go to work. When they become self-supporting, they are in a position to marry and establish homes for themselves. Usually parents are involved in the approval of a mate and in helping their children set up their own homes. As the young people have children, the parents become grandparents and continue to be involved as the family changes its organization over the years. In many families, the children's leaving home appears to cause only a mild disruption. Parents can even find it a relief to have the children off their hands and to be free to do the things they would like to do together.

When a person in the late teens or early twenties begins to behave in strange and failing ways, it should be assumed that the stage of leaving home is malfunctioning and that the organization is in trouble. The trouble will take different forms depending on the structure of the organization. In single-parent families a mother often lives with her own mother and raises children. As the children disengage, mother and grandmother are left as only a dyad and face a reorganization. Sometimes the mother is a lonely single parent, and if the only members of her organization are herself and her child, the child's leaving is a major disruption.

In two-parent families, the parents are faced with only each other, after many years of functioning in a many-person organization. Sometimes parents have communicated with each other primarily through a particular child and have great difficulty dealing with each other more directly. When the child leaves home, the parents become unable to function as a viable organization. Sometimes they threaten divorce or separation. The emphasis in this work is on problems in the offspring, but at this stage of family life problems can appear in one or both parents. When divorce occurs, or a middle-aged parent develops a depression or other symptom, it often coincides with the children leaving, and the problem is a response to an organizational change.

Sometimes the difficulty in the family becomes extreme when the first child leaves; sometimes not until the last one is leaving; and at times, it is a middle child who is in some way special to the parents. The problem is a triangle between the parents and a special child who is the bridge between them; when that child begins to leave home, the family becomes unstable.

The issues that the parents did not deal with because of the children must now be faced. All the marital themes that were communicated about in terms of the child must be dealt with differently when the child is no longer going to be active in the triangle.

When a family is in real trouble because a child is leaving home, there is one way the trouble can be resolved and the family stabilized—the child can stay at home. Yet, as young people reach their late teens and early twenties, the social forces of the community, as well as physiological changes, exert pressure on the family to disengage the young person. School or work is expected, as well as social life outside the family. The young person may stay at home for months or even years, but the expectation increases that the offspring will have a life outside the family and the parents will be left facing each other.

A Solution

One way the young person can stabilize the family is to develop some incapacitating problem that makes him or her a failure, so that he or she continues to need the parents. The function of the failure is to let the parents continue to communicate through and about the young person, with the organization remaining the same. Once the young person and parents fail to disengage, the triangular stability can continue for many years, independent of the offspring's age, though the onset of the problem began at the age of leaving home. The "child" can be forty years old, and the parents in their seventies, still taking their crazy son or daughter from hospital to hospital and doctor to doctor.

There are two ways the family can stabilize: The parents can use an official institution to restrain their offspring, so that he or she does not become independent and self-supporting. By placing the young person in a mental hospital or other social control institution, or by arranging that a doctor heavily medicate the offspring, the parents keep the family stable. The professional community can become an arm of the family to restrain the offspring and maintain them in a handicapped state. For example, I can recall that, years ago, when electric shock was more popular, a mother would threaten a daughter that if she did not behave she would be taken down to the doctor for shock treatments. With rich families, the offspring is sometimes placed in a private institution for years, and the family is stable as long as the incarceration continues. A naïve therapist talking to a young person in an institution can believe that he is an agent of change, when he has actually been hired by a family to stabilize the organization so that change does not occur. The parents can visit the institution regularly and keep involved with the offspring, without the inconvenience of actually living with and taking care of him or her.

The other way the family can stabilize by means of a failing offspring is for the young person to wander about in a failing life. He can be a vagrant on the road and serve as a stabilizing agent in the family, as long as he regularly lets the parents know that he is continuing to fail. He can do this by writing to them regularly and asking for money, by letting them know he is in jail, or through some other unfortunate circumstance.

There are borderline situations, where the young person is failing in one sense and not another. He can live on a commune as a deviant and be a failure in the eyes of the parents. Or, a more common situation these days, he can join a deviant religious cult. Within the cult he may be a success at begging or recruiting new members, but as far as the parents are concerned he is still a failure. Often they not only commiserate with each other for their unfortunate offspring but even hire people to kidnap them from the cult and deprogram them. The focus continues to be on the offspring.

Whether dependent on an institution arranged by the family or community, or on an institution sought out by the young person, the offspring is defined as a failure by the parents, and they communicate about him as if he has not left home. For example, the parents can blame each other for causing the problem or argue about what still might be done. The offspring cannot be left out of their plans as could a successful offspring earning a living. The parents also do not change their relationship with each other; it continues frozen, as if they cannot move to the next stage of family life any more than the dependent offspring can. Their difficulties with each other do not get resolved because when an issue between them comes up, the child is introduced into it just as if he were in the room. For example, a father can complain that his wife did something that irritated him and he didn't mention it to her. When asked why he did nothing about it, he will say, "Well, I know my wife is worried about our son." The concern and preoccupation with the young person prevents an organizational change because the triangle persists unchanged.

Although the family crisis and failure of the young person usually occur in the late teens or early twenties, it can occur later. Sometimes a child who has left home collapses back when his youngest sibling leaves the parent's home. For example, a woman in her late thirties had been out of the home for several years. She began to behave bizarrely, and her parents set out to help her by hospitalizing her and planning her return home to be cared for. This event coincided with the family's youngest child leaving home for college. Because of the older daughter's failure and return home, the family continued to be an organization with a child at home.

When one approaches a mad young person with an interest in organizational change, it is evident that such change does not occur with institutionalization but rather with normal behavior in the community. Therapeutic change therefore occurs most rapidly when the family is encouraged to push the child into normal activities immediately—that is when action in the family happens.

The Cycle

One of the ways to describe the situation is in terms of a recurring cycle. As the young person reaches the age of leaving home, he or she begins to succeed in work or school or in forming intimate relations outside the family. At that point the family becomes unstable, and the young person begins to manifest strange and troublesome behavior. All family members seem upset and behaving in deviant ways, but when the offspring is selected as the problem his behavior appears more extreme, and the other family members stabilize and appear to be reacting to him. The parents, who are divided over many issues, become so divided that they cannot deal with the young person, who begins to take charge and have power over the family. If the parents begin to pull together to deal with their child, it is not unusual for him or her to gain support from more distant relatives, such as the father's mother, against the parents. As the wider kin system comes into conflict with the parents over the young person, the parents become more unable to control him or her, and the behavior escalates. Outside experts are turned to for help, and the expert typically is used by the parents to restrain the offspring with medication or custody; the family stabilizes itself by such restraints. Conflict often increases, however, as family members blame each other for what has happened. The expert then typically attempts to rescue the young person from the parents and so joins him or her in a cross-generational coalition against them, thereby undermining their executive position. This mad situation becomes cyclical when the young person is released from restraint and begins once again to function in the community. As he or she begins to take preliminary steps to succeed in work or school or in forming intimate relations outside the family, the conflict and instability appear again. The young person begins to behave eccentrically, the family says it cannot deal with him, and experts are called. The young person is sent back to the place he was sent before. The second time, everyone knows where he belongs--the place he went the first time. Once again in the institution, the young person is treated for a period and then sent home. The situation is stable until the young person starts to succeed in work or school, the parents threaten separation, the family becomes unstable, and the cycle repeats. The goal of the therapy proposed here is to end that cycle, to get the young person past that eccentric episode and successfully functioning outside the family, with the family reorganized to survive that change.

Failure in Intimate Relations Outside the Family

Ordinarily, a young person forms intimate relations outside the family which in time become more important than the relations within the family. There is a transition from one's family of origin to a new one that is created. Usually, the family is a base from which one tries different relationships until ultimately a mate is chosen and a new family begun.

When it is necessary for the young person to remain involved at home, procedures are developed for preventing and avoiding intimate relationships outside the family. The boundary around the family of origin becomes impermeable, and the young person stays within it. Attempts to get involved outside are aborted, and ultimately the only involvement is within the family.

Typically in these situations, the young person is unable to develop friends outside the family. The person is shy and withdrawn, avoiding all peers, or associating only with lost and unstable young people in short friendships, and so on.

At times, a young person in this situation will get married, but such a marriage tends to be of a special kind. Instead of establishing a new family with the marriage, the spouse becomes co-opted into the family of origin. That is, some parents will permit a marriage when it is clear that the spouse will not take their child away but merely be a compliant addition to the family. Then the child has still not left home.

Failure of the Family to Change Eccentric Behavior

Agents of social control are brought into a family to deal with a problem young person when the family cannot contain the difficulties developing within it. When the parents are about to separate or do harm to each other, the child will make trouble in the community in such a way that the parents are forced to deal with the community intrusion. This can cause them to stabilize by uniting them against the community. It is like a nation starting a war with another nation when internal dissension threatens total disruption.

The problem young person will either make trouble or simply become apathetic and unmoving, requiring the parents to remain together to take care of him or her. When siblings or other relatives insist that parents do something with the "vegetable," the situation becomes unstable. Or outsiders may make comments which embarrass the parents to the point where they arrange therapy, so they can say they are doing what should be done. If the therapy is only custody, medication, or long-term insight therapy, the family can stabilize and the parents can succeed in claiming that they are doing all they can, while not being threatened with change.

Therapists are often surprised at how tolerant parents have been of deviant and eccentric behavior. For example, a young man burned the palms of his hands with cigarettes and called himself "Christ." His parents dismissed this behavior lightly as merely mischievous. There can be a large disparity between the community's shock at eccentric behavior and the family's acceptance of it. Sometimes this is because the strange behavior developed slowly, with each stage of it accepted, so that the next one did not seem extreme. Sometimes the family is actually shocked by what is happening but will not admit it because they do not wish to concede a problem when they believe nothing can be done. If the family comes to public attention, it means the community is asked to resolve the extreme behavior of the young person. It also means that the family has been caught in a runaway change which has caused the previous stability to fail.

A communication description of this class of young people is presented in the following outline.

1. FUNDAMENTAL SOCIAL PROBLEMS (present in every case)

    a. Failure of the young person to disengage from the family or of the family to disengage from him or her. A social base outside the family is therefore not developed because the young person fails to establish enduring intimate relations.

    b. Failure of the young person to succeed in work or school, and so continuing support is required from other people.

    c. Failure of the family to contain and change eccentric behavior, and so agents of social control are activated in the community.

2. SPECIAL COMMUNICATION PROBLEMS (may or may not be present at a given time with a given person)

    a. Disruptive and discourteous communication

    (1) Threatens to harm self or is violent toward other people.

    (2) Acts in a confused and uncertain way, requiring that normal discourse be stopped and something be done, but also makes the doing of anything difficult or impossible.

    (3) Unpredictable eruptions of bad temper for unclear reasons, causing uncertainty and social confusion.

    (4) Drinks or injects drugs irresponsibly, and then behaves in a helpless and physically incapacitated way or with rude and aggressive behavior.

    (5) Generally breaks rules of social courtesy in either subtle or gross ways. May interrupt a conversation or disrupt a

      household by walking the floors all night and sleeping all day.

    (6) Is disobedient to authority, whether parents or community authorities. Often is disobedient in a way that appears to be involuntary, and so the authorities hesitate to use the usual sanctions against disobedience.

   b. Deviant communication: acts

    (1) Criminal acts, such as stealing and other delinquent behavior, are done without apparent self-gain or in a seemingly random way.

    (2) In physical appearance can be starved and look like a skeleton or may be obese in an unpleasant way.

    (3) Wears strange clothes, or appears unclean or too clean, and in dress and behavior attracts attention in a way that frightens or antagonizes other people.

    (4) Walks and moves in stilted and strange ways that make people uneasy.

    (5) Refuses to speak or move.

   c. Deviant communication: words

    (1) Will talk with odd speech mannerisms and sometimes in strange languages with made-up words.

    (2) Will write in a peculiar manner, both in the content of the statements and in the improper way the writing is placed on the page.

    (3) Talks or listens to imaginary people.

    (4) Will frame situations in peculiar ways. For example, will say that in this social situation the time, place, purpose, or people involved are really not what other people say they are.

    (5) Will communicate about physical ailments when there is no evidence for them or they seem bizarre.

The Professional Failure

One can be distracted by the bizarre nature of the behavior or offenses of problem young people and overlook the main theme that runs through their lives—failure. When they approach success, they do something that ends it. Success and failure will vary with the definition of a particular family, but success is generally defined here as behaving competently in work or school and successfully forming intimate relations outside the family. Essentially success is defined as being self-supporting and able to form a family of one's own. It does not mean that a person is a failure if he or she does not marry and have children, but it does mean that one should be able to have intimate relations outside one's family of origin.

It is typical of these eccentric young people to fail at the point where success is imminent. A typical time to begin to behave strangely is just before high school graduation. For many people graduation from high school is a symbol of success and a first step toward emancipation from the family. Often the young person will quit high school a few weeks before graduation, commit some strange delinquent act, or exhibit bizarre behavior which causes institutionalization and failure to graduate.

In many families graduation from high school is a minor matter, whereas graduation from college is the moment of success. In such families the young eccentric does not begin to exhibit the "inappropriate" behavior until just before graduating from college. Often he or she avoids one course that is required for the degree, simply quits during the last semester (saying that college is irrelevant), or attempts suicide just before taking an examination required for graduation.

It should be emphasized that success is defined by the particular family in different ways. In some families, just going away to college is defined as success, and the young people collapse in the first semester. The collapse takes them back home, and they have failed to go to college. In other families even college graduation is not a sign of success, because graduate school is expected. The young person is therefore not a failure until he or she leaves school just before receiving a graduate degree. Failure is defined as the time when training is to be completed and the young person becomes self-sufficient in the view of the family. That training may range from the vocational, lasting a few months, to the medical or legal, which takes many years.

When work, rather than school, is the arena for failure, the young person setting out on an eccentric career just does not find a job. Often he behaves in some peculiar way at job interviews so that he will not be hired. When he does get employment, it is clearly below his abilities, as when a bright young person takes a menial job. He or she may continue to work and make some income, but the family defines the job as indicating failure, and therefore the young person has failed.

Sometimes the young person works for the father or some other relative, and the implication is that he or she cannot handle a job where competence is really expected. In such cases the eccentric behavior and the failure come about after the young person is defined as a success, because he shifted from a job with a relative to a job outside the family.

In some families the doing of any paid work is defined as success, while in other families success is doing a certain kind of job at a certain level of pay. Often the eccentric young person manages quite a good job and threatens to be a success, but then he or she loses it (only to get another one later) and is defined as a failure because of his or her continuing failure to stay regularly employed.

A Communication View

The kind of behavior exhibited by a young person who is stabilizing a family by failing can have great variety and still function to prevent family disengagement. What is important for therapy is to develop a way of thinking about the problem that clarifies how to bring about change. An organizational framework and communication description tends toward this goal more than other theoretical approaches do. The first requirement of a communication description is that it be at least dyadic and preferably triadic—that is, for every behavior by a person that is communicative, it is *to* one or more other people. Therefore, a young person who communicates by wearing strange clothes is giving a message with a social function. It is not merely an expression of the person or a report about his or her thought processes, but both a message and a response *to* others. As an example of the difference in point of view, I recall a psychiatrist doing therapy with a young man who would not talk or go to the toilet. He wet himself and fouled his pants and so was a twenty-two-year-old youth in diapers. The therapist gave the young man a pan to urinate in, and the young man began to wear the pan as a hat and walked about with it. The psychiatrist took this as a random act expressing the young man's confusion, but from the communication view it would be assumed that wearing the pan as a hat was a message to others in that social situation. It is characteristic of such young eccentrics that they manage to decline to do what they are told, but in a way that leaves other people puzzled over whether the issue is disobedience.

Organizational Protection as a Basic Motivation

Disobedience is an issue with eccentric young people, but before considering it the therapist should first accept the fundamental premise that eccentric and mad behavior is basically protective.[1] No matter how strange, violent, and extreme the behavior, it functions to stabilize an organization. Being disobedient is in itself a way of forcing a group to organize with more stability.

Perhaps an example will illustrate this point of view about madness. I was once asked to give a talk to the staff of a psychiatric ward; the people

---

[1] I owe the emphasis on the young person's protection of his family to Cloe Madanes. See C. Madanes, "The Prevention of Rehospitalization of Adolescents and Young Adults," to be published.

who gathered in the day-room were a mixture of nurses, aides, psychiatrists, social workers, and psychologists. They were of different sexes, ages,
and races. I stood waiting for the group to settle down as they pulled up
chairs and arranged themselves. At that point a young patient wandered
into the room looking confused and uncertain. He wore striped pajamas
and a wrinkled bathrobe. A bearded staff member said to him, "You can't
come in now, Peter, this meeting is just for the staff." He took the young
man's arm and led him out of the room. When the staff member came
back, the staff gave a little laugh, sharing embarrassment at the intrusion.

I waited for everyone to get settled before I began to speak, and at that
point Peter wandered back into the room. The staff member stood up again
and said, "Peter, the group therapy meeting isn't until one o'clock. This is
a meeting of just the staff." He took the young man's arm and led him from
the room. When he came back, he smiled, and the people in the group
chuckled with him. As they all turned to me expectantly, Peter again wandered into the room. Everyone laughed out loud. Someone who seemed
to be in charge said to an aide, "Take him out." A large aide escorted Peter
out and then came back and sat down. The young man did not enter again.

As I looked over that group and thought about what had happened, I
was sure that my explanation of why Peter had made his entrances and
exits was different from that of the staff. Of course a range of explanations
is possible. The most common idea within a medical setting would be that
Peter was disoriented as to time and place and that he wandered almost
randomly into that particular room. An alternate explanation would be
that the young man's entrances were partly random but at least partly an
expression of hostility toward authority and therefore toward the staff who
symbolized authority. The strange costume which had been put on the
young man, as well as his confused and rather idiotic manner, would provoke most people to look on him in a patronizing, rather amused way.

Let me describe what I thought the young man did for me and the staff.
As I watched the staff gathering for the meeting that day, I sensed severe
bad feeling among the people there. Usually there is tension and covert
conflict among the people who work in a mental hospital, but it seemed
especially severe on this ward at that time. The staff were gathering reluctantly, and their manner expressed a distaste for me and for each other.
Obviously there were personal and factional conflicts among them, as anyone could see by their sullen behavior.

I felt the bad feeling of that group and became more and more reluctant
to lecture. I wondered what I might say to lighten the grim mood or relieve
the desperation. I knew there was nothing I could do.

At that point Peter began his entrances and exits. By his third arrival and
departure, everyone laughed, and the group had been transformed. They

were amused that a visiting speaker was delayed by Peter. Everyone was pulled together into a stable and amiable group by his actions. The dissension was no longer evident; everyone was friendly toward me and toward each other as we chatted together. I felt relieved to be talking with a pleasant group. Peter had done his job and did not need to return. He had done what neither I nor anyone on that staff could have done. The eccentric young man had brought order and some degree of harmony to an organization where there had been little or none. It is the argument of this book that the madness of young people has that function in mental hospitals and families.

It is best to assume that eccentric young people who stabilize a group by sacrificing themselves are doing so consciously and willingly. This assumption prevents a pointless attempt to give the eccentric person insight into what he or she is doing. He knows what he is doing and how he is doing it better than a therapist who might point it out to him. It is a sacrifice by a person who is willing to make a clown of himself, do himself harm, or do whatever is necessary to do his job. Attempting to persuade such a young eccentric to give up that sacrificial career typically fails. On rare occasions a therapist can simply persuade such a young person that the therapist knows the seriousness of the family situation and is competent to deal with it. The young person will become normal and leave his parents to the therapist. Only competent action causes such persuasion to occur, however, not talk or promises of trying to do one's best.

Deviant Communicative Behavior

One can become so fascinated or provoked by the strange movements, words, and behavior of young eccentrics that one overlooks their function and fails to focus on change. It should be kept in mind that distraction from family conflict is one of the purposes of such strange behavior. For a group to be stabilized by a deviant, the deviant must perform in such a way that his or her deviance is the focus of attention. If mildly eccentric behavior is not sufficient, the young person can threaten suicide or spread gasoline around the foundation of the house and play with matches, so that the group must organize in a functioning way to deal with him.

It would seem apparent that a group containing a young eccentric is not functioning well; otherwise a deviant would not be necessary. Often this is not immediately obvious. A daughter can be starving herself, and the family will arrive to see a therapist with a walking skeleton, presenting her as the problem. The parents and siblings appear to be reasonable people, sacrificing time and worry over their starving daughter. Yet it can be assumed as a fundamental premise that the organization of the family is malfunctioning, or the daughter would eat normally. One way to make this malfunctioning more evident is to have the parents require the daughter to eat. The situation changes from kindly parents and a compliant child into total confusion, with no one in charge except a screaming skeleton. Sometimes the nature of the organization's difficulties becomes apparent only when the young eccentric becomes more normal; in this case, when the young skeleton begins to eat and gain weight.

Although a scientific description of the deviant communicative behavior of a problem young person in the family is incredibly complex, a therapeutic description can be simplified. For therapeutic purposes, the behavior can be simplified into two main functions: (1) The social function: The young person stabilizes a group of intimates by his or her eccentric behavior. It is this function which is the main issue for therapeutic interventions. (2) The metaphoric function: Every deviant act is also a message to the members of the group and to outsiders. The act can be seen as a metaphor, often a parody, of a theme important to the group. Usually it is a group issue which is conflictual.

A young man who burns nail holes in his hands with cigarettes can be expressing something about religion in his family. A young man who puts a pan, given him to pee in, on his head as a hat is expressing something about a clown. The robot walk of an eccentric can indicate the group is too rigid in rules. A violent young person is signaling the issue of violence in the intimate group where he lives.

The metaphoric function of eccentric behavior is complex and often difficult to understand. Every act has multiple meanings, and one can overlook one significant message while emphasizing another. Verifying what the messages are about can be quite difficult, because inquiry and exploration of meaning are often not welcome to the family or staff group. The eccentric behavior typically expresses a theme which the group would rather deny and conceal. Group consensus to verify the meaning of a message is therefore not practical. The group usually responds to an inquiry with metaphor, which leads to more metaphor, and so on.

Just as the family does not welcome a translation of the message expressed by eccentric behavior, neither does the hospital staff nor the therapist. For example, an eccentric who randomly steals is likely to be in a family where covert dishonesty is occurring; the family members know what the young person's acts signify, even though they may protest that they do not. Usually family and staff would rather define eccentric behavior as meaningless and organically caused, because its meaning is not welcome to the group.

At one time it was thought important to explore the meaning of metaphoric behavior in the family. It now seems wiser not to do so. The metaphoric communication can be a problem to the therapist, since bringing out meanings that are not welcome to the family (or staff) will antagonize a group whose cooperation is needed to bring about change. It is therefore important that the therapist not point out what he thinks the meaning of the behavior is: everyone knows it in any case, so there is not much point in making it explicit. The wise therapist will receive the meanings and keep them courteously to himself as a guide for what is happening. If the therapist does this, the eccentric and the family will become clearer in guiding the therapist.

The metaphors also offer the therapist warnings about certain eventualities that might occur if change is threatened. For example, if a young person ineffectually attempts suicide so that it is called a "gesture," the therapist should take that gesture to mean that suicidal issues are relevant among the people in this family. If the young person is threatening to set the house on fire, there are explosive issues in that family.

Even though such guidance can be helpful, however, the primary concern of the therapist should not be these metaphoric issues, as would be the case if he or she were doing research. Even the act of exploring metaphoric meaning in order to verify an idea is likely to arouse a resistance which can cause therapeutic failure (this is why insightful interpretations or confrontations to face "reality" can be fatal to successful therapy).

Again, just because a message in the form of eccentric behavior may be helpful in stabilizing a group, the message is not one the group is going to want to have expressed in an explicit way. If a mother is having an affair which threatens her marriage, a daughter might express that theme by peculiarly seductive words and behavior. The parents would not like to have it pointed out that the behavior is relevant to mother's conduct. Similarly, if a young woman, when hospitalized, talks about an abortion in a delusional way, it may be relevant that she is from a Catholic family and that her mother is burdened by many children. It is best to assume that the family is aware of the meaning of the young woman's behavior and will not welcome the therapist's explaining what is "really" being said by the girl's act. Eccentric behavior is always both helpful and threatening, just as it often touches on themes of serious desperation in a comic way.

At times people have said that madness is something to be admired, or that the mad and eccentric are more creative and alive than other people. They are said to be the rebels in a repressive society. Some authorities have even said that the mad know more about the secret of life than other people do. Admiration of the mad is not part of the therapeutic approach recommended here. The mad are failures, and failure is not admirable. To encourage madness, as some enthusiasts do, is to encourage failure. Arranging a place where eccentric people can be eccentric does not lead to normality.

Granting that madness is not admirable, one can still acknowledge the interpersonal skill of many mad young people. Their skills had best be respected by the therapist or he will be made to look foolish. It is also best to assume that the mad act of a young eccentric is positive, in the sense that it is an attempt at something better. It is a struggle to get out of an impossible situation and take a step forward. The result may be disaster because of the response of the community, but one should give credit to the mad young person for attempting to better his or her lot and the lot of his or her family.

THE ISSUE OF RESPONSIBILITY

Where there is madness, there is irresponsible behavior, by definition. People are not doing what they should do, or are doing what they should not do, according to accepted rules of social conduct. What differentiates mad and eccentric behavior from other behavior is not only its extreme form but the indication that the person cannot help himself and is not responsible for his actions. This inability to help oneself is also communicated by the ways the continuing acts lead to repeated failure and misery. It is characteristic of problem young people that they do something that breaks social rules and then qualify the act with an indication that it is not their fault. The drug addict lives a deviant life and indicates that his compulsion forces him to these acts. It is not his responsibility because he cannot help himself. Similarly, the girl starving herself says she is not responsible because she has no appetite or is repelled by food. The eccentric thief steals what he does not need, indicating that he is helpless to stop.

The truly mad are most expert at doing something and qualifying it in a way that indicates they are not responsible for the act. Sometimes they indicate that they are not really themselves but someone else, or that the place and time are not what others say they are, and therefore the act is not their doing.[2] A young person can refuse to get a job and say it is because he has millions of dollars in funds hidden away; in this way he indicates that he does not know what he is doing.

For the therapist, it is important to acknowledge that a problem young person is behaving irresponsibly and must be required to take responsibility for his actions. It is equally important to note that the people around the eccentric are behaving irresponsibly. When there is nutty behavior, the eccentric will say it is not his fault because a voice from another planet told him to do it. The parents will each say they are not responsible because it

---

[2] For a description of schizophrenia from this point of view see J. Haley, *Strategies of Psychotherapy*, Grune & Stratton, New York, 1963.

is the fault of the other parent, or the influence of evil companions, or drugs, or heredity. The experts who are called in often blame the parents, or "illness," or genetics. They do not acknowledge that their interventions compound the problem. When the young person is locked up, the psychiatrist will deny responsibility for committing him, saying it is the judge who did it. The judge will say he is not responsible for giving a person an indefinite sentence because he must depend on the advice of the experts on mental illness. So no one takes responsibility for what has happened or for doing something about it.

When no one takes charge or assumes responsibility, it means that an organization is in confusion, with no hierarchy marking clear lines of authority. When the hierarchy of an organization is in confusion, mad and eccentric behavior occurs and is adaptive. The mad behavior will tend to stabilize the organization and clarify the hierarchy. When normality returns, the organization again enters confusion. To correct the mad behavior, it is necessary to correct the hierarchy of the organization so that the eccentric behavior is not necessary or appropriate.

STAGES OF THERAPY

Given this view of the problem, the therapy of young eccentrics can be outlined in the following stages:

1. When the young person comes to community attention, the experts must organize themselves in such a way that one therapist takes responsibility for the case. It is better not to have multiple therapists and modes of therapy. The therapist *must* be in charge of dosage of medication and, if possible, of institutionalization.

2. The therapist needs to gather the family for a first meeting. If the young person is living separately, even with a wife, he should be brought together with the family of origin. No blame should be placed on the parents. Instead, the parents (or mother and grandmother, or whoever it might be) should be put in charge of solving the young person's problem. They must be persuaded that they are the best therapists for the problem offspring. It is assumed that the members of the family are in conflict, and the child is expressing that. By being required to take charge and set the rules for the young person, the family members are communicating about the young person as usual, but in a positive way. Certain issues need to be clear:

a. The focus should be on the problem person and his behavior, not on a discussion of family relations. If the offspring is an addict, the family should focus on what is to happen if he ever takes the drug again; if mad and misbehaving, what they will do if he misbehaves again in the way that led to the hospital before.

b. The past, and past causes of the problem, are ignored, not explored. The focus is on what to do now.

c. It is assumed that the hierarchy in the family is in confusion. Therefore if the therapist, with his expert status, crosses the generation line and sides with the young person against the parents, he will make the problem worse. The therapist should side with the parents against the problem young person, even if this seems to be depriving him or her of individual choices and rights, and even if he or she seems too old to be made that dependent. If the young person does not like the situation, he or she can leave and become self-supporting. After the person is behaving normally, his or her rights can be considered.

d. Conflicts between the parents or among other family members are ignored and minimized, even if those involved bring them up, until the young person is getting back to normal. If the parents say they need help too, the therapist should say that that can be dealt with after their son or daughter is back to normal.

e. Everyone should expect the problem person to become normal and not excuse failure. The experts should indicate to the family that there is nothing wrong with the child and that he or she should behave like others of the same age. Medication should be eliminated as rapidly as possible. Going to work or school immediately should be expected, with no delay for day hospitalization or long-term therapy. It is going back to normal that brings about family crisis and change. It is the continuation of an abnormal situation that stabilizes the family in misery.

f. It is to be expected that as the young person becomes normal by going successfully to work or school or by making friends, the family will become unstable. The parents may threaten separation or divorce, and one or both may become disturbed. One of the reasons for the therapist fully siding with the parents at the first stage of therapy, even to the point of joining them against the child, is to be in a position to help them at this stage. If the therapist cannot help the parents, the problem young person will commit some mad act, and the family will stabilize around the young person and his eccentricity once again. Institutionalization needs to be prevented at this point to keep the cycle of home-to-institution-to-home from continuing. One way to put it is that the therapist replaces the young eccentric in the family, and the young person is then free to become normal and go about his business. The therapist must then either resolve the family conflict or move the young person out of that conflict so it will continue more directly and not through him. At that point the young person can continue to be normal.

3. The therapy should be an intense involvement and a rapid disengagement rather than regular interviews spanning years. As soon as change occurs, the therapist can begin to recess and plan termination. The task is not to resolve all family problems, only the organizational ones around the problem young person, unless the family wants to make a new contract for other problems.

4. The therapist should occasionally check with the family to follow up what has happened and ensure that positive change continues.

In essence, the therapy approach is like an initiation ceremony. The procedure helps parents and offspring disengage from each other so that the family does not need the young person as a communication vehicle, and the young person establishes a life of his or her own. Two extremes have often failed. Blaming the parents as a noxious influence and sending the young person away from his family typically fails. The young person collapses and comes back home. The opposite extreme—keeping the young person at home and attempting to bring about harmony between child and parents—also fails. This is not a time of coming together but a time of disengagement. The art of the therapy is to bring the young person back within the family as a way of disengaging him or her for a more independent life.

A therapist can define the simple goal outlined here if he or she is able to think in simple organizational terms. Achieving the goal can be a complex endeavor and requires all the skill and support the therapist can develop.

Chapter 3

Social Control and Therapy

When young people are put in institutions, they have in common the fact that they are failures. They are not succeeding in work or school and must be supported. However, the problem they present when they come to community attention is not that of failure. They are locked up because they disturb the public with behavior that indicates hallucinations or delusions, take heroin or other illegal drugs, steal or otherwise break the law, or because their parents say they cannot control them. Some of them threaten to harm themselves or others, and some behave in lost, neglected, and helpless ways. All of them require that the community do something about them. The people who take that action are agents of social control, such as the police and the people who work in medical and psychiatric centers.

When a therapist takes on a severely disturbed young person, he usually finds agents of social control in charge. Doing therapy with mad young people means continually dealing with issues of custody, restraint, and medication. A major aspect of the therapy is negotiating with colleagues in social control settings, such as psychiatric hospitals, drug rehabilitation centers, halfway houses, jails, and juvenile halls. Problems can arise between the therapist who wishes to change people and the social control agents whose job it is to quiet, reform, custodize, or eliminate those people who offend society.

Young people are ingenious in finding ways to be deviant and live marginal lives, but relatively few of them make enough difficulty to announce their presence to social control agents or therapists. These young people are generally put in one of two legal categories: they are either defined as criminals or labeled "mentally ill." The criminal offenders have committed some delinquent act and are put in custody for the good of the community, although it is also argued that custody has some rehabilitative purpose. The medical offenders called mentally ill are of two types: either they are troublemakers whose families cannot manage them, or they do nothing to support themselves and their families give up taking care of them. People are not usually put in mental hospitals because they have symptoms such as delusions and hallucinations, but because they make trouble or are apathetic and will not take care of themselves. In recent years the diagnosis of "manic-depressive" has become fashionable, possibly because there is now a treatment—lithium—that has been partially successful with some depressed people. Young people who are in this category manage to be at two extremes: they are troublemakers when manic and apathetic when depressed.

The legal offender and the medical offender are not clearly different kinds of people with different behavior. Sometimes the behavior is so similar that it is a mystery how one career was chosen rather than another. Often it seems to be the social situation rather than the acts of a person which determines whether he is called a criminal or a lunatic. A policeman may decide the category of the person by where he takes him for custody, and sometimes family and police collaborate. Often the choice is based on social class; the wealthy are more likely to be classed in the psychiatric domain while the poor become part of the criminal system. If a young person steals a car, it can be either a criminal offense or a symptom of "poor impulse control," depending on the wealth of the offender's family. There are also borderline instances where it is a toss-up whether the problem is criminal or medical, as in the case of drug and alcohol abuse.

One of the curious differences between the diagnoses of "criminal" and "mad" is the idea that a criminal is responsible for what he does and makes a free choice to misbehave. Even if he wastes his life going in and out of jail, that must be considered a rational decision; otherwise there is no point to a legal system that assumes he made crime a choice. He deliberately does his criminal acts; therefore his punishment is deserved. The staff of a prison can be severe with prisoners with an easier conscience than the staff of a mental hospital. The "mentally ill" are said not to be able to help what they do. When a patient misbehaves in a mental hospital, the staff can only punish him reluctantly, under the guise of help, since they define themselves as healers as well as community protectors. Drugs, shock treatment, deep brain probes, and lobotomies are always considered medical treatment, and it is denied that they are used for disciplinary purposes.

Because of the theory that the criminal made a conscious choice of what he did, penology professionals do not welcome traditional therapists. Therapy concerned with "unconscious" processes seems unwelcome among the keepers of criminals. They consider it their job to persuade the felon to misbehave no more; therefore they focus him on work or school. They are also usually reluctant to involve the criminal's family in a meaningful way. They prefer to believe that he made his own choice rather than that the crime resulted from difficulty in a family.

The criminal offender is usually tried in a law court under rules which society developed to protect both the community and the offender. When someone is defined as ill or mad, the task of the community is more complicated. Custody is used, as with criminals, but there are also chemical restraints in the form of medication. The dilemma is that something must be done about someone who makes the kind of trouble that does not allow a legal trial and sentence. The rules of justice are not easily applied when it is not clear that a crime was committed or when sanctions like those brought against criminals do not seem appropriate. If a young person strolls around a neighborhood in the nude singing nonsense verses, the police will be called and are likely to take him to a psychiatric hospital. The young person can be held in the hospital for what amounts to an indefinite sentence and might spend his or her life in custody essentially for being a public nuisance. A therapist who attempts to do something about the young person and his or her family must deal with social control agents, who have the responsibility for seeing that he or she does not bother the community again. The psychiatrists, nurses, aides, and social workers in the institution have their ways of dealing with the problem young person; a therapist oriented to the family has quite another way. Often the confusion between social control procedures and therapeutic acts causes conflict among the professionals in dealing with each other. Just as family members will struggle with each other over who is right and who is wrong in dealing with a mad offspring, so will professionals quarrel when they take on the problem. Success in therapy can be determined at least as much by what happens among professional colleagues as by what happens within the family.

The problems facing therapists in this situation can be described in terms of both the institutions they must deal with and the premises and theories evident in the community control approach.

Social Control Institutions

Therapists have different problems with different institutions. As a general rule, the more removed the institution from the community, the more difficult the therapeutic task.

The most impossible place to attempt therapy is in a total institution where an offender is completely removed from the community. Except in large cities, these places are usually isolated from the community and far from the family and friends of the inmate. A socially oriented therapy is not practical in the abnormal situation of total custody. It can begin only at the point when the offender is being released.

Just as penitentiaries are usually far from the community, so are mental hospitals. These hospitals are usually large places where those unwanted by society are kept. Contemporary ideas enter with difficulty because of the size and rigidity of the staff. The institution tends to be staffed by professionals who are trained to work in hospitals and do not understand the point of doing therapy in the community. The emphasis is on persuading patients to join the culture of the hospital. Such a goal can be irrelevant to the ways the person must behave in ordinary life. A staff can forget, or never clearly understand, that the task is to change the person in the community where his problem is. Many of us used to sit and talk to patients in mental hospitals several times a week, for years, with the idea that the talk would somehow make them better able to live outside the hospital in the community. We had the idea that if we said the right things (those that gave insight and a corrected emotional experience) the person would go off and live a normal life.

As another illustration of the withdrawal from reality by the staff in mental hospitals, I recall two residents who reported to a staff meeting about the way they had established a therapeutic community on a ward. They discussed what they did, how the staff responded, the democratic processes, and so on. During the discussion period, someone asked them if more patients had been discharged from the ward since the therapeutic community was established. There was a silence, and the two young men looked stunned. It was not merely that they did not have the discharge figures; the idea had simply never occurred to them. Their actions on the ward were not in the context of the hospital as a place to change the ways people lived in the community.

Although mental hospitals are making brave attempts to reform and develop new approaches, they are hampered by the vast inertia which characterizes any large bureaucracy. For several years more contemporary psychiatrists have been attempting to involve families in the admission and discharge of mental patients, so that the life situations of the patients are brought into the hospitals.[1] One can watch such an attempt begin, and then vanish when its proponents leave that institution. The ward often returns to a traditional mode that has existed for a hundred years.

---

[1]   Henry Harbin, "A Family-Oriented Psychiatric In-patient Unit," *Fam. Proc.*, 18: 281–291, 1979.

In recent years the state hospital population has been reduced as mental health centers have developed in the community and chemical restraints have been more widely used. At times the attempt to empty the hospitals has been a misfortune. People who were chronic cases, in that they had been locked up for years, were suddenly dumped into the community. They were often exploited, and some were incapable of caring for themselves, particularly when heavily dosed with medication. If clinicians were specially trained to return people to the community after years of institutional life, the task would be difficult enough; not to have trained clinicians and simply to put people out is inexcusable. I recall doing therapy with patients who had been locked up ten years or more. Their social inexperience was immediately evident when they went outside the hospital. For example, one man had not ordered a meal from a menu in a restaurant for ten years and approached the task with uncertainty, if not panic.

The inability to function in the community after being locked up is not necessarily related to "mental illness." A convict released from prison after twenty years is often a lost soul in the community, without family or friends, and he can seek to return to the institution.

The state mental hospital is hardly defensible as a form of therapy[2] but it is also not defensible to release chronic mental patients into the community without guidance. A basic goal is to succeed in therapy with young people to avoid locking them up, so that twenty hears later they will not be social misfits unable to live in the community.

An important difference for therapists between the criminal and the medical offender is that criminals do not voluntarily go into custody (unless one defines a badly carried-out crime as a search for custody). They are sentenced by the court. Medical offenders are classed in two categories: the involuntary and the voluntary. The involuntary class includes people committed by the state on the advice of psychiatrists. The line between involuntary and voluntary patients, as well as between open and closed wards, is not always clear, but the distinction is important to a therapist attempting to cooperate with a hospital. Locked custody tends to embarrass psychiatrists; thus a pretense can develop that it is not happening. The therapist attempting to deal with a patient in a hopsital must also deal with the pretense.

Both the legal and medical systems have experimented with part-time custody as a means of creating a better relationship between institution and community. Inmates in prison spend their nights in jail and work in

[2] Assembly Interim Committee on Ways and Means, California Legislature, *The Dilemma of Mental Commitments in California: A Background Document*, Subcommittee on Mental Health Services, California, 1967.

the community during the day. Psychiatric institutions do the opposite; people are kept in the hospital during the day and sent to their homes at night. This keeps them occupied in something that is not self-supporting during the day, in contrast to the prison program, which involves inmates in normal work or school.

Another alternative to total custody is the halfway house, which is used in both the criminal and psychiatric systems. These are places where the person can recover from being in a total institution and slowly integrate into normal living again. Sometimes it is forgotten that they are halfway houses, and they become dead-end houses for some of the inmates, who become part of the culture and never quite return to normal community living.

Sometimes without custody, and often after it, the criminal offender is placed in the community under supervision. He is watched for a period of time, and if he avoids trouble he is set free. Medical offenders are on "parole" in visits home with their families and in trial visits before release. If the misbehavior recurs, the person is placed back in full-time custody.

Private Mental Hospitals

In the medical offender category there is a special class of institution which is a private enterprise. The criminal class does not enjoy private prisons, but the medical offender can be placed in a private hospital. These places tend to be for the rich who can pay high rates, or for those with appropriate medical insurance. Families feel less guilty about placing an offspring in a private hospital than in a public institution, because they feel he or she will be better cared for and because they will have more influence if they are paying the bill. A typical way for a family to stabilize is by paying someone else to restrain the problem young person, preferably somewhere far out in the country.

University Psychiatric Wards

Criminology departments in universities have not been allowed to have private prisoners in order to train staff to work with felons in a private place on campus. University departments of psychiatry, however, have been allowed to arrange a place for inmates for training purposes. These are private institutions, yet they are public in that the training is often funded by the government, or the universities are state supported. Usually the staff holds patients on a voluntary basis, but they can also use legal custody procedures. When the patients fail in such training institutions, the state mental hospitals receive them.

Unfortunately, training needs sometimes determine whether custody occurs or not. University wards, private hospitals, and state hospitals need a certain number of inmates for their training programs and to meet their overhead. When there are not enough patients, it can be decided that the ones currently available need total custody. In private hospitals, a public relations task is often done to persuade families to pay for the custody and therapy of a family member for as long as three years, which happens to be the time the residents need to train in doing "deep" therapy with the inmates. The financial condition of families and the insurance limits tend to set the length of hospitalization and the "depth" of therapy.

Psychiatrists and staff in hospitals do not like to think of themselves as agents of social control, but rather as healers of the sick. Their problems come when financial needs or community pressures require them to heal the sick whether the sick wish it or not. While accepting the burden, the psychiatric profession expresses the idea that they would rather not have responsibility for the marginal people of society. For humanitarian reasons, however, they would rather not let anyone else have that burden. Often they feel misunderstood, since they think of themselves as having the difficult task of dealing with mad people who threaten suicide or other violence, police who insist that something must be done, families who want members locked up, patients who insist there is nothing wrong with them, and civil libertarians and sociologists who are shocked at the conditions in hospitals and call them psychiatric penitentiaries. To be both a healer of the sick and a jailer is stressful and paradoxical, and the psychiatric profession suffers as much as it benefits from its obligations. It is a mad world inside the ward for both staff and patients.

Premises of Social Control

By definition, an agent of social control has the task of bringing peace to the community. Whether the agent acts in a kind and humane way or ruthlessly, when he is removing a troublemaker to protect the community, the primary goal is the peace of the neighborhood.

Certain assumptions are expectable in agents of social control. First of all, they assume that the problem is an individual rather than a social situation. The psychiatric diagnostic categories and the criminal classification system contain no social units larger than a person. If a whole family erupts into violence, or both spouses in a married couple act strangely, one person is typically selected to be diagnosed and quieted by custody or drugs. To put more than one family member in custody is unusual, just as medicating a whole family is unusual. The system is built on the idea that the source of trouble in a community is a troublemaker.

Generally social control agents not only focus on an individual but are also antifamily. Sometimes the relatives are just ignored, and so the consequences of social control action on the total family group are not noticed. A person will be plucked out of his family and hospitalized without any concern for what happens to that family when it loses a member, even temporarily. Or such agents will heavily medicate a troublesome woman without considering the effect on the way she raises her children. A man will be medicated so that he will quiet down and cause his wife less trouble; what will be ignored is that the medication can have unpredictable effects and cause him to be unresponsive in a way that gives him more difficulty with his wife.

Social control agents often assume the family is the noxious influence that caused the problem. Typically they are rescuers of family "victims." The antifamily stance of many drug rehabilitation centers is partly due to the fact that some of the staff are ex-addicts who are in difficulty with their own families and who therefore do not welcome family participation in therapy. They prefer therapy groups of peers, such as fellow addicts, rather than of relatives.

There are also psychiatrists who join families against eccentric offspring, assuming an organic or hereditary cause, who therefore do not blame the parents for poor parenting. They tend to sympathize with parents for having a child who will always be defective.

In summary, agents of social control represent the community, and their primary job is to do something to quiet troublemakers and other social deviants. Only secondarily is it their task to help the deviant. They tend to identify one person rather than a social situation as the problem, and they ignore the family or consider it a noxious influence. These premises, and the institutions which develop from them, handicap a therapist who seeks to bring about change.

Difference Between Therapy and Social Control

The goal of a therapist is to introduce more complexity into people's lives, in the sense that he breaks up repetitive cycles of behavior and brings about new alternatives. He does not wish to have a problem person simply conform, but wants to place in that person's hands the initiative to come up with new ideas and acts that the therapist might not have even considered. In that sense the therapist encourages unpredictability. The therapeutic job is to bring about change, and therefore new, often unanticipated, behavior.

The social control agent has quite the opposite goal. His task is to stabilize people for the community, thus he seeks to reduce unpredictability. He wants problem people to behave in expectable ways, like others in the community, so that no one is upset by them. It is not change and new behavior that he seeks, but rather stability and no complaints from citizens.

There is inevitably a conflict between a therapist whose job it is to encourage people to behave in new ways and a social controller who wants them to behave according to society's rules in predictable ways. The therapist needs to take risks, while the social controller wants to reduce risks. When the therapist says, "Let us take this person out of custody, off medication, and back into the community," the social controller says, "Let us not be irresponsible, let us proceed with caution." Since there is a time and tide in the therapeutic enterprise, and the therapist must take advantage of timing, caution is not always welcome. Often there is an optimum moment when parents will accept an offspring back home or when a job opportunity arises, and the therapy can fail if action is not taken then.

A therapist needs flexibility in other ways. If medication is used, it is best to be free to give or withhold it, to change it, to use placebos, to medicate more than one family member, and so on. Medication should be part of the strategy of change, as should any form of restraint. If medication is used only to quiet someone, or because there is an administrative or ideological rule that such a person must always be medicated (or medicated for set periods of months), the therapy is in trouble. A typical situation is one where parents want the young person medicated because they cannot agree on how to control him. If the psychiatrist medicates because the parents want the young person quieted, it is different from medicating for strategic reasons; for example, as part of a bargain that the parents will cooperate in therapy.

Therapists need flexibility, whether it is in moving someone in and out of custody or on and off medication. The social controller feels a different responsibility. He does not wish to let a mad young person out of custody or off medication prematurely. The problem for the therapist is that cautious delay stabilizes the social situation and prevents change, because the family and community organize around the young person as an invalid, which makes the therapist's work more difficult. The longer he or she is in custody and treatment, the more the young person settles into the career of a mental patient, not only within his family but also with the deviants he associates with in treatment settings. There is also a stigma attached to anyone institutionalized; this affects job applications and school acceptance. The prophecy of social controllers that a person is handicapped and must remain in custody or on medication for life is often fulfilled by the "treatment," which socially handicaps the person for life. In time a mad young person becomes a professional patient just as other people become professional criminals. Institutionalization becomes his or her career.

Conversely, according to social controllers, some therapists rush too quickly into the normal situation, causing a relapse and making life more difficult for the patient and family. There must be rehospitalization, additional expense, and more time away from the ultimate job or school. The therapist in turn argues that sometimes a relapse is a necessary part of the therapy. When a young person improves after a first offense, it does not mean that he will stay normal. As the problems in his family increase, he may relapse. If the family is helped to solve its problems at that point without social control, it is able to reorganize so that further relapses are unnecessary. Change, in the sense of getting past a stage of development, can be prevented by interventions intended to avoid relapses.

Another difference between therapists and social controllers is that the social controller welcomes other helpers, while many therapists do not. The therapist must deal with a problem young person's family, which can be difficult. If custody is used, he must also deal with the people in the institution. He has trouble both in getting the experts out of the situation and in getting the person back into community life in a normal situation. The social controller prefers to isolate the problem person from the community, and he values custody as a way of dealing with the person without family interference. He also welcomes all other experts, whether they are doctors, nurses, group therapists, art therapists, or any other experts who are willing to work in the hospital setting.

The attitudes of the therapist and the social controller differ in one other way. The person in a social control setting tends to develop a pessimism about anything being done with problem young people. He lives constantly with failures, seeing the recidivists who fail again and again. In that situation, one loses hope that anything can be done and welcomes a physiological theory that assures one the failure is not one's doing. The therapist, in contrast, has sufficient success so that he has hopes of improvement and looks forward to the possibility of normal behavior in problem young people. The therapist becomes exasperated with pessimists, since it is only people with hope who take those extra actions that sometimes make the difference between success and failure.

A Classification of Social Controllers

Although contemporary psychiatry and modern criminology argue that great advances have been made and that changes have taken place in the problems of institutions, a few people still feel that there is a quality of being back with the dinosaurs when dealing with social control. In that sense a classification is possible, which ranges from social controllers who are the most old-fashioned and difficult to deal with to the more modern staff members of institutions.

Pithecanthropus   The most extreme form of social controller is the psychiatrist or penologist who accepts the premise that a problem young person has a physiological defect. This type argues that the problem is genetic, therefore nothing can be done. Worse, they implicitly suggest that nothing *should* be done. The problem persons should be in custody where they will not breed and reproduce their kind. If forced by civil libertarians to release a person, this type prefers incapacitating medications, or, as Gregory Bateson put it, "chronic intoxication by chemotherapy." When a young woman was recently rehospitalized after a number of previous stays in that mental hospital, the doctor there said that she really should kill herself and get it over with. He expressed a typical view of the Pithecanthropus. This type has a similar theory about criminals, namely, criminal behavior has a physiological cause and is unchangeable. Attempts at rehabilitation are therefore pointless.

Therapists should avoid dealing with the Pithecanthropus and not attempt negotiations. To educate them is impossible. One can only do one's best to keep people out of their hands.

The Cro-Magnon   This type assumes there is a genetic defect, and quite probably lifelong custody will be necessary. They also try to be more liberal, however, and suggest that perhaps in some cases there was really a miserable infantile experience that has scarred the person forever. This type is willing to release an inmate if he or she is heavily medicated. Reducing the medication is against his philosophy. Even when it is pointed out that the medication causes irreversible neurological damage, the Cro-Magnon says that that is better than life in the hospital; besides, the person is already physiologically damaged anyhow because of the genetic defect. This type will allow a therapist a chance to prove that therapy is pointless, but at crucial moments, such as when custody or medication is the issue, will prevent change. Therapists should avoid this type if possible, but when they must be dealt with, it is important to listen to them and appear naïve, so that they will let the therapist have a chance "to find himself wrong."

The Ancient   This type always says there is probably a physiological or genetic cause for a severe disturbance in a young person, but he also likes to feel there is an intrapsychic cause, such as an Oedipal problem. He does conversational therapy inside an institution. The therapy is expected to take many years. Sometimes it is estimated that the therapy required for recovery takes as many years as the person is old when he or she enters the institution. Therefore, twenty years of therapy for a twenty-year-old is likely to be done. This type assumes that the problems can be solved in the institution, and only after the person is normal for a long time will he or she be discharged. Usually this type inhabits expensive private institutions where he or she does therapy with problem persons from rich families. In past times they avoided the use of drugs, but now they use medications to "make the person accessible to therapy" whenever the person makes trouble on the wards of the institution.

Usually a therapist with a family orientation is not involved with this type, since they inhabit hospitals in out-of-the-way places. Claiming a client from one is difficult because the institution's solvency is at stake if the patients begin to leave and return to their families in the community.

The Pragmatist   This type is quite common in the modern psychiatric hospital and essentially has no theory. He believes his teachers when they say there may be a genetic or biological cause to a problem, but he also believes his analyst who says the problem might be psychodynamic, and he likes an interpersonal theory that says a person's peers are important, and to keep up to date he reads a book on family therapy so he can talk about that if the subject comes up. Generally, in action, he simply medicates people and turns them out of the hospital as soon as he can. If they come back, he increases the medication and sends them off again, until ultimately they can hardly walk because they are so full of drugs. Mad behavior is a mystery to this type and, as with any mystery, superstition sometimes takes over. So he tries magic periods of time, such as three months' hospitalization before discharge, or six months on medication no matter what changes. Usually this type has been taught nothing in psychiatric training other than to listen to patients, encourage them to talk about anything, and make sure they take their medication.

This is the most helpful type of person in authority for a therapist to deal with. He will let a therapist take on a problem person as long as it does not make trouble for him or ask anything in particular of him.

Although these types of social control agents inhabit psychiatric hospitals and prisons, that does not mean there are not also therapists in such places. Many psychiatrists work with problem persons in the context of their families; they do not merely hope that a pill will solve human problems. Many social workers, psychologists, and nurses also have a therapeutic rather than a social control view, whether they work in hospitals or prisons. Total institutions, however, can organize everyone's behavior in unfortunate ways. Just as parents find themselves acting in nontherapeutic ways without wanting to, so can staff members find themselves acting in nontherapeutic ways without wanting to. Psychiatrists in particular can be forced into social control postures when that is their least interest. I recall one young psychiatrist who left a city and sought a job far away because he could not find employment other than the kind which forced him to give regular doses of medication to unfortunate people without doing anything else for them.

A therapist can be tempted to struggle against people in a hospital in order to save a problem person from agents of social control, but that is an error. To negotiate and clarify who is in charge is essential; to use the person as an excuse for a quarrel with a colleague, or to prove a point to him, produces the same kinds of conflicts as those in the family, where members attempt to save the problem offspring from other members. Such conflict can create the problem the therapist is supposed to solve.

INCREASING THE PROBABILITY OF SUCCESS

Therapy with difficult families not only requires skill, it requires a situation which makes success probable. Certain circumstances increase the chance of success with a problem young person and are more important than chronicity or length of hospitalization:

1. With inmates in custody, a therapist should not begin therapy if there are no plans for immediate discharge. There have been many years of failure with inpatient therapy. To bring in the family once a week to talk with their incarcerated child in family interviews is not only untherapeutic, it can be pointlessly painful.

2. With inmates in custody, the therapist should have power from the upper administration to establish a therapeutic plan. It is best to respect the hierarchy in any organization. The lower-echelon people will cooperate when the upper administration approves.

3. Part of the plan for an inmate should be a discharge date set by a therapist and the family. Discharge should not be based on a ward rule, a set sentence, or a committee made up of the various in-house therapies. Ideally the therapist should be able to ask the parents to decide when to take their offspring home. That gives them the power in the situation in the view of the offspring, and they start with an advantage in their plan to take more charge of the young eccentric at home.

4. The therapist who begins therapy with the family inside the institution should carry on after discharge to the community. A change of therapists from inpatient to outpatient is often a problem. The family needs the support of the therapist who lays the plans out with them and follows through with them to success.

5. The therapist needs to control medication. Either the therapist must be a physician who can himself medicate, or the therapist needs a physician available who will medicate according to the needs of the particular therapy and its stages rather than according to some ideological dream.

6. The therapist needs to control rehospitalization. There should be cooperation from institutions not to rehospitalize without clearance with the therapist. If the family is to contain the problem and solve it, they should not be able to stabilize easily by hospitalization.

7. No other therapists should be involved with the family without the permission of the primary therapist. The family should not be pulled in different directions by different experts.

In summary, what is needed is simple: the therapist needs to be in charge so that no one in the family is placed in an institution and nothing is injected into a family member without permission. To put the family in charge, the therapist must be in charge of the family in the professional community.

A final case example illustrates one of the wrong ways for a therapist to deal with a fellow professional in power in a social control setting.

A twenty-one-year-old woman was hospitalized on a university psychiatric ward after she made an ineffectual suicide attempt. After two weeks in the hospital, a social worker therapist took charge of the case and met with the family to make plans with them for taking her home. The first family interview involved twelve people, including siblings and more remote relatives. The family agreed that she should go back to college immediately while living at home. They chose the following Friday as the day of discharge. The social worker thought she had administrative approval for this plan. At this point, however, a first-year psychiatric resident, recently put in charge of the ward, entered the picture. He declined to allow the patient to be discharged, saying that it was up to him, not the family, to decide when the girl should return home, and he felt she should stay in the hospital. He was not concerned about the threat of suicide. His objection was that the young woman refused to talk to him in her individual therapy interviews. She also would not participate properly in the group therapy and other treatment programs of the ward.

The social worker asked her supervisor to sit down with the resident and discuss the problem. They sat together and the young psychiatrist was adamant. He said the woman would not be discharged until she was willing to talk with him and to participate in ward activities. He offered the Catch-22 argument, namely, that only if she admitted she needed to be in the hospital would she be allowed to leave; if she did not think she belonged there, she would have to stay. The resident was rather supercilious and made it clear that his status in the situation gave him the power to determine what was to happen.

The supervisor became exasperated with what seemed an improper interference with a carefully made therapeutic plan. He advised the social worker to drop the case and obtain a different one from a different ward. The social worker canceled the therapy, and the young woman was discharged a few weeks later without a plan. The parents were uncertain about whether they would put her in the state mental hospital.

This example illustrates the basic dilemma of the therapist who must deal with colleagues who have social control power. To agree with their position can cause the therapy to fail. Yet to disagree and struggle against them produces the same kind of organizational conflicts one is trying to change in the family. The unit for the therapist dealing with problem young people consists of the family *and* the professionals involved. The therapist must be as patient and ingenious in dealing with his colleagues as he is in dealing with difficult families. It is incorrect to get angry at a powerful grandmother and provoke her to pull the family out of therapy; that is also true about provoking a colleague with power.

In the case of this resident who would not release the young woman until she would talk with him, the villain in the situation was not the young resident. The fault was with the supervisor, who became irritated with the resident for not cooperating after the first steps with a family had been successfully taken. The supervisor, who was myself, could probably have persuaded the resident to release the young woman or could have exerted authority to have him do so, even if she wouldn't speak to him. Looking back now with a more objective view, I can see that I lost sight of the fact that the unit of therapy included not only the young woman and her family but the ward staff and myself as well. Not only was I irritated and impatient with the interference, but I fear I was also using the young woman to prove a point to the resident. It was the young woman who lost. If I had behaved more responsibly, there would have been less risk that she might ultimately spend her life in a state hospital. Professional experts have the responsibility to avoid conflicts among themselves which are similar to those in which families are involved. It should be kept constantly in mind that a major function of mad young people, whether within the family or among professionals, is to be a vehicle of struggle and to be sacrificed.

Chapter 4

The Therapist
Support System

When dealing with the family of a mad young person, a therapist should assume that the members of the family are likely to be more interpersonally skillful than he is. The therapist can increase his chances of success by arranging a setting that gives him an advantage. Ideally the setting should be a one-way-mirror room with a knowledgeable supervisor watching and telephoning in suggestions. The use of videotape allows the interviews to be studied at leisure so that issues can be clarified and strategies planned.

The professional setting of the therapist, particularly his supervisory relationship, is of basic importance. There is a reciprocal relation between the supervisory structure and the family structure. If the authority relationship between supervisor and therapist is clear, the hierarchy in the family will be more easily restructured. When the family heirarchy is in particular confusion, as it is with madness, it is especially important that the hierarchical arrangement of supervisor and therapist is clear and firm.

Although it is often emphasized in the field that the important aspect of a therapist's support system is his personal life, that is not emphasized in this work. Presumably any person does better work if he has a stable personal life. If his personal life interferes with his work, he must deal with it. Granted that some therapists, like other people, need therapy when they are in trouble, I do not think it should be assumed that personal therapy will improve a therapist's ability to do therapy. I do not know of any research evidence that suggests that a therapist achieves better results if he has had personal therapy. In fact, my experience is that the therapists who have had the most personal therapy are often the most difficult to train to do effective therapy, since they are so wrapped up in their own personal affairs. The therapist support system emphasized here is the professional situation, not the personal one.

Cotherapy

Some therapists believe that they receive support from a cotherapist and that mad families are so difficult that more than one therapist is necessary. Various arguments are offered, ranging from the idea that cotherapists support each other and exchange ideas, to the notion that cotherapist arguments are good for a family to observe, to Carl Whitaker's idea that, with two therapists, one can administrate while the other can be as extreme as the family.

There are several objections to the use of cotherapists from the point of view of this work, in addition to the fact that the cost is twice as high and, according to outcome reports, the outcome is no better than with a single therapist. The primary one is in relation to the skill of the family. With cotherapy the family has a relationship to deal with, and it is in the relationship area that they are expert. It is not merely that they have two people to influence rather than one, but that variations increase geometrically with two experts in relation to each other, particularly when there is an ambiguous hierarchical relationship between them.

With one therapist, there is typically a single supervisor. With two therapists, each one often has a supervisor (and there is sometimes a supervisor for the case as well). Typically, cotherapists are of different professions, as are their supervisors. The supervisors often have an ambiguous hierarchical relationship between them, such as that between a psychiatrist and social work supervisor. Conflicts in the family can be a reflection of conflicts between cotherapists, which can be a reflection of conflicts between their supervisors. The professional network is as complex as the extended family network in relation to the case. Opportunities for misinformation and manipulation abound as people with power multiply.

Cotherapy is usually done for the comfort of the therapist, rather than for the need of the family. Should a therapist really find company necessary, it is always possible to place a fellow therapist behind a mirror to observe. Sometimes the person can be introduced at the beginning of therapy, and the family can be told that he or she will be out of the room most of the time. Then he or she can enter and assist, or stay out, depending on how well the in-room therapist is doing.

Colleagues or a supervisor behind a one-way mirror are valuable as consultants for difficult problems. They can help plan a strategy. They also give the therapist a base from which to orient himself in contrast to the sometimes bizarre ideas in the therapy room. Still, when the therapist works alone in the room, he has the advantage that he can give a directive without delay. He can make use of ideas that arise immediately out of the action and do what needs to be done at an appropriate time without hesitation.

Supervision

The task of a teaching supervisor is not only to help the therapist succeed with a particular family but also to teach a way of doing therapy. Often therapists have ideological backgrounds from previous training which interfere with their attempts to do successful therapy. A supervisor cannot always discover what a therapist's ideology is by talking with him. What he says and what he actually does during therapy can be quite different, just as what a family member says occurs in his family and what can be observed are often quite different. A therapist needs to observe a family to see what happens in their interaction, and a supervisor needs to watch a therapist in action to determine what his ideas are and how he operates.

Conversations between therapists and supervisors will be presented here to illustrate the supervisory process. These conversations took place just before the first interview with a family as part of a planning session. In the first example, the supervisor and therapist did not know each other except as acquaintances in the same clinic. The therapist, Dr. Gary Lande, was a psychiatrist in training as a child fellow at that time. Supervisor and therapist become acquainted by talking about the family and planning the general approach. Their working relationship occurs in relation to the particular family they must deal with rather than in relation to general ideas about therapy. The conversation reported here is verbatim, with occasional cuts and editing to eliminate redundancies and irrelevant matter.

HALEY: The girl is now in the hospital?
LANDE: She's been hospitalized for the past two weeks.

HALEY: What was she put in for? Do you know?
LANDE: Talking crazy, delusions. She believed the doctors had two of her fetuses locked up someplace and weren't letting her have them. She was hearing voices, I believe.
HALEY: She was making trouble of some kind.
LANDE: Yes. She had the parents pretty upset.

The destination of the therapy will be determined by the choice of problem, and the problem of the girl could be described in many different ways. Certain information that might be relevant for a diagnostician or a researcher is not relevant to a therapist and can even be a handicap. When the therapist mentions delusions and hallucinations, there might be a discussion of their nature and meaning. This would be a supervisory error. Discussing the problem in that way can orient the therapist to thinking in that way. With such ideas prominent in his mind, he can greet the girl thinking of her as a mental case with delusions and hallucinations. He is likely then to think that the problem is her and that she is a defective person, which could cause him to underestimate her interpersonal skills. If one wants to place the problem within the family, it must be defined as a problem the family can deal with. A "troublemaking" problem is something the parents can do something about. Hallucinations and delusions must be the domain of "mental health experts" rather than of the family. One can incapacitate the parents as authorities over their offspring by how one defines the problem that is to be resolved. In this case the supervisor emphasizes the trouble the daughter causes, and the therapist responds appropriately to that orientation.

It is also important to note that the query about why the young woman was put in custody is the only mention of her past history in this conversation. When the supervisor shows no interest in the past, the therapist too is helped to show a concern only with the present when he deals with the family. The conversation continues:

HALEY: And she is how old?

LANDE: Eighteen.

HALEY: She is in what position in the family?

LANDE: From what I can understand, there are two older children. I think the oldest must be twenty-one. I'm not sure where they're living or what the situation is. The youngest is in second grade—about seven or eight.

HALEY: There are how many?

LANDE: I think seven children.

HALEY: They're all supposed to show? (*At the interview.*)

LANDE: I asked them to come.

Although an interview must be conducted to determine the family structure, sometimes one can guess the type of structure on the basis of general information. Given the position of this young woman in the family, it is possible that she is in the position of a "parental child." This is a child who is neither of the parent's generation nor allowed to be of the child's generation because she is burdened with the care of younger children.[1] Caught

[1] See S. Minuchin, B. Montalvo, B. Guerney, B. L. Rosman, and F. Schumer, *Families of the Slums*, Basic Books, New York, 1967.

in the difficult position of having responsibility for but no power over younger children, the parental child sometimes develops symptoms. Such a position indicates that one or both parents are abdicating responsibility, or that the parents are so divided that they can offer no leadership, and they impose too great a burden on the daughter. In this case the daughter's position as a parental child seemed evident from the behavior of the children in the first interview. The siblings had not seen her for two weeks, because children are not allowed on a psychiatric ward. The way the little children greeted this problem daughter indicated a probable parental child position. The conversation continues:

HALEY: What have they been told about why they're coming here?

LANDE: They've been told that the best kind of follow-up (meaning posthospital therapy) recommended for Annabelle would be for the whole family to be seen together. Since the parents have been to the marriage counselor already, and to a TA group—they seem to join and leave very rapidly. The parents themselves seem to have some awareness that something is wrong between them, and they go for help and then they leave, they go for help and then they leave. I don't know exactly how long ago that was.

(Long pause.)

There is a long pause while the supervisor is thinking about this unclear statement of the therapist and wondering how to respond to it. The question for the supervisor is whether he is misunderstanding what the therapist is saying, whether the therapist is making a confused statement, or whether there is a possible ideological problem which will have to be dealt with in the supervision.

One idea that can cause difficulty for a therapist is the notion that people need to be made aware of how they deal with one another, what their problems are, and what is behind those problems. This assumption—that people do not know something and that the therapist can help them discover it—comes largely from the theory of repression. That theory encouraged therapists to make people aware of what was out of their consciousness by offering them interpretations. This interpretation procedure can be a misfortune to a therapist who is dealing with the skillful family of a mad young person (as well as with other families). It is best to assume that whatever the therapist might point out is already known by the family, even though they might not wish to concede it explicitly. Their problem is not what they do not know but their inability to stop behaving as they do. The therapist who makes interpretations to them arouses resistance that can cause the therapy to fail.

This therapist says that the parents "seem to have some awareness that something is wrong between them." This is a puzzling statement since, if they have been to marriage counseling and other therapy for their marriage, they must know that something is wrong between them. Possibly the therapist has an insight-oriented ideology and will point out the obvious to families. This would be patronizing, and disastrous when doing therapy with people who know how to take advantage of a patronizing therapist and not change.

It turned out that the therapist did not have such an insight view, but the supervisor did not know that at this time and faced the possibility that he might have a difficult supervision task. He dropped the issue, planning to return to it later. The conversation continues:

HALEY: Is the date set for her to come out of the hospital?

LANDE: I talked to the resident about that on Friday and tried to get some control over that. Their feeling was that she should stay at least a couple more days, until the insurance runs out. (*Laughs*) That was when she would be better. That she was on thirty milligrams of Stellazine, and it was finally beginning to work, maybe. They weren't sure of that. Their complaint was that she had loose associations.

Not only should the insurance company not set a discharge date, it is also best if the staff does not do so, but lets the parents make that decision. After all, it is the parents who are going to live with the person. More important, a major goal is to correct the hierarchy in the family, with the parents in charge rather than their offspring. When the experts have the discharge decision, and the young person wishes to leave the hospital, he will turn to the staff as authorities and ignore the parents. In a conversation about discharge between family and experts, the young person knows where the power is and is more respectful to the professionals than to the parents. If, however, the parents have the power to decide when they will receive the young person back home, the situation is quite different. The offspring must persuade the parents that he or she will not make trouble and will meet their requirements. The parents thereby have an initial advantage, and control begins to shift from the professionals to the family, which is the goal of therapy.

LANDE: The idea at the hospital was that she probably wouldn't be able to go back to school and that maybe she should be in day-care.

HALEY: Do you know what she was doing before? Was it high school or college?

LANDE: Yes, twelfth grade.

HALEY: What's your idea about what she ought to do?

In a teaching situation, it is best to ask the therapist for a plan. If he does not have one, the supervisor can offer one. If he does, the supervisor should try to go along with it, since it will be followed with more enthusiasm if it is the therapist's own plan. The same principle applies when the therapist asks the family for a plan and hopes they will come up with one he can support.

LANDE: Well, my plan, my beginning plan was to—that's why I talked to the resident—instead of him telling the parents where she was going to go, I was somehow trying to use the first or second sessions, while she's in the hospital, to talk about what they're going to do as a family about her leaving. My plan was—on the surface—to look like they were going to be involved, more involved with her, which is what they have always been, but in a process of getting her out of the house. So, you know, if they decided that she was going to go to day-care, then at least she wouldn't be at home. To move somehow, to get them involved in helping her get out of the house. That would be my kind of goal, in general.

The merit in what the therapist suggests is that he has a stragetic plan; he is assuming that he must arrange what is to happen rather than merely respond to the situation in a non-directive way. The demerits of his plan are that it involves a deception that could fail and that the short-term goal, if achieved, would defeat the long-term goal.

If a therapist tries to separate the daughter from the parents by getting her out of the house, it should be assumed that the parents will not be deceived about the purpose of the move. They will know the therapist wants them to be apart from their child, and they are likely to respond negatively, since they will believe they have been blamed as a cause of their child's problem. Instead of helping the parents take charge, such an approach undermines their authority with the implication that the child is better off out of their house and away from their influence.

A more serious demerit of the plan is that the long-term goal is to achieve normality for the young person by disengaging her from the family to be self-supporting. This goal cannot be achieved if the young person is considered "ill" or "handicapped." A defective young person is kept at home by parents—only a healthy one is released. Therefore, to define the young person as needing a day hospital might get her out of the house during the day, but it keeps her at home because it defines her as unable to take care of herself.

There are other objections to a day hospital. To keep a young person from work or school for a treatment program that prevents such activities puts her further behind her peers each day and defines her more and more as a deviant. In this case, the young woman was expected to graduate from high school in a few months. If placed in a day-hospital program, she would have to miss school and might have to repeat her grade the following year, if she made it back to school at all. While repeating, she would be stigmatized as a mental patient who had failed in school and fallen behind her classmates. She would also begin to socialize with the deviant kinds of young people who habituate day hospitals instead of associating with the normal young people in her high school. In that way she could begin the social career of a mental patient. If such a destiny were necessary, that might be a misfortune, but to plan such a destiny seems unwise.

It is more reasonable to arrange that a young person go immediately into the normal situation that he or she left when put in custody. If in high school, that is the place to go; if at work, back on the job immediately before the job is lost; if in college, back to classes. However far the young person has progressed toward self-sufficiency before failing, that is the point to begin after custody.

There are yet other reasons for pushing immediately for the normal situation. Whatever caused the crisis will become evident when the situation is reconstituted. If, for example, the parents were about to separate when the young person began to be self-sufficient, then going immediately to that point can evoke the parents' marital issue again. The problem situation can be recreated and dealt with differently. One cannot learn about past causes of a problem by talking about them; one learns the person's theories about such causes. It is when the family faces the situation that the cause of a crisis appears, and often families would rather talk about the past than create that situation again.

Often when the family returns to its normal situation the problem has been solved because of the changes that took place during the crisis. The problem behavior of the young person is no longer necessary, because the situation has changed. Yet at times the problem behavior continues because the treatment situation now requires it. A therapist should always try to bring about success in the normal situation and go to abnormal arrangements only when the try for normality fails. To put the matter another way, the therapist should separate the social control issues, such as institutionalization and medication, from therapy by getting the young person back to normal functioning. It should always be assumed that if the family conflict is dealt with correctly, the young person will not need to fail and will function normally. When one accepts the idea that behavior is *adaptive* to a situation, then one must arrange a normal situation to achieve normal behavior.

Sometimes families and professionals need to be persuaded that going back to work or school immediately is reasonable. For the medically oriented, an analogy helps: one can say that in the past a person who had an appendix removed stayed in bed for weeks. Now he is up and functioning the next day.

The conversation continues:

HALEY: I think one of the things to avoid is day-care, if you can, or any connection with treatment, because that defines her as abnormal. It's very hard to get out if she is defined as abnormal. You can only get out of your house if you're normal. So even though it keeps her out of the house part of the day, it still keeps her in the family because she is the defective one whose parents have to take care of her. I think you should make it appear that you're having the parents decide, while "spontaneously" getting them to decide to get her back in school.

LANDE: Would that take precedence over somehow kind of beginning in some light way to redefine what's going on in the family? In other words, who is normal and who is not?

HALEY: No, I wouldn't do that.

For a supervisor, this statement is also a worrisome one. At one time in therapy it was thought wise to persuade the whole family that everyone was a problem, rather than just the problem person. This was supposedly a way of taking the pressure off the "victim." Such an approach proved to be a misfortune. Parents who came in with one child who had failed were persuaded they had failed with all of them and were even abnormal themselves. After putting the parents down in that way, the therapist would ask for their cooperation and be puzzled by their resistance.

The therapist here could be proposing a compromise: he wishes to suggest that not only the problem person but the whole family could be abnormal, thereby redefining the problem as a family one. But he wishes to do it in "some light way" so that the parents will not be antagonized. There is no light way to suggest that everyone in the family is as crazy as the daughter; either the parents will feel guilty and depressed and therefore be uncooperative, or they will spend their time proving the child is the only crazy one in the family. If the parents get upset because of the accusation, the offspring will go into more extreme crazy behavior to show she is the problem. The therapist will have produced more crazy behavior in response to his attempt at a rescue.

The conversation continues:

LANDE: Don't go near it?

HALEY: If they go into it, you have to deal with it. But I think you should put it on a very practical basis. She's going to come out of the hospital, and how is everybody going to receive her, and who is going to be home when she's there? What are her plans when she's over her convalescence?. . . .

LANDE: So keep it in terms of how she's about to be normal in a day or two, and how are they going to . . .

HALEY: As much on a day-to-day living as possible, and as much as possible away from who caused it or who upset her. It makes me a little uneasy when you say the parents must be aware that they have something wrong between them, because I'm sure they're aware that they have something wrong in their marriage. The problem will be how to handle that courteously, not to help them be aware that they have a problem in their marriage. I think I would worry about it if they have a history of going somewhere and dropping out and going somewhere else. It may be that people kept confronting them with their problem, or it may be that that's just their pattern, and we'll have trouble hooking them.

LANDE: Maybe one way to do that would be to—hopefully—when I find out what the father and mother do, find out that they're competent in something, and kind of deal with them as competent parents and how they together are going to deal with their daughter.

HALEY: Yes, particularly if they've got a couple out of the home or have done well with any of them.

LANDE: Right.

The prognosis for the therapist is good. He has shifted to a more positive approach and is searching for ways to find competence rather than pathology. The conversation continues:

HALEY: They will come in assuming that they are going to be accused of driving this daughter crazy, even if they have not been, because the very act of bringing them in accuses them of that. Otherwise, you would just see the daughter. So, you're in a morality play in which they're proving their innocence even though you are not making accusations. This makes a funny situation for them, because they cannot prove their innocence unless you make an accusation. If you don't make one, they have real difficulty. If you do make one, they'll say, "Aha, I knew it all along," and they won't come back.

LANDE: So, if I really go along with their normality and health also. That they've helped two other children very successfully, now how are they going to use their resources to help this child.

HALEY: That's right.

LANDE: So even though the etiology may be in the family, leave that out.

HALEY: They know that. That wouldn't be any great discovery to them. Your working process will be getting them to decide when she comes home, what she's going to do, and getting them to hold together in getting her to do what she should, in the room or out of the room. And getting them to treat her like a girl who needs to get back to school and accomplish something in life, rather than a girl who is sick. Really, what you push for is to define it as a behavior problem, ultimately, if not in the first session, rather than an illness problem. And, if she says something screwy, like loose associations—in the first session you really should try to understand it. Later, you might not. But you should treat it like she's just not communicating clearly rather than that she has sprung a brain. And that they should get her to communicate clearly so they know what the hell she's up to. Try to get that into a kind of misbehavior—other people can communicate clearly, why can't she?

LANDE: What about if they bring up the thing about the medicine, the medication?

HALEY: They'll bring it up at the first and at the end (*of the interview*) probably. I think in the first session you've got to go along with it. At a certain point when she's ready for a fresh start, then she can come off it. I would define it as temporary in some way, so they don't think this is a lifelong thing. Then it's only a question of when she comes off, and how she comes off, whether a little bit off each day or off in one schlump. But say that can be worked out in the future. You've got to accept them saying that she's the patient and the whole problem, while at the same time saying this is temporary.

At this point the family arrived and the conversation ended. The issues discussed at this ending point are crucial to the conduct of the therapy.

The problem for the expert, particularly the medical expert, in a medical setting, is to redefine the problem so that the family can deal with it. If the problem is a medical one, only doctors can treat it. In that case, the parents can justifiably back off and pay the professionals to take responsibility for a problem offspring. When that happens, the young person tends to adapt to medical institutions rather than to normal living. It is important, therefore, to define the problem to the family in such a way that they not only can, but are obligated to, solve it themselves. The therapist must have the parents focus on the child to change him or her; that way they continue to triangulate with the young person, but in a positive way and with the help of a therapist who is bringing about their disengagement. So the first step must be to make the problem something the parents can do something about. A behavior or disciplinary problem is something they can deal with. Similarly, they can deal with motivating an apathetic offspring to take action to do something.

Medication is a special problem with such an approach. One gives medication to the ill, not to people with behavior problems. The medication must therefore be defined as a behavior control device, which it is, and not as a medicine for an illness, which it is not. More important, it must be defined as temporary. If it is defined as for an illness, like diabetes, it is implied that there will be lifelong use for a handicapped person. The more the emphasis on medication, the more the family cannot be put in charge of the problem. A particular difficulty is the fact that it is usually the parents who insist on the medication. They feel helpless about controlling the young person's behavior and disagree with each other about what to do, so they want someone to dope the offspring. Different ways of dealing with medication will be discussed in this work. Here one needs to emphasize that medication can be used to gain an advantage or to make the therapy difficult, if not impossible. For an advantage, and risking the damaging neurological effects, one uses the fact that the parents want their offspring medicated—they will come to therapy to get that medication and will cooperate if the therapist will cooperate by medicating.

In this approach it is important to begin by emphasizing that the problem young person is the whole problem. Such a focus gives leverage for winning the cooperation of the family and bringing about change. The young person is willing to make himself or herself the problem, so the therapist should accept that. The young person needs to be defined as a temporary problem, however, rather than as a person with a lifelong handicap.

At this point in the conversation, the supervisor and therapist have a working relationship. The therapist has shifted to a positive view and is ready to define the problem as the girl's misbehaving. The past is not relevant, and the custody and the medication are considered temporary. The parents need to get their daughter under control and back to school as quickly as possible. The difficulties in the marriage and other family problems will be dealt with as part of dealing with the problem daughter.

Living Separately

Another conversation between a therapist and supervisor illustrates how to think about beginning with a young adult who is older and has lived away from home. In this case the therapist, Dr. Charles Fishman, brought in a young man and his family. The young man had been away from home for four years in college and had married, so he had been living separately from his parents for several years. In his last semester, just before graduating, he began to act strangely and came back to his parents' city, where he was hospitalized. The wife came with him and stayed with the parents while he was in the mental hospital.

The young man's family of origin had a number of psychiatric patients in its history, a fact that interested the therapist. The supervisor showed no interest in that since it was not relevant to the therapy, and since to discuss it would focus the therapist on the young man's pathology. What is most relevant to the therapy is how to plan where the young man is to live when he leaves the hospital. The conversation takes place just before the family arrives for the first interview.

FISHMAN: He's been in the hospital almost two months. They've worked him up really extensively. He's on tremendous amounts of medication.

HALEY: Right now?

FISHMAN: Yes.

HALEY: Do you have control of that medication?

FISHMAN: I will, yes.

HALEY: Starting when?

FISHMAN: As soon as he gets out. He's going to stay here, I think, and live with his folks. And the plan is to have him go to a day hospital.

HALEY: Ideally he should go right back and finish college. Now he can't go back and go to college if he's full of medication. What are you thinking about for this interview? How would you like it to end when they leave today?

FISHMAN: Well, some kind of understanding of what's going to happen when he gets out of the hospital.

HALEY: What is it you want to happen?

FISHMAN: Well, I want him to be increasingly autonomous.

HALEY: That's not a happening. It's a state of some kind (*laughs*). I think it would be a good idea if you got them to set a deadline of how long he is going to live with them. If you get an agreement with them that he really is married and should be living in his own place. But because he's handicapped at the moment he's going to live with them (*the parents*), if that is the arrangement. Find out if that is. If that's what they're going to do, then get them to agree on a deadline when he is to move out with his wife to live on his own again. So that when he comes out of the hospital it is only temporarily into his parents' house. This is crucial.

FISHMAN: Mm-hmm.

HALEY: It's not permanently into his house until he's better, or something like that. It's with a date set for him to move out of his house into a place with his wife. Your goal is to move him out of there and have an autonomous unit with his wife. Previously he must have moved out and collapsed back. You've got to move him out again, because collapsed back it will stabilize there and go on forever. If that's the situation, which it might not be. I wouldn't explore with them very much of what happened or why it happened, I would put it on how your job is to help him get on his feet. And what is it that he wants to do, and his wife wants him to do, and they can all help him do it. If they want to explore the why or even the family history, I would cut it right off. You're starting with a lot of handicaps here. You're starting with him married and collapsed back, so that's confused. You're starting with him advised to go to a day hospital which defines him as abnormal. And you start him after two months in the hospital with everyone stabilized with the idea that he is really the patient now. And with a family that has a history of patients. So there's a lot of arguments for stability with mental illness in this family.

FISHMAN: Yeah.

HALEY: I think the general approach should be to agree that he's the problem: the parents are not the problem, the wife is not the problem. And since he's the problem, what can be done to get him on his feet?

In the first interview the therapist set a date with the family for the young man and his wife to move out of the parents' home into a place of their own. They chose April Fool's day. When the day arrived, Dr. Fishman overcame the difficulties and skillfully moved him out with his wife.

An Operational Emphasis

Another verbatim conversation between supervisor and therapist about another case emphasizes the relationship between them as well as some technical issues about supervising in this situation. Essentially it is a monologue by the supervisor orienting a psychologist, David Mowatt, Ph.D., to this approach, just before he is to interview a family.

HALEY: Okay, let's clarify the situation with you and me. What I would like to do is make this a responsible supervision. Sometimes in supervision I'm just a consultant. In a responsible supervision, if this therapy fails I fail as much as you do. In that sense it's a different kind than the usual. I'll try to be here every session or see that somebody is here. I would like you, when you take this on, to have an attitude that you'll go to the mat with it. That you'll either cure this guy or you'll die, whichever comes first. That may mean some weekend work, or some crisis time. It might call for more from you than the usual case. Because if you're not going to hospitalize him or medicate him, then you have to do more, the parents have to do more, everyone does.

In this supervision I'll call you on the telephone during the interview. I always call reluctantly, and as little as possible. So if I call it's not that I just wish to pass the time of day. Since you can never tell from behind a mirror what's really going on in a room, because the mirror screens out many emotions, I would rather you take what I say as only a suggestion. You don't have to do what I suggest. But if I say, "You have to do this," then you have to do it. That means I know something is going to blow the case so they won't come back, or something. But ordinarily, use your judgment. If I suggest something and you don't feel quite right about it, either don't do it or excuse yourself and come out and talk about it. Because I can have ideas about what is going on which may be off.

I think in starting with the family it's always fair to define your position first. Say what you would like to do. One of the ways to start is to say that you brought this meeting about because you'd like to help them get their son on his feet, and as rapidly as possible. You'd like to help them take charge of this, so that the family can deal with the problem, so that he can get back to normal. Or some statement like that, which makes it clear that you're going to try to contain this problem within the family, and that you're going to help them deal with this problem. I think you should make it clear that you have an agreement with the professional community— that you have an arrangement with the hospital and they're agreeable about what you're doing. You explain to them that as far as medication is concerned, you're a psychologist and so you will not medicate. But you will have a psychiatrist here who will prescribe medication. So that it's clear that you've made the professional arrangements—you want to sound organized. Because you've got to organize the professional community involved before you can help the family organize. You need to tell them that you're doing that, even if it's in an offhand way, like, "I have a good relationship with the hospital, and this has been arranged." Then I think you should try to tell them what you'd like to achieve by the end of the first meeting. You'd like them to decide on when he should come home from the hospital, and at least some of the rules at home—the rules for how he is to behave when he gets home. Your attitude in this should be siding with the parents. You're polite to the son, but you really don't define him as having many rights at this point. He's abdicated his rights by going into the hospital. And he will try to say it ought to be done this way or that, and you say, "It's up to your parents right now until you get on your feet." I think your attitude toward him should be to expect him to be normal. You're really trying to define him, as misbehaving.

There's no excuse, I think, for this guy to be in a day hospital and auditing classes at college. He should either be in college and studying, or he should be working and supporting himself. The middle ground of half-assedly doing things is what you don't want, and he should not want, and the family should not want. I don't know how that might come up in the session, but as it comes up you should ask if he wants to be in school or working. Actually, I wouldn't put it to him, I would put it to the parents. . . .

MOWATT: I was going to ask you that, that was my view, that it should be asked of the parents what do they want for him.

HALEY: Right, and if they want him in college, I would discuss with them whether they want to go on paying tuition as they have been if he isn't studying and doing well. Or do they want to get him out to work if he isn't going to school properly. Treat it like it's a normal situation rather than a mad situation as much as you can. You should assume that you're helping them work on the rules for dealing with him as a way of working on their marriage. You start with the parenting, and if you can get them to agree on the parenting then you can get to the husband-and-wifing later, and get them to agree on how to husband-and-wife. If they bring up any disagreements between them about him, you need to say, "I'm sure you've had disagreements, but starting when he comes out of the hospital you better be in agreement. I want you to agree. That's what we're here for." You politely turn it off if they each want to go into how they did it wrong in the past. Generally, you want to turn off the past and say this is going to be a fresh start for everybody. This is their last son at home, I understand?

MOWATT: Yes.

HALEY: I think you need to define it, in some way, just so they hear you, that he'll be leaving home ultimately. And that they must want to help him get on his feet so he can go on his way. That is, you don't want to define this as him getting along with them and staying with them. You want to make it clear that ultimately he's moving out, and this is the first stage of that. If they bring anything up about how he should go away to college, then you should immediately reassure them that he should not go away to some place that makes them uncomfortable about where he is, and they don't know what is going on.

One of your difficulties is going to be putting the parents in charge of a guy as old as this one. When he's younger, it's easier. And if they say that, or he says that you're treating him like he's younger, then you should say, "I think your parents should treat you like you're younger until you get on your feet." So you make it clear that isn't going to be a permanent arrangement. Is the family here yet?

MOWATT: Yes, they just arrived. Everyone is here but the brother who is living outside the home and is married. I left it that we might want to include him at some future time.

HALEY: I think generally it's a good idea to include all the siblings at this time. Because part of the brother managing to live outside the home can be the fact that this young man is at home.

MOWATT: You would include him in the first session?

HALEY: And probably his wife. Not so much that she might be involved, but she could give a more objective statement about the situation. At times an in-law will help in clarifying the situation if you're puzzled, because sometimes they say what is on their minds. Of course, sometimes they're just very polite and stay out of it. One more thing, don't forget to introduce the nature of this special room to everyone. Show them the mirrors and the cameras and inform them they are being observed. It's up to you whether you say you have a supervisor back there or a colleague. You just need to say that someone is there.

MOWATT: Should I introduce you to the family?

HALEY: No, they will never meet me. Sometimes if a family really wants to meet the supervisor, you can say that they can do so after the therapy is over and they are over the problem.

Although some supervisors prefer to join the therapist in the room, that is not recommended in this approach, particularly not with a family as difficult as this one. The family is at a disadvantage when they know the therapist is in collaboration with someone who is not there for them to deal with. If the supervisor enters the room, the family can not only estimate his range but can play therapist and supervisor off against each other more easily. The supervisor who remains remote can support the therapist, and the therapist's influence is increased. Often when the supervisor enters the room, the therapist is put at a disadvantage because the family tends to turn toward the higher-status person for direction. The therapist must recover each time the supervisor exits after an intervention. A primary reason for the supervisor not to enter is that the therapist must do the job, no matter what guidance he gets from the other room. The more responsibility is put on him to do it, the more he will deliver, which is also true of mad young people and their families.

Chapter 5

The First Stage

Therapy with a problem young person is best thought of in stages. The first stage is arranging a return home from an institution correctly so that the person does not immediately return to custody. In cases where institutionalization has not occurred, the first stage is getting the family past the crisis and the young person back to a normal situation.

The second stage deals with the crisis brought about by the inevitable relapses of the young person. To say "inevitable" may be too deterministic, because sometimes the relapse does not occur. In the usual course of events, however, the young person returns to normal and in a few weeks erupts again. The problem is to contain the eruption within the family, without custody. If the eruption leads to a return to custody, the therapy must begin again as if nothing has been accomplished. It is extremely important in this situation to prevent a second institutionalization. (In the case of a chronic problem, when the person has been in custody many times, the return to custody is less of a setback.) Preventing the cycle of in-and-out institutionalization is the main task of the second stage.

The third stage of therapy is disengaging the young person from home, perhaps by a physical move out of the house. It is possible for the young person to be disengaged from the family triangle while still living at home and going to work or school, but the physical move often ensures that change.

There are two repeating cycles involved in the system of mad young person and family. The first occurs within the family, the second in the relationship of family and community. Within the family, the typical sequence is that the two parents, or two other adults such as mother and grandmother, threaten separation. This separation may be in terms of a divorce, or it may be that one of them collapses and the threat is separation by hospitalization or custody of one of the parents. As the threat of separation occurs, the young person erupts into mad behavior or some extreme action that requires the family members to remain together to deal with him or her. Usually the young person is put in custody. When he or she returns home and begins a normal life, the family members threaten separation, and the young person erupts and makes trouble again. This repeating cycle takes different forms in different families. In one family the parents might talk about divorce, while in another the mother might just say, "I'd like a vacation by myself," which is a threat of separation in that family. The young person reacts to these events in an extreme way, as if life depended on the state of the parents and their marriage. By making trouble or by failing to leave the triangle with the parents because of some incapacity, the young person stabilizes the parents. A move by the young person toward normality, in the sense of work, school, or intimate relations, provokes the threat of separation, and again a failure that stabilizes.

When the young person erupts into troublesome behavior to stabilize the family, the community becomes involved. Agents of social control go into action and institutionalize. Ultimately the young person is released back home. As long as the young person is labeled by the community as handicapped, either by medication or by custody, the stability continues. To keep this cycle going, the family members must each participate, and the agents of social control in the community must offer their aid. The task of a therapist is to end both the cycle within the family and between family and the community institutions.

It might be mentioned in passing that the decision about which family member is institutionalized can seem arbitrary. In some cases it is one of the parents, or other adults, at this stage of family development. When a therapist enters a family in crisis, he can think that any one of the members is behaving strangely enough to need action. Usually the young person is chosen for custody, and at that point the parents and other family members look more normal and the young person more extreme, so that the decision to hospitalize the young person appears to have been a sound one. A sociological explanation for choosing the young person could be offered, however. When everyone is upset and someone must be defined as a failure, the young person is less essential to the family and so most vulnerable. Often the father is supporting the family and must keep his job. The mother is either working or taking care of other children, or both, and is needed. The young person has no function of a practical nature and is therefore the expendable person. Once the young person is chosen, he continues his new "job" in the family by being handicapped.

A therapist who deals with this problem situation should not underestimate the power of the triangle. It is as if three planets were held together in orbit by unseen bonds. When one breaks out of the orbit, the other two do not remain bonded but also begin to break out of orbit. It is as if there must be either a triangle or destruction. One can overlook this bonding by being distracted by what people say. The young person will say that he or she is sick of the parents and wants to leave. The parents will say that they wish the child were gone—on his or her feet and away from them. Talk of a willingness to separate has nothing to do with the actions taken. Faced with a continually failing young person who remains on their doorstep, the parents will protest that they are sick to death of him and wish he would go away or die. That statement is made, however, when he is handicapped and living with them. A quite different response occurs if he moves toward normality and self-support.

The classical triangle which involves a problem young person is one where a parent crosses a generation line and sides with the child against the other parent. An alternate form occurs when a grandparent crosses the generation lines and joins a child against a parent. This "pathological triangle" is typical with problem children. When dealing with such a cross-generational coalition, a common procedure is for the therapist to join the more peripheral person as a first step and get him or her involved with the child. For example, when a mother is joining a child against the father, the therapist has the father join the child in some endeavor which leaves the mother out. At that point the mother objects to what the father is doing with the child, or to the way he is doing it, and the therapist shifts to the struggle between the parents as a focus. At that point the child is symptom-free, and the therapist is dealing with the marriage.[1] This kind of intervention can be used with routine children's problems as well as with severe problems of young eccentrics, as in the case of a heroin addict who will be described later. With families with a greater range of skills, however, such as families with a mad member, that way of conceiving the triangle is simplistic.

With a family in which a mad young person is sufficiently disturbed to come to community attention, one cannot simply assume that the triangle is one where one parent is joining the child against the other, who is more peripheral. One finds that both parents are joining the child against each other in a "double bond." Mother is in a tight coalition with child against father, but so is father in coalition with the child against mother. Therefore the therapist cannot simply put one or the other in charge of the child. It is better to proceed by focusing on the parents agreeing about what the

---

[1] For a description of these stages in an interview involving the usual children's problems, see J. Haley, *Problem-Solving Therapy*, Jossey-Bass, San Francisco, 1976.

young person should do. This keeps the communication between the parents about the child and his problems active, as it has been before, but in the new context of agreeing on how he should change. They shift from complaining about how badly he behaves to planning what he is to do.

One can also assume that the madder the young person, the more cross-generational conflicts he is caught up in. These can include each parent saving the child from the other, but grandparents and experts in the field can be involved as well. The wider context of family and community is obviously relevant to the problem, but for therapeutic purposes it is usually best to begin with a focus on the central triangle and produce a change in that. As that change occurs, the wider network becomes active and relevant. To move the young person out of the triangle with his parents without a misfortune is a challenging endeavor. The therapist who enters that system will find himself receiving more of an education there than with any other type of therapeutic problem. As change is threatened, the therapist will find his or her character tested by the intensity of the involvement.

Often the triangle is changed by substituting parts. The therapist can take the place of the problem young person with the parents; at that point the eccentric is free and can become normal. The therapist must then find a way to free himself without attracting the young person back for a relapse or involving a sibling as a replacement. At times one of the parents begins an affair, sometimes with a younger person, and the marriage triangulates around that person; in that way the problem child is freed from the system.

Whether substituting himself for the problem child as a deliberate tactic, or focusing on the marital dyad in order to free the problem child, the therapist should keep in mind that the goal is not necessarily a happy marriage after the child has become normal. The goal is not to make a happier marriage, unless that contract is negotiated, but rather to make a marriage which does not include the young person who should be leaving home and leading his or her own life. The therapist should also keep in mind that divorce of parents with a severely disturbed child, after the child becomes normal, is unusual. The threat of it is there, but it usually does not happen.

It is paradoxical that as problem young persons become more helpless and handicapped, they become more dominating in the family.[2] The parents, divided themselves, cannot exert authority, and the young person tends to decide what is to happen. The authority of the young person over the parents, particularly her or his power by helplessness, is what signifies a hierarchy in confusion. When the parents succeed in joining together

[2] This idea was developed by Cloe Madanes. See C. Madanes, "The Prevention of Rehospitalization of Adolescents and Young Adults," to be published.

and exerting authority, the young person becomes normal. At that point he threatens to leave home, which can divide the parents so that again they have no joint authority. The threat of the young person leaving home is a powerful deterrent to the parents exerting authority over what is to be done.

THE FIRST STAGE

A part of the goal in this approach to therapy is to correct the hierarchy in the family so that the parents are in charge. In the first stage, when the young person is coming out of an institution, the parents are placed in full charge by the therapist, with little or no emphasis on the rights of the young person. It is an exaggerated authority which is encouraged in the parents, and the young person often protests that it is tyranny.

It should be specially emphasized that putting the parents in authority in this extreme way might not be at all appropriate with younger people, no matter how mad they are. From age eighteen on, if the young people do not like the parental authority, they can leave home and support themselves. Younger children, however, are trapped at home, so a different approach is needed. With the younger adolescent, it is more reasonable to put the parents in charge, but with emphasis on his rights in terms of decisions and privacy.

With the problem young adult, the therapist can put the parents in charge with more confidence that tyranny will not be a problem. The point is that putting the parents in charge and setting rules for the problem young person has little to do with parenting or authority. It has to do with resolving the differences between the parents that incapacitate them as leaders in the family. Their discussion of rules is a way of communicating with each other about the problem child and resolving their differences. As they begin to communicate directly, the young person is freed from being the communication vehicle between them. The freedom of the problem young person does not come from his participating in family decisions, it comes from the parents talking directly to each other and not requiring the young person to misbehave to keep their marriage stable. As a typical example, the young person does not have to express strange ideas about sex if the parents are dealing directly with each other about sexual issues. They can do this first when setting rules for the problem young person, and later in relation to each other. Having the parents communicate with each other more directly and correcting the hierarchy in the family are simultaneous processes. By asking the parents jointly to take charge of an incompetent offspring, the therapist is forcing them to reach agreement by communicating with each other about what should be done.

Excerpts from interviews illustrating this typical process of the first stage of therapy can be offered. The therapist is Gary Lande. The family is a large one, with seven children present in the first interview. The problem young person has been in the hospital for two weeks.

The therapist has suggested that the parents plan when the daughter is to come home and what she will be doing when she leaves the hospital. She was hospitalized when she acted strangely during her last semester of high school.

MOTHER: I'd like to see now what situation would be best for you to complete whatever healing that you need right now. You know . . .

ANNA: My healing is I'm too fast.

MOTHER: What I'm trying is to make you completely well. You know, and—ah, I don't know.

ANNA: What do you mean "completely well"?

MOTHER: Well, I'm not sure whether . . . I don't know. I want the advice of all the . . .

FATHER: Well look, are you completely well? That's what she means.

ANNA: Yes.

FATHER: You're not, honey.

ANNA: Don't tell me I'm not.

FATHER: Then will you tell me what you are? Then what do you mean?

ANNA: I know what I am. I know what I can do, and I want to do it.

The confusions around the issues of madness are made greater by the medical model which the family is caught up in. To be in a hospital with doctors and nurses, and to be called ill when there is nothing physically wrong, is a mystification of the problem. The mother continues to try to clarify the situation. In the following statement, when she talks about "whatever situation" the girl might go into, there is an implication that she might not go home.

MOTHER: What I'm talking about is the transition from the hospital to—whatever situation is best for you to go into. I'm not . . .

ANNA: The best for me to go into is home . . .

MOTHER: I'd like to know what *you* want to do. I'd like to know what the people in the hospital who have been caring for you recommend. Then I'd like to express what I'd like, what I think about it.

ANNA: In other words, you're trying to plan my life.

MOTHER: No. From all those things I think that would be a good way to make a decision about what to do.

(Later in the interview.)

LANDE: I agree there are all kinds of decisions, but maybe we could talk about the ones that are going to come first. You're going to come out of the hospital sometime this week, right?

ANNA: Right.

LANDE: So where is your daughter going to be going when she comes home? . . . the pragmatics, you know, at a very simple level.

ANNA: I could go to my high school, but I missed three weeks of school there and I can't catch up.

MOTHER: She's coming home. As far as we know, she's coming to our house.

LANDE: She's going to be coming to your home?

MOTHER: Yes.

LANDE: Okay. And who's going to be there when she comes home, to meet her?

SON: Everyone right here will be there.

MOTHER: How do you mean, "Who will be there to meet her?"

LANDE: Let me just . . .

ANNA: Arnold will be there to meet me.

LANDE: Arnold is?

ANNA: Arnold is my love.

(Laughter from the children.)

LANDE: He lives near you?

ANNA: Yes.

LANDE: I think what we have to do today, and do things in order, is that there are some very important, practical decisions that are not profound, but we must make them. This transition period, as you're both saying, I think is important. How is Annabelle going to move from the hospital and get back into her normal kind of life?

MOTHER: Right.

LANDE: So one thing I hear, which everyone seems in agreement about, is that part of being normal is going back to school. And I couldn't agree with you more.

The therapist quickly defines going back to school as part of being normal and also suggests that she should go directly back to school. This is done in such a way that it appears to be part of both the family plan and the thera-peutic plan, and it is therefore taken for granted and need not be discussed or negotiated. In contrast, if the therapist expressed doubt that the mad daughter was in condition to go back to school, the family could easily organize around keeping her at home as an invalid or even putting her in a day hospital or halfway house. By saying he agrees with the parents, the therapist defines the parents as taking the initiative in the situation, which is what he wants to happen. As the interview continues, he finds out who is living at home and the position of the problem girl there.

LANDE: Living in the house, you're the oldest girl, right?

ANNA: Yes.

LANDE: Do you help Mom out at all?

ANNA: Yes, definitely.

MOTHER: Yes, definitely.

ANNA: I'm the second momma.

LANDE: The second momma.

CHILD: (*In the background.*) I'm the third.

MOTHER: I'm not so sure about that, but she does get along well with the children. They really like her. They really have a good time with Annabelle. They really missed her.

LANDE: You've all been missing Annabelle over the past two weeks?

ANNA: Yeah, man. You should hear them when I call up. Susan says, "When you coming home? When you coming home? When you coming home?"

LANDE: How does that feel to hear that?

ANNA: Man, it makes me depressed.

LANDE: To hear that?

ANNA: Yeah.

LANDE: How do you feel now that you're coming home?

ANNA: I feel so happy.

LANDE: You have a reception committee. (*Referring to the little girl sitting on her lap.*)

ANNA: Yeah.

The therapist asks the young woman how it feels to hear the younger children asking when she's coming home. This is an error. It was intended to bring out some of the warm feelings of being desired at home, so it had a positive purpose. But in dealing with a family with such interpersonal skills as those of the family of a mad person, it is better not to allow them an opening to indulge in metaphors. Asking how someone feels does that.

To put the matter another way, when the therapist asks the family to confine itself to practical issues and rules or bits of behavior, he is on safe ground.[3] When he asks for analogies, like feelings and meanings, the family is an authority in those areas while he is not, so they can take advantage of such communication to attack each other in subtle ways. When this is done,

---

[3] The idea that "digital communication" rather than "analogic communication" should be emphasized when doing therapy with these families was suggested by Cloe Madanes.

the therapist has encouraged it, no matter what he intended. The therapist is on safer ground if he simply never asks anyone how they feel about anything. As the conversation continues, one can observe how the father becomes defensive about the daughter being depressed about coming home, and how the daughter takes advantage of this metaphoric opportunity to "double-bind" her mother.

FATHER: What are you depressed about when you hear them say that?

ANNA: I'm depressed that I can't come home when they say, "I want you to come home."

FATHER: I see.

ANNA: And if I don't go home, I'm gonna sit crying.

SON: You're going home. You're going home in a couple of days.

FATHER: Well, we don't know when you're coming home. We haven't gotten any real official word from the hospital.

LANDE: I think part of what we're deciding right now is related to that.

ANNA: *(As mother begins to cry.)* Go ahead and cry, cause you can cry. Seriously, I learned from the old ladies in the hospital that tears can't come out no more because they held their tears in too long when they wanted to cry.

MOTHER: I'll be happy to have you home, too.

ANNA: There's ladies your age who can't have tears, Mom. I seen them.

When the therapist inquires about feelings, the mother begins to cry. The daughter responds to her in a curious way. She sympathizes with the mother and encourages her to cry. At the same time she classes her with the "old ladies" in the hospital who cannot cry. Apparently the mother is concerned about being younger, as the daughter says later, so the mother is in a difficult position. She cannot accept the sympathy of her daughter because the daughter is classing her as an old lady, but at the same time she cannot get angry at the comment because the daughter is sympathizing with her. This bind was made possible by the therapist, who asked about feelings. He begins to shift and succeeds in siding with the mother in the interchange that follows.

LANDE: *(To mother.)* It must have been a pretty tense period for you?

ANNA: Yeah, without my help.

MOTHER: It's been a pretty sad, you know, sad period for me.

ANNA: It's been a pressuring period.

LANDE: *(To mother.)* Does "pressuring period" describe it? What would you call it?

MOTHER: Sad.

LANDE: Sad.

(Later in the interview.)

MOTHER: Does the hospital give us any recommendations about what would be the best after they've studied it? What would be the best situation.

LANDE: No. At one important level they've made one of the recommendations, and that's why everybody is here today.

MOTHER: Mm-hmm.

LANDE: So, this is their basic referral. I've talked to her doctors and the social worker several times last week. We've been in very close contact. So the basic idea in terms of follow-up and all of that is made. But there are very important things about school and things like that.

(Later in the interview.)

FATHER: There are a couple of big decisions that we have to make before Anna comes home. Or should be made. One is what she's going to do about school.

LANDE: I agree with you.

FATHER: And what is going to happen with her and Arnold. By that I mean particularly the hours they keep and things like that. I think, you know, she is going to need plenty of rest and she shouldn't be under any pressure.

When a therapist wishes a family to follow certain actions, it is sometimes best to phrase what he wishes to happen as if the family had initiated the idea. Then he is in a position to agree with them. In a discussion later in the interview the therapist agrees with the idea that the parents should set up certain rules for the daughter as they have proposed, even though they have not proposed that.

LANDE: I think a lot of important things are being brought up by everybody. But it seems that we're talking about when Anna's going home, which everybody is interested in, and somehow you're saying that certain kinds of rules have to be set up, and I agree. In other words, who is going to decide what time Annabelle can come home, what night she can go out, and what her other responsibilities are. I think we have to come to some decision, because until that's made, her going home is going to be . . .

ANNA: Wait a minute. Can I make a request or a suggestion, or ask a question?

LANDE: Is it about this idea, Annabelle?

ANNA: Yes. Mom, see, you're wearing my shoes?

MOTHER: Yes?

ANNA: That's cause you're trying to go back and be younger. *(Laughter from everyone.)* I'm serious.

MOTHER: I wore your shoes because I thought they looked the best with my dress today.

ANNA: See, see.

MOTHER: Well, I hope you're wrong. But let's leave that for a little while.

The young woman is probably quite right about the mother, given what was learned later in the therapy. However, that is irrelevant to the therapy at this point. If the therapist explored how the mother wanted to be younger, the mother would be put lower in the hierarchy and the mad daughter put higher at a time when the mother needs to be encouraged to take charge.

ANNA: All right, Mom, all right.

LANDE: I think we should come to some understanding, the three of you, so I can make my recommendation to the hospital about when you can leave.

(Later in the interview.)

LANDE: I would guess in this period of convalescing and Annabelle getting back to her normal self, that you two are going to have to do a lot of decision making.

MOTHER: Yes, I think so too. Our experience in the past hasn't been good about it, I don't think. In other words, Annabelle has pushed for more freedom, a great deal more freedom, than maybe a person her age could handle. And I always, for quite a long time—Dick was in the other direction, very restrictive and not willing to listen a great deal to what they really wanted to do. And I—I really was kind of in the middle.

A research point of view, or a pathologically oriented therapy, would appreciate this statement of the mother's and explore further the disagreement between the parents about the problem young person. Yet such exploration typically leads to failure in the therapy. Any exploration, even a benevolent one, about the bad feelings or problems between the parents can prevent them from resolving their difficulties with each other by taking charge of the problem child. Perhaps the mother offers this topic because she has had experience with therapists. When the therapist makes it clear that he is not interested in the parent's difficulties with each other, but rather in solutions, the mother orients in that direction. A similar process occurred between therapist and supervisor: when the therapist found the supervisor primarily interested in solutions and positive aspects, he shifted to that orientation.

LANDE: The problem is now, though, that you all don't have to make a decision for the next three months, month, year or two years. We're talking now about the immediate—Annabelle coming home sometime this week. What night can she go out? What night she can't go out. What time should she be back? If you could now, right in the present . . .

FATHER: Okay. Let's talk about that. My understanding is that on the school nights, when they have school the next day . . .

LANDE: Will you talk to your wife? (*Encouraging them to discuss this together.*)

Since the therapist wishes to encourage more direct communication between father and mother, he asks them to talk directly to each other. As they do so, the tension and disagreement between them become evident. Talking to the therapist about something does not bring out the issues in the way that talking directly to each other does. A therapist needs to be skilled in arranging to be central at times, so that everyone talks to him, and arranging to be peripheral at times, so that family members are required to deal with each other.

FATHER: Okay. We've had an understanding they should be in like ten or eleven o'clock on those nights. And when they go out any length of time at all, it's on the weekends.

MOTHER: How about me? (*Father has not tried to talk to her as therapist asked.*)

FATHER: (*Turning to her.*) Look, I'm just talking. Anybody can answer what I have to say. Did you hear what I said?

MOTHER: What you're recommending now is what?

FATHER: (*Angrily.*) I'm just trying to talk about what I thought we were supposed to be doing already before she came here.

MOTHER: (*Patiently.*) Okay. But how about now when she's going home?

FATHER: Well, I'll get to that. I don't think if she would do that it would be much more of a problem. I don't know what the doctors will allow her to do. But first of all . . .

LANDE: I think what's important—let me try to support you. I think what is important is what you two decide now, see. In other words, what plan do you have when Annabelle comes home Wednesday, Thursday, Friday, or whatever day, and she says, "I want to go out, and what time should I be home?" You two have to decide what the answer to that question is going to be.

When the therapist sides with the parents and defines them as authorities over the daughter's life, the daughter is likely to object. Part of the art of this approach to therapy is to succeed in joining the parents while not antago-

nizing the daughter to the point where she refuses to cooperate in the therapy. It is best if the therapist makes two factors clear: that what he is doing for the daughter is benevolent and not simply a matter of disregarding her interests, and that what he is doing is helping the parents, which is also what the daughter wishes to have done.

ANNA: Why can't I decide the answer?

LANDE: I think your parents are pretty involved in this, in this period of your coming home, until you're back into school and back to normal.

ANNA: See, I'm already an adult.

FATHER: We've had a big problem, you know. The kids think at this age they should run their own lives. Okay, maybe they should have more to say about it than I've allowed them to, but it's a continual battle.

This is not a therapy where there are discussions about the philosophy of child rearing or about the nature of effective parenting. It is focused sharply on the immediate situation with this offspring.

LANDE: Yes, I can see that. We're talking now not about something that happens in a year, we're talking about this first day or two days. You need some sort of battle plan.

MOTHER: Yeah, a plan of action.

LANDE: A plan of action.

(Later in the interview.)

MOTHER: I think for the first week I don't even know what you can handle.

ANNA: But it's not your problem, Mom.

LANDE: Annabelle, it is your parents' problem. I have to disagree. I think this is very much—this period—you getting back together is your parent's problem.

When the parents began to have difficulty with each other, the father offered the problem to the doctor. The therapist gave it back to him. The daughter entered the arena to say that she should decide things for herself. The therapist had to set that aside and put the responsibility back on the parents. The father tried a philosophical discussion, and the therapist shifted it back to specific bits, or precise issues, and he shortened the time to the next few days rather than a lifetime approach to child rearing. Again, the daughter tried to take the responsibility from the parents and put it on herself, and the therapist shifted it back to the parents. Most of the work of the first stage is the therapist patiently shifting the responsibility for authority to the parents.

One way to focus the issue on parental authority is to have only the parents present in the second interview. At the first meeting it is most important to have everyone present to see what the family is like and who is involved, and to have everyone hear the therapeutic plan. To next see the parents alone defines the hierarchy as one where the parents are in charge and making private executive decisions.

Before the second interview, the therapist and supervisor talked about what to do in the interview.

LANDE: Would your feeling today be to limit the parents to mainly discussing what curfew, and what she's going to be doing, and who's going to be home?

HALEY: I think you should have them lay down some rules.

LANDE: For the next period of time.

HALEY: See, ostensibly what you're working on is rules for the girl. Actually you're working on an agreement in their marriage, but you need to put it in terms of the girl.

(Later in the conversation.)

HALEY: One of the ways to solve it is to suggest to them that they make rules not for how she ought to behave, but for what they'll put up with. Make that distinction. It isn't a question of deciding how late she should stay out. It's a question of whether mother is uncomfortable if she's out after eleven. If she's out after eleven and her mother is uncomfortable, then she should be in at eleven. The important thing is how mother feels, not how this girl feels. If the girl wants to go back to school or doesn't want to go back to school, they should think in terms of what's best for them as parents. They would feel better if their daughter graduated from high school. Therefore, the girl should graduate from high school.

(Later in the conversation.)

HALEY: Once she flips, they tend to overcompensate and be nicer and kinder to her when it's the very time when they should be firm. If you say they should be firm, they don't really feel that because she's ill, and so on. But you have to present the argument that if they take a clear position themselves, then a confused daughter can take a clear position. If they're confused themselves, she is going to be confused. So they have to work out something between them, something that they both agree on. Like, the day the girl comes home from the hospital, can she go out that night? They should have a plan; yes or no she can go out. It should not be whether it's good for *her* to go out. It should be whether *they're* comfortable. That's the distinction.

LANDE: Is this a general thing with families?

HALEY: No, with these families at this time . . . You need to impress them with taking a normal position with her like they would with other kids. That will be best for her. Because they don't know how to deal with her, you know, when she's flipped.

(In the interview room mother, father, and therapist sit down together.)

FATHER: I guess we're here to kind of firm up what we ought to do with Anna when we get home with her, you know.

LANDE: It sounds like that would be an important thing.

FATHER: I think it is, and we've talked quite a bit about it since we left— off and on—I don't think we've really come up with anything real firm because I don't think we know quite what's good for her and what isn't yet.

The opening comments of the parents are a sign that the first interview was successful. If the second interview begins with the parents defending themselves from ideas that came up in the first interview, then the therapist has erred. They must have been blamed if they still carry a desire to correct misunderstandings and absolve themselves. When they begin the second interview by getting down to business in this way, the therapist can accept it and go on. Later in the interview the therapist clarifies the issues about the girl returning home and the parents being prepared for her.

LANDE: Let me pick up on something you said. Because I think Annabelle's going home is going to be very dependent on when you two come to an agreement, and that's what, as you said, we set up the session for, on a set of rules and regulations. I think when you two feel comfortable and you've come to an agreement, then she would be ready to go. Because I think this is something she'll need very much. So if . . .

FATHER: I think she needs it, but I don't know exactly what you mean. Do you think she believes she needs it?

LANDE: I'm not sure that's as important as you two agreeing with each other on what would make you two feel comfortable when she comes home. I think that's going to be most crucial.

MOTHER: I think what you're saying is that one of the problems is just that we may not be together in Annabelle's direction, and that would be important to her right now.

Again, the mother offers a problem between the parents which the therapist does not accept.

LANDE: I'm saying that it's going to be important when she comes home—in other words, if at the end of this session . . .

MOTHER: She knows what to expect.

LANDE: Right. At the end of this session you two feel that you're in agreement about, let's say, what time she comes in and whatnot, over the next couple of days, and you feel good about it. I don't think it's as important what Annabelle thinks about it, because she's eighteen and you're her parents.

MOTHER: Mm-hmm.

LANDE: If we can come to an agreement at the end, and you feel good about it, then she may be ready to go home tomorrow. She'll be ready to come home when we all come to this agreement.

FATHER: O.K. I guess I'm having some fear that it isn't going to be that simple, but I hope you're right. Because she can really be hell to try and manage if she don't want to do something.

(Later in the interview.)

LANDE: She's coming out of the hospital, and I think this is a time when she needs very firm rules.

FATHER: O.K., she keeps saying things like this, though: "I'm an adult. I don't need people telling me what to do. I don't like this hospital because they keep telling me what to do." And I know she needs direction.

LANDE: If she didn't need direction right now she wouldn't be in the hospital; so part of her problem is that she needs direction. At the point that she shows—whenever that is; in a week, or a month, or a year—that she's an adult, then obviously things would get renegotiated.

(Later in the interview.)

MOTHER: I really feel that I need some trust to be restored, that I have a right to expect Annabelle to really show me that she *is* capable of being trusted, because I have had some evidence that she couldn't be. I'm not sure if that's the best way to put it. But I'm scared, I guess. I'm really scared of what's happened before. You know, I feel maybe overly protective now, in that I would like her to see her friends, at least for a while, at home.

(Later in the interview.)

FATHER: I have some real concerns about this boyfriend of hers. This guy has had sexual relations with her, and they've had drugs together. That's way out of my value system. I really don't know how—I really feel angry about him right now.

LANDE: Well, for instance, if Annabelle says tomorrow, "Can I go out and see Arnold?" how are you two going to respond? This has to be in the plan.

FATHER: Here's the way—just to be frank about it, I called Dr. Marsh at the hospital when she first went in. She was—you know, she had a lot of anger and she was really fantasizing a lot. She was afraid she was pregnant. She thought she was being brought there to have an abortion. She had all kinds of weird ideas. Yet she was menstruating; she wasn't pregnant. But anyway, it had become very obvious, you know—then she—she had told her mother earlier about some of the things between her and the boy, and I wasn't aware of it. And I kind of found out what the hell was going on while she was in the hospital. And within the last week or so she's talked to me about it. And apparently she has been promiscuous with other boys earlier.

LANDE: If I'm hearing you correctly, you're not entirely comfortable with her relationship with Arnold?

FATHER: I am not at all!

LANDE: This is something that you two really have to . . .

FATHER: Well, we've talked about it a lot.

LANDE: What's going to happen when Annabelle comes home?

FATHER: I want to talk to *you* about that. Because I talked to Dr. Marsh and I said, "Hey, look, I find this has happened. That's way out of my—I don't see it at all. What I'd like to do is tell this guy to shove off and don't come around again. I'm going to kick the hell out of him." You know, I didn't say it in those words. But anyway, he told me—he said he didn't think that was wise to do right now in her state because he didn't want to change her environment a lot. Okay, so I haven't done a thing. I haven't said a word to him, and I didn't even like what he said.

The father's comment illustrates how an expert can incapacitate a father, but an equally important issue can be emphasized here. Why would a mother and father not be able to agree about setting rules for the daughter? When a high-school-age daughter is staying out until four in the morning and smoking dope, why can't the parents agree on rules and enforce them? The issue with the boyfriend can be used to illustrate how a marital difficulty causes parents to be unable to deal with a daughter's misbehavior.

When mother and father are not getting along, father can turn to his daughter for emotional company. He will therefore tend to be jealous if the girl goes with a boy outside the home and will be overstrict about the boy. In these interviews it was clear that the father consistently thought that punishment for the girl should be depriving her of the boyfriend. The mother, in a natural competition with her daughter, will prefer to divert her daughter from her husband to outside the home and will therefore encourage the relationship with the boyfriend. The parents will be unable to agree on how to deal with daughter and boyfriend when there is misbehavior. (There will also be mixed feelings in both parents about the issue: father will also wish daughter to have a boyfriend, and mother will prefer that father have an interest elsewhere when she is not getting along with him.) An inability of the parents to deal with the marital issues forces confusion into their function as parents. The therapy can focus on the rules for the daughter and in that way deal with the issue of agreement between the parents.

LANDE: This is remarkable to me that you two are so rightly concerned with Annabelle's feelings and Arnold's feelings and Dr. Marsh's feelings, and I think you give yourselves short shrift as parents. I think what you're comfortable with and what your feelings are come like third or fourth. To me, you have very powerful and strong feelings about your daughter. She's coming out of the hospital—but you put your feelings low in order.

FATHER: The reason I'm doing that is that I feel partly responsible for the state she's in. I don't feel that probably I've done a good job, or she wouldn't be like that. So, you know, I'm looking for some direction.

(Later in the interview.)

LANDE: So for the next week—before we end, I would feel real good about Annabelle being discharged if you have like a daily log of what she is going to be able to do or not. I'm trying to be very concrete so . . .

FATHER: Fine. I like to operate like that. I think that would be great.

LANDE: I'm like you. I kind of like to think and have the specifics and the details. It makes life easier for me. So tomorrow Annabelle, if she comes home, and says, "Can I go out?" the answer you agree on is . . .

MOTHER: Would you agree to this? I would say, "No, but Arnold or anybody else is welcome to come to the house."

FATHER: Yeah.

Mother and father are now talking to each other and being reasonably specific. One must expect, however, that as they make a decision, they will then tend to take it back. As the father says, "On the one hand, but on the other hand." The therapist must be patient enough to spend forty minutes on a parental discussion of what time a young person should be in at night. The issue is not the parents making a decision but their communicating together. After reaching a decision, the mother begins to take it back later in the interview.

MOTHER: I don't want to get to be so darn suspicious that the poor kid can't move either. I mean that . . .

FATHER: That's true. But, on the other hand, for her own sake, I think we have to, you know, kind of redirect her a lot. And I think she's really been misleading us a lot. But on the other hand, we should have been smart enough, I should have, when some girl comes in at three, four, or five o'clock in the evening (*meaning* A.M.), you know, and all you do is just go into an uproar about it the next day, and nothing more, and it happens again and again—you should know that something is going on.

Once the parents decide on a rule, then there is inevitably a similar struggle and difficult discussion of how they might enforce the rule. It is best if the therapist first gets a rule clear and then deals with how to enforce it. Later in the interview this comes up.

FATHER: Except this, the kids won't do it, and how we get them to do it is where we had the problem.

MOTHER: It's what happens when the rules are broken.

LANDE: What's going to happen? You say ten o'clock and Annabelle, I don't know, throws a tantrum or . . .

FATHER: I'll tell you what she's done before. First she'd just walk out of the house, and then, you know, we would have to, you know, go find out where she is and get her back. Maybe. And sometimes she won't come back.

LANDE: Well, what are you two going to do when she starts walking out of the house?

FATHER: Well, I don't know.

LANDE: Could you still physically . . .?

The therapist is asking the father if he can physically restrain his daughter. This is a necessary question. The discussion is brief here, but in some families the discussion must be lengthy. If the young person is not to be reinstitutionalized, the family must deal with violence and threats of violence at home. Therefore the therapist must plan with the family how to contain potential violence.

FATHER: Oh, hell, yes. There's no problem with that. You know, the thing is whether that's good for her mental state or not, you know, you get her all in an uproar.

LANDE: This is the strangest thing. You two worry so much about her mental state, I worry about you two as parents. This is a very stressful period for you two.

(Later in the interview.)

LANDE: I think she's going to—your wife is going to need you very much to help her through this period of Annabelle's coming home. I don't know if you hear that. It's a very bad time.

The therapist uses the problem of the daughter to bring the parents closer together.

FATHER: I guess I don't, because in the past it hasn't been that she's wanted my help at all, I don't think.

MOTHER: Oh, that's not true.

FATHER: Well hey, every time I do something you tell me it's wrong, and I can't do anything. And it just ends up that nothing gets done.

MOTHER: Well I have to disagree with . . .

FATHER: And I think we've been pretty damn consistent about it. You know, like, "You come in by eleven o'clock." We give them a time to come in, and it isn't varying very often. It may be only a half hour at the most from night to night.

(The therapist shifts away from the disagreement to agreements.)

LANDE: How are you going to help your wife when Annabelle keeps asking to go somewhere and your wife says, you know, she shouldn't go? How are you going to help her deal with that?

FATHER: O.K., I would tell Anna to get back in here and stop that. That's what I usually do.

(Later in the interview.)

LANDE: What happens if she somehow gets you to feel guilty? "I'm eighteen. I'm grown up, and you're treating me like I'm fifteen."

FATHER: Oh hey, we hear that, you know, all the time from the three older ones. They put every problem they ever had and everything back on their parents. They really have this—try to put the guilt on us a lot.

LANDE: I think it would be a good idea tonight—if Annabelle is going to go home tomorrow, maybe tonight when the kids are in bed and everything has quieted down, if you two together, without the kids, for about an hour would sit down and on a piece of paper—we find, in general, that these things just work better—really kind of firm up the things you two decided here, and any other things about what's going to happen over the next three-day period or four-day period. Just really make sure that you both are on the same team.

This task for the parents is to help them reach agreement about their daughter. Perhaps more important, it also requires then to spend some more time communicating together. The more they talk together, the less the girl needs to perform their differences. A task between sessions also keeps the therapist present during the week, since they are thinking about him when they do or don't do the task.

At the third interview, the parents are asked to come with the girl to present their plan to her. One can assume the girl will attempt to undo the plan, and the therapist must support the parents. Supervisor and therapist talk before the third interview.

HALEY: Let's review a little. You had a session alone with the parents and they were going to have her home once they agreed on the rules. And she did come home Friday?

LANDE: Friday, right.

HALEY: Then what happened? What have you heard over the weekend?

LANDE: I called them Saturday afternoon to find out how things—if going home went O.K. I asked to speak to the mother, and I spoke to her. So far things are going much better than expected, she said. But Anna got on the phone and was kind of angry about the parents setting the rules. I acted very dumb about it. She was very angry, she didn't want to come in. I said, well, we could talk about it on Monday. She didn't want to come in and I said "It soulds like you have a problem with your parents. If I were you I'd want to try to work it out. You're living at home." Then she mentioned something about the medication. She wasn't happy with that. There were a lot of four letters words.

When there is a conflict between the parents and a problem young person, the therapist can feel caught between them, trying to side with the authority of the parents while having the best interests of the young person in mind. Sometimes it helps to have more than just the two factions in the room, as this therapist prefers and discusses later in the conversation.

LANDE: The other thing I'm worried about is that I'm worried with just three people in the room, and I had thought maybe just to ask them to bring another sibling arbitrarily, maybe another adolescent. I'm worried about being able to join—joining with the parents is one thing; I don't know how I'm going to be able to join with her *and* her parents.

HALEY: Well, that's the art of this business.

LANDE: Now I know how to do it. (*Laughing.*)

(*Third interview with the family, parents and Anna present.*)

ANNA: You look kind of casual today compared to my mom. She looks dressed up. (*To mother.*) You know that design you have there? Well, with my psychiatrist at the hospital, it was complete and it had the cross up. It looked like the paint was dripping, and it looked like there was a dead bird hanging up there like this. (*Illustrating a design on the front of a dress by lifting her arms and letting them hang.*)

LANDE: We don't go for that kind of stuff here. *(Laughter of all.)* We're much more informal than that.

ANNA: Yeah, it looks like it.

LANDE: So how does it feel to be home?

ANNA: It feels confusing because I got too many restrictions on me now.

(Later in the interview.)

LANDE: Are you very, very clear in your mind what exactly—not generally, but exactly—your mom has in mind?

ANNA: What my mom has in mind?

LANDE: Yeah. She's very concerned about how certain things are going to go for you.

ANNA: Well, let me see, I don't know exactly, but I think . . .

LANDE: Why don't you ask her, if you don't know exactly? You see, it's important that if she has something in mind . . .

ANNA: *(To mother.)* All right, what?

MOTHER: What am I concerned about?

ANNA: Are you concerned about drugs? Are you concerned about my social life?

MOTHER: I'm concerned about drugs. I'm concerned about, uh—you being able to carry maybe the weight of some ridicule.

ANNA: Oh man, I can carry ridicule. Man, I've been ridiculed ever since I was three. I can carry it. I can ridicule right back. It doesn't hurt me.

LANDE: *(Leaning forward and talking to the daughter.)* Why don't you ask your mom, what about drugs?

ANNA: Yeah, what about drugs?

MOTHER: What about drugs? Well, let's say you have experimented with them. And I think most of the kids who are on drugs like the company of someone else who is too.

ANNA: And they'll want my company.

MOTHER: Yes. They'll want you back with them.

ANNA: Too bad for them. That's all I can say. *(Laughs.)*

MOTHER: That sounds great. It really sounds great.

(Later in the interview.)

LANDE: You'd like to see what? Because I'm confused about what you . . .

MOTHER: On drugs?

LANDE: Yeah.

MOTHER: No drugs.

LANDE: Well that's . . .

ANNA: No drugs, but I would still like to smoke marijuana because it's, you know, a nice nerve calmer. Like if you have a hard day you need something to calm your nerves. Mom and Dad can have a martini, but what can I have?

FATHER: You know that's an old—we hear that cliché, you know, all the time about marijuana and martinis. But, by the way, I don't have a martini hardly at all.

ANNA: I noticed.

FATHER: We don't even have much alcohol in the house, for a long time.

LANDE: You're both saying, or you're saying, that you're agreed about this—no drugs.

FATHER: Yes sir. I sure am.

ANNA: But see, I'm the one that wants it, and they're the ones that don't. Like I don't want drugs. All I would like is marijuana, you know.

(Later in the interview.)

LANDE: You would probably be wondering how the first day went at school and a lot of things, so it would seem to be important that you know what time to expect her.

MOTHER: Yes.

LANDE: I think you need to kind of establish with Annabelle what time she is . . .

MOTHER: Yes. But classes are over at one-thirty, aren't they? One-thirty is your latest class? Isn't it?

ANNA: I don't know, because my last class is art.

FATHER: Anna, you know why we need to know is important, because we'll be looking for you right away.

ANNA: Well I don't know, but listen. Will you listen to me for a second? My last class is art, and therefore art is lunch. But I can't eat my lunch in time, so I come into class usually late, and I told the teacher I would usually be late. But I can make up the work I missed. So I'll probably hang in there . . .

FATHER: What did the teacher say? Did she agree to that?

ANNA: Yeah, she agreed. My teachers are cool. They know what I'm talking about.

LANDE: You know, Anna, I think what's happened is this is getting too—your parents are just asking you what time you're going to be home. You're not giving them a straight answer.

ANNA: I don't know. That's why.

FATHER: Well, O.K., well look, we can decide now. You don't have to work extra time in art.

ANNA: Yes I do, yes I do, because I'm a slow worker in art.

FATHER: All right, let's say then that you will not work any later than two o'clock in art.

ANNA: Fine.

FATHER: And you'll be home at a quarter after two.

ANNA: That's the time class ends. And I'll be in there late, and class will end at two o'clock, and I won't have the work done. Then I'll fail art, and art is a major!

LANDE: Annabelle, they're talking—I think what your parents are asking is just about tomorrow.

FATHER: We're not talking about the whole year—tomorrow, Tuesday.

LANDE: They're not talking about the whole year.

ANNA: Oh, all right.

FATHER: Because I think tomorrow is going to be hard enough without working overtime.

ANNA: All right. Well then, I'll just come home after the class is over, and I don't know what time that is.

FATHER: It's two o'clock. You just said so.

ANNA: Well that's what usually . . .

FATHER: All right, O.K., it will be two o'clock or very close to it. We'll expect you home at a quarter after two, then.

ANNA: All right, well, if I'm late don't worry about it, because you know . . .

FATHER: Well, we probably will worry about it, then. We'll expect you . . .

ANNA: Well, I have to go—see, I have to—would you let me talk, and listen to something?

FATHER: Yeah. Go ahead, go ahead.

(Later in the interview.)

LANDE: What you two have to also decide is, now what if she is ornery enough not to go along with you? What do you . . .?

MOTHER: And we catch her?

LANDE: And you find out about it. You see, you two have to agree what—she doesn't know what consequence yet. You see, it's still . . .

ANNA: Why are you putting all these rules on my parents? *(Mother laughs.)*

LANDE: I'm just trying to help you out of the confusion. Because I can see how confused it is from your point of view.

FATHER: You know that's going to happen. He's really helping you, Anna, when he does that.

ANNA: He's not helping me at all!

(Later in the interview.)

FATHER: Your privileges of seeing Arnold would be . . .

ANNA: Oh, good . . .

FATHER: . . . taken away.

ANNA: Just so I can see Arnold.

FATHER: No, they would be taken away, if you were smoking marijuana.

ANNA: All right, then, if you're going to take away Arnold, man, I'm just gonna smoke marijuana.

LANDE: So you two—is this something you agree with?

MOTHER: Well, I definitely think some privileges should be taken away.

LANDE: Do you agree with your husband's suggestion?

MOTHER: I'll have to think about it for a minute. Yeah, I guess so. If it's that effective, yes.

(Later in the interview.)

LANDE: O.K. Do you feel that you two have set that up with her?

FATHER: That she will call? I'm not so sure.

LANDE: If she doesn't come, what's going to happen?

FATHER: No, we have not.

LANDE: Because I can see maybe you don't see it, Annabelle, but sitting behind you here, you two are trying so hard to be very flexible with Annabelle. Really, it's coming from the heart. I can feel that. But I can feel, sitting over here, how it's—because you're trying so hard, it doesn't come off as clearly. In other words, as Annabelle, I would have trouble knowing exactly what I should and shouldn't do still. I could tell my parents are really trying very hard to be very careful and loving to me, but I wouldn't know what I was supposed to do.

(Later in the interview.)

MOTHER: *(To Anna.)* Okay. If you don't call on time . . .

ANNA: What's on time?

MOTHER: At two-fifteen.

ANNA: In between two and two-thirty is on time.

FATHER: No. Two-fifteen.

ANNA: In between two and two-thirty is on time.

FATHER: In between two and two-fifteen.

ANNA: Alright, and then what?

MOTHER: At two-fifteen you're to call me. And if you don't call by two-fifteen . . .

ANNA: What if you're on the phone at two-fifteen?

FATHER: *(To mother.)* Tell her what it is, will you?

MOTHER: Then you have to help with dinner as well as help with the cleanup after dinner. If you don't come home on time, you don't have any visitors that night.

ANNA: That sounds all right. Just as long as I don't go crazy while I'm doing it.

LANDE: I think with these very clear things nobody could go crazy. This is the kind of stuff that keeps people right on line.

(Supervisor and therapist talk before the fourth interview.)

LANDE: She called Thursday morning to tell me that she was quite upset because Wednesday night she had told Annabelle she couldn't go to a movie. Annabelle gave an argument, but the mother felt that Annabelle was about to listen. Her husband was out working. At the point the mother was about to get things under control, the eighteen-year-old son, Henry, came in between and told the mother that she was wrong, and that Annabelle should be able to do anything she wanted and stay out to any hour she wanted. The mother reported that they both kind of ganged up on her and said she was a terrible mother and had no right to tell them what to do. The mother felt pretty overwhelmed and terrible about the whole thing. She called me, very distraught. She was very upset and began talking about how bad the marriage was. And she had thought about leaving. At which point, I suggested we should have a meeting pretty soon and not let it go over the weekend.

HALEY: So this was an issue over going to a movie. It wasn't over coming home from school?

(Later in the conversation.)

HALEY: So, what has appeared is that if mother tries to enforce some sort of rule with the girl, the brother, the older brother, now appears as siding with daughter and making life difficult. In this interview you're going to try to hold the brother out of that situation so mother and father can deal with daughter, right?

LANDE: Right.

When the problem young person begins to obey the parents and the parents are sufficiently united to take charge, there is a reaction from other people involved in the situation. In some cases it is individual therapists or other professionals who begin to object to what is being done. At times the grandparents or other members of the extended family, who have been sta-bilized by the previous structure, begin to intrude. A common reaction is that of a sibling. If the problem young person has siblings, a sibling typi-cally intrudes when the hierarchy begins to stabilize with the parents in charge: the sibling attacks the parents, joining the young person against them and saying they are not respecting the rights of the young person. The parents become uncertain and divided, and the therapeutic plan is under-mined. The intrusion of a sibling at this point is typical enough to be expectable, and one of the reasons for having the whole family present in the first interview is to observe the siblings and determine which one might later create difficulties. The correction of the hierarchy with the parents in charge is a change, one that the siblings do not necessarily welcome. If the parents insist on more correct behavior from the problem young person, who has been the focus of attention, they are likely also to begin to insist on more from a sibling when they are free to focus on other aspects of the fam-ily. Sometimes the sibling has been making problems which seem minor in comparison to those created by the problem young person, but once that major issue is settled the parents turn to the more minor problems. At that point they often encounter a sibling coalition against them.

One of the ways to deal with the problem is the way used here. The ther-apist has the parents criticize the sibling for inadequacies, putting him down in the hierarchy. Then the therapist discusses with the sibling whether he wants to take responsibility for his sister. The goal is to persuade him to stay out of the problem and shift the responsibility back to the parents.

(At the fourth interview parents, daughter, and brother are in the room with the therapist.)

LANDE: What about this? Does Henry devote enough, or too much, time to the family? How do you as parents see that?

HENRY: We want to get into a real heavy family thing, you know. I guess ninety percent of my time is devoted to the family.

LANDE: Right now, ninety percent of your time. And you're won-dering . . .

HENRY: No, that's what we would like to get into.

LANDE: Who's we?

HENRY: The two executives of the family.

LANDE: They would like more of your time?

FATHER: No, I don't think we would.

MOTHER: I don't think so. *(Laughs)*

FATHER: I would like to see you follow some rules so we can have some order around . . .

HENRY: Along with rules comes a lot of time, man.

FATHER: It don't take you any time to say, "Hey, I'm going over here."

HENRY: Oh, O.K.

FATHER: It don't take you any time to say, "Hey, I'm taking the car." It don't take you any time to hold reasonable hours that we've asked you to do and you've refused to do.

HENRY: Yeah, that does take time, right there . . .

FATHER: Does it take time to come in at midnight rather than three o'clock in the morning?

HENRY: Oh, come on, man. How many times do I . . .

(Later in the interview.)

LANDE: So, you're really caught between helping your mother and father and helping your sister?

HENRY: Yeah, right. So then it's up to me to make the decision on what's good for Anna, right? And since I have decided I don't really know what's good for Anna, I'll just stick with their rules. I thought, you know, I knew how to handle Anna. The thing is this thing came up Tuesday, and I didn't know how to handle Anna. All I could think of doing was freaking out on her, and, you know, I think that's probably the last thing she needs is someone to freak out on her. So then, as far as I'm concerned, I don't know how to handle Anna.

ANNA: I couldn't believe what you guys did *(the parents)*. After I did that, you started screaming and grabbing at him. He started screaming and grabbing at me.

MOTHER: I didn't scream. I just picked him up and . . .

ANNA: You screamed. You screamed.

HENRY: You screamed, Mom. Everyone was screaming.

ANNA: I was screaming, trying to get out of the way of everybody.

LANDE: *(To son.)* So you're saying it's a little too much for you to take that responsibility?

ANNA: It's a responsibility he took on himself.

HENRY: It's a responsibility that I wouldn't want to handle, man. That's what it is.

(Later in the interview.)

LANDE: *(To son.)* Why don't you bring your chair over by me and sit back, and we'll relax and kind of be the odd men out here. We'll listen on.

HENRY: I'll be more than happy to fall asleep.

LANDE: Let these folks kind of worry about tomorrow and what not.

(The therapist seats the son beside him, outside the family circle, and turns to talk to him while the parents and the daughter deal with the daughter issues.)

ANNA: What have you guys got planned for me tomorrow?

MOTHER: Well, I think we'll have to make out a list of what things are necessary to be done, and then we'll give you your choices, without trying to . . .

ANNA: I'll clean all the bathrooms tomorrow.

MOTHER: I don't know about that.

ANNA: I'd rather clean all the bathrooms tomorrow and clean my room, and be free from the house all the other time.

MOTHER: What do you mean by free from the house?

ANNA: Out.

(After the interview, supervisor and therapist in a conversation.)

HALEY: As far as the goal to be accomplished in that interview, I never saw it done as well. The goal was to move the young man out of the situation and focus on the three of them, and that young man was moved out in actuality and visibly and physically.

LANDE: Off dreaming about his girlfriend doing his wash or something.

HALEY: He was sitting over there combing his hair, out of it, while all this was going on. It's extraordinary. Now the stage that I see—I don't know how you're seeing this, it's going smoothly and so well. It's going at the level of "Let's just get everything back together again." Whatever the hell disrupted this whole thing, we don't really know yet. And I think what you need now is to begin to push that girl toward more independence, and that will begin to unstabilize it. But this time you push it toward more independence step by step and it won't unstabilize in a mad way.

(During an upset that week, the mother had mentioned to the therapist on the telephone that she was thinking of separating from her husband. This was not brought up in the interview with the sibling present, but supervisor and therapist had discussed what to do if separation was brought up.)

HALEY: If one of them starts talking about separation, I think you should say that they shouldn't even consider separation at this point. That they have an obligation to their daughter, and that she's not going to be with them very long, but they should at least stay together long enough to help her get out successfully and on her own feet. That should be the attitude about it. Again, somewhere in the session, you need to say something about her ultimately leaving home.

The separation issue came up in the next interview, which was the fifth interview. The parents say that all is going well with the daughter and then bring up their problems with each other. The parents and daughter are present in the interview with the therapist.

LANDE: How have things been going?

FATHER: All right. I think things have been a lot quieter since the explosion we had last week. Anna seems rather subdued and quiet tonight. She hasn't taken her medicine yet today. I don't know whether that affects her or not. You were napping this afternoon, weren't you Annabelle?

ANNA: Mm-hmm.

FATHER: I haven't seen her quite so quiet since she came home from the hospital. But that's good.

LANDE: How do you see it?

MOTHER: Her quietness?

LANDE: Just how are things in general?

MOTHER: Oh well, things, I think—she has been very responsive to all our limitations. She's been very good.

(Later in the interview.)

MOTHER: There's been some difficulty with this business with my husband as far as—I don't believe we do come to agreements well.

LANDE: About Annabelle?

MOTHER: Yes, about Annabelle, and it will have to go into the other children sooner or later. We've been kind of concentrating on Annabelle. Saturday night I didn't think that we carried it out well. I raised quite a fuss because I didn't think we carried out what we had agreed to do.

FATHER: I'd like to talk about that a little if I can. I don't think that's the way it is at all. I've never been able to make my point.

MOTHER: I feel uncomfortable as far as talking like this in front of Annabelle.

LANDE: You feel that this is something between you and your husband?

MOTHER: Yes.

(The therapist sends Annabelle out to the waiting room.)

FATHER: Well, what did you want to talk about with her gone?

MOTHER: Mainly, what I'd like to know is how jarring would it be for Annabelle right now if my husband and I separated?

(The therapist is startled—the therapy had been going so well.)

LANDE: How jarring would it be for Annabelle?

MOTHER: Psychologically, you know.

LANDE: This is something you two have discussed?

MOTHER: We've been discussing it for several months.

FATHER: Well, that's one way to put it. I think that's something you've been threatening to do for quite a while.

MOTHER: All right, then it's something *I've* been discussing for several months.

LANDE: I'm wondering if you're asking me to give you an answer about

Anna, or whether it's time to start dealing with some marital issues, and not just Anna.

MOTHER: I have to be honest and say that I think I've dealt with the marital issues for quite a while. I'm really interested in your opinion about Anna.

LANDE: What would happen to Anna if you leave your husband?

MOTHER: Yes.

LANDE: (*Long pause.*) That's like the sixty-four-thousand-dollar question. I tell you, if I could give you a straightforward answer I'd give it to you. I can't, I really can't. I think you two have to—number one, decide what's good for you two.

At this point the therapist must tell the parents that they are obligated to stay together until their daughter is on her feet. The issue is not a moral one in relation to separation and divorce. It is simply that the therapist must break the cycle in which the problem young person becomes more normal, and their marital difficulties appear and separation is threatened. The therapist must intervene in the family system to break this cycle. He must arrange that the parents stay together when the adolescent is behaving normally. As the parents deal with each other directly, they need to communicate less through the daughter, so she has the opportunity to disengage and achieve her independence. At that time the parents can stay together or not, as they choose, without the daughter being involved in that issue. The supervisor telephoned the therapist and told him to advise the parents to stay together until the girl graduated from high school, which would be in a few months. Therapists who have been trained to be a consultant to the family and to be nondirective often find it difficult to take the responsibility of telling parents not to separate. They hesitate to take charge to that extreme. This therapist succeeds in asking the parents not to separate, but he puts it gently.

LANDE: My answer would be that right now, to deal with an issue that's been going on for months or years, when your daughter has just come out of the hospital and things are going really nicely now, but there's not a solid foundation yet just from the weeks gone by—I think it's important that at least for the time being that you two can work together effectively enough and stably enough that Annabelle can get on with the things she has to get on with.

With this threat of separation, the first stage is ending. It might be helpful to review some of the steps necessary when helping a family reorganize after such a disturbed episode.

To establish a functioning structure with a clear hierarchy:

First, the experts who have been brought in to deal with the problem must resolve their organizational confusions. It is most effective to have a single therapist with *one* supervisor and a clear hierarchical relationship between them.

Next, the therapist must arrange that the professional community let him be the authority on the case and that there not be other professionals involved.

When the professional network is correctly organized, it is possible to organize the family with the parents in charge. As this process begins, the problem young person will attempt to insist on taking charge. She or he must be gracefully set aside. Another way the young person will attempt to take charge is by using strange metaphors which others cannot understand. These must be blocked off.

As the young person begins to accept parental authority, a sibling will often attempt to confuse the hierarchy by preventing the parents taking charge, as happened in this case, and he or she must be set aside.

Much of the work of the therapy is negotiating disagreements between the parents so that they can jointly take charge of the family instead of attacking each other.

Finally, as the family stabilizes and the parents are in charge, a split between the parents threatens, which could disorganize the family and cause the young person to erupt and save it. The therapist must hold the parents together and bring about at least temporary stability.

By this fifth interview the daughter was back in school, working part-time, and going completely off medication. These are the signs that the first stage of the therapy is ending and trouble is about to begin. It can be expected that there will soon be a crisis, and that will be stage two of the therapy.

At this point the first stage has been completed. The problem young person has been properly brought home from the mental hospital, and the family is ready to deal with the issues that precipitated the crisis in the first place.

A note about some variations in this therapeutic approach is in order for therapists dealing with a variety of kinds of families. This family is a typical one in that the parents are hesitant and ineffectual and their mad daughter has taken authority over them. The parents had to call in outside help to deal with her. The strategy of the therapy is to place the parents in charge by persuading them to take the necessary actions. The daughter is placed further down in the hierarchy not so much by being put down herself as by the fact that the parents are placed higher. These parents are intelligent, functioning people who can cooperate in this approach. In some cases parents are so helpless and ineffectual that they do not respond. For example, with some drug problems the parents seem so passive and helpless, and the addict so skillful in dealing with them, that asking them to take charge in the beginning is asking too much. Sometimes one of the parents also has a serious problem, such as a drinking problem. In such cases another approach is for the therapist to put the addict down. As this is done, the parents are placed higher by the fact that the addict is placed lower than they are by the expert.

As an example, I recall how Paul Riley, a skillful therapist, dealt with a heroin addict and his parents. The parents seemed helpless and passive. The interview began with Mr. Riley asking the addict to take off his cap. This was done politely, but it was clear that an issue was being made of the problem son being discourteous while the parents were not. The addict was twenty-seven years old and considered himself superior to other people in many ways. He listed the important jobs he had had over the years. Out of this discussion came an emphasis on how he had been unable to keep a job while his father had kept a job for twenty-one years and his mother for seventeen. The addict countered that he did not wish that square life-style. Mr. Riley countered that the style the addict had chosen had landed him in jail and with an addiction for which he now sought help, while the parents continued to live and work in the community. This kind of step-by-step putting of the problem young person down in relation to the parents is a beginning which can later lead to the parents initiating more authoritative acts on their own. The task of the therapist is not to be warm, empathetic, and permissive, but to be negative to the addict while still keeping him involved in a cooperative way.

Historians of therapy may recall that John Rosen, with his *Direct Analysis*,[4] emphasized the importance of the therapist's taking charge of a mad young person. He was criticized by nondirective therapists who sat passively and listened to such young people (and failed in therapy with them). I once reported a case in which a young man insisted he was God, and Dr. Rosen said, "I'll have to show you who God is," and he had his assistants force the young man to his knees.[5] By the 1950s it had become clear that mad young people exercised authority inappropriate to their willingness to take responsibility, and the therapist needed to take charge. In those cases, the therapist often succeeded in establishing a hierarchy where he or she was in charge and the mad young person was not; but then the young person was sent home, where nothing had changed. At home the young person again took charge in a mad way while the parents responded helplessly and the hierarchy continued to malfunction. Only later was it realized that correcting the hierarchy in the artificial setting of an institution or with nonintimates was not the point. The hierarchy needs to be corrected in the intimate group where the young person lives.

---

[4] J. N. Rosen, *Direct Analysis*, Grune & Stratton, New York, 1951.
[5] J. Haley, *Strategies of Psychotherapy*, Grune & Stratton, New York, 1963.

Chapter 6

Beginning Correctly in the First Interview

A first interview with the family of a mad and eccentric young person is not like other, more routine, therapy interviews. To come together with such a family without a plan is to invite misfortune and difficulties. It is not best for the therapist to be exploratory and merely wait to see what will happen.

If a young adult is in a mental hospital, a drug rehabilitation center, or a jail, there is no need to find out what the problem is, since it is self-evident. The young person is in severe trouble in the community, and the family is malfunctioning. A similar assumption appears at times with a younger problem child: if an anorectic child comes in as a walking skeleton, the issue is not what the problem is but what is to be done so the child does not die of starvation or from a disease because of lowered resistance.

Obviously the goal with a young adult in custody is that he or she leave the institution and live in a normal way, with the family and professional community surviving that change. The therapist does not have to explore what the problems and goals are; he must take charge. As he takes charge, exploration occurs and information is gathered about the specifics of the situation, but exploration is not the point of the interview. In fact, an exploration can lead to difficulties and cause the therapy to fail. Usually the therapist must be able to tolerate working with less information than he would like to have as he is intervening.

As in many therapy situations, the more extreme the problem, the more obvious the strategy. If a young person is in custody, the issue in the first interview can be clearer than if the young person is behaving in a mad way but has not yet activated social control agents. When institutionalization first takes place, the young person and family are uncertain and unstable, and so the therapist has leverage. With a first custody, the young person usually wants to get out, which gives therapist and parents an advantage. By the second or third admission, the young person has learned to take advantage of custody, or the threat of it. The family, too, has learned to make use of custody. When the child is first taken from the family, neither the child nor the parents are certain what to do in this crisis; therefore they follow directives that lead to change. Once the family has learned to use the institution to stabilize itself, however, change is more difficult. The therapist asking to place the young person immediately back into the community is asking the family to reexperience instability and stress.

Although therapist and family have more leverage in the situation of first custody, that does not mean that custody should be used to facilitate therapy. The stigma of being in an institution can outweigh any advantages. Moreover, one cannot predict whether a person can be freed from social control agencies once they are activated, because such organizations have purposes and needs of their own.

When the young person is not institutionalized, and sometimes even when he is, there are certain rules about how to recruit the family to cooperate. That is, sometimes the young person is presented as a problem, and the family needs to be brought into the therapy. Certain procedures increase the probability that the family will cooperate.

First of all, they should be asked to come in to help their son or daughter, not to have "family therapy." Few people want family therapy, particularly when they think it means exploring their past and all their guilts and problems. A willingness to help the offspring is usually present, however.

The young person should not decide how to conduct the therapy. Whether the family is to be involved or not should be decided by the expert in therapy, not by a mad young person. At this stage of leaving home, the family needs to be involved in the therapy whether the young person wants to have that happen or not. Sometimes the young person is reluctant to involve the parents because he is protective of them. Only if he sees that the therapist is competent will he show a willingness to let the parents be exposed to the therapist.

The therapist should not expect the young person to bring in the family. The therapist, as expert, should take that responsibility, personally contact the parents, and ask them to come in for an interview with the problem young person. If they are reluctant, they should be asked to help by providing information and guidance to the therapist; they should not be criticized. Just as the therapist should not expect a mother to bring in a reluctant father but should invite the father directly, so should the therapist not expect the young person to bring in the parents but should invite them directly. That makes what happens in the interview the therapist's responsibility, not the problem young person's.

Assumptions

Certain social assumptions are helpful to a therapist doing a first interview. Even though these assumptions may not always hold, and there may be occasional exceptions and surprises, still it is better to discover the exception in the occasional case than to err by uncertainty and lack of planning in every case.

1. It should be assumed that the hierarchy in the family is in confusion and that there is a marital impasse of more than usual severity. The way a therapist begins the interview, even the matter of whom he speaks to first, should begin to correct the hierarchy.

2. The problem person should be assumed to be organically sound and intelligent, if only covertly so. He or she is failing as a way of protecting the family and should be approached with patience and respect, but not allowed to disrupt the interview. Normality and a medication-free life should be expected. The therapist should express that view to indicate that the family can survive normality.

3. It should be assumed that the young person's leaving the family by becoming normal and self-supporting is a serious threat to the family, no matter how much the parents protest that that is their wish. The family needs to be reassured that the young person will not leave home unpredictably and irresponsibly, but only under the direction of the parents.

4. The parents will offer the young person as the problem rather than the family. The therapist should accept that while knowing that the parents are also aware that the family is a problem.

Expected Difficulties

Although families have similar organizations, each is unique and will present different content in the interview. It is sometimes difficult to see the similarity between a seventeen-year-old girl in a loud and noisy battle with her parents over drug use, and a quiet male graduate student who becomes apathetic just before his oral examinations. The therapist needs to separate the content issues from the organizational ones and to recognize the important patterns and sequences in the situation. The intellectually abstruse philosopher son who is incapacitated by his concern with sin can be functioning in the same way organizationally as the retarded son incapacitated by the difficulties of tying his own shoes.

When the young person and parents are in a struggle, it is difficult for some therapists to achieve coalitions with both generations. The therapist must side with the parents at this time of crisis while also maintaining an alliance with the young person. It is an error to side with the young person against the parents, but to join the parents and ignore or antagonize the offspring can cause disruption of the therapy and can mean the therapist has been outwitted by the young eccentric, who can continue to fail.

The therapist needs to listen to the young person for guidance, no matter how seemingly mad his statements. At the same time the therapist should not let the mad behavior interfere with the interview when important family issues are arising. The problem young person knows the family issues well; that is his job, and the therapist should let him be the guide to the important problems. Yet he must not let the youth present his directions in such a rude and offensive way as to interrupt and prevent the aims of the interview from being accomplished. That is, the mad young person has two tasks: one is to help the parents by being a failure and causing trouble when they are in difficulty so they will pull themselves together to deal with him; the other is to help the parents by guiding the therapist toward what needs to be done. The therapist must accept the guidance while preventing too much disruption.

The parents need to be supported in their correct position in the hierarchy—being in charge of the children—even though they may be behaving inadequately or incompetently. The therapist has the problem of arranging a correct hierarchy at a time when the people of upper status are struggling with each other in such a way that they are incapacitated and cannot offer executive leadership.

The Social Stage

As with any other interview, the family must be made as comfortable and as much at ease as possible. The special circumstances of the situation are the uncertainty of the parents about what is expected and their expectation of blame. If the young person has been charged with a crime, the parents can more justifiably feel that the fault lies in him, not them. If a mental hospital is involved, the parents are usually more uneasy. They are not sure if they are being blamed by being asked in for the interview; they are not sure whether they will also be thought to be crazy; they are uneasy about what will come out about what led to the crisis and hospitalization; and they expect that the professional staff will be on the side of the young person because they have been associating with him and hearing his views rather than those of the parents. It is therefore important that the therapist treat the parents and other family members with respect and special courtesy. It needs to be made clear from the way the therapist introduces himself or herself, and how he or she asks the family members to take off their coats and be seated, that no one is to be blamed.

Besides the issue of blame, the problem of hierarchy must be dealt with during the social stage. The parents should be talked to first, the children later. It should be made immediately clear that this is not going to be an interview of a "patient" in front of his family, but that the family members will all be involved, and the expert will be joining the parents in dealing with their problem child.

At this stage the physical nature of the room should be made clear, if necessary; for example, the presence of one-way mirrors and observers, video cameras and microphones, and so on.

Generally the social stage is one where the family is made at ease and helped to recover from any misunderstandings and apprehensions so that the business of the therapy can be conducted. If the problem child makes a difficulty immediately, or if the parents say something about the problem immediately, the therapist should suggest that he would like to meet everyone before dealing with the problems. If the problem young person is particularly upset and uneasy, the therapist should reassure the *parents* about the situation and make it less threatening to them. As the parents feel more at ease, the problem child will usually quiet down and not be obstreperous as a way of helping them.

Ordinarily in a first interview, when the family is at ease, the therapist will ask about the problem. With this extreme situation, the therapist should make an orientation statement to the family instead.

The Orientation Statement

Just how the orientation statement is begun will depend on how the family came to the therapist. If they have been sold on therapy elsewhere and have arrived to begin it, that is one situation. If they have arrived in an involuntary way because their child is incarcerated and they have been asked to come in, then a different beginning is necessary. In either case the therapist should express some appreciation about everyone coming and then state the agenda of the meeting and the goals of the therapy. This is not a situation in which the therapist wishes to be ambiguous or mysterious to see how the family responds. It is not a time for long silences, waiting to see what the family offers. The therapist needs to make a clear statement, and the family can then agree or disagree with his position.

The particular phrasing of the therapist will vary with the social class of the family, the ages of the people involved, the number of family members, and so on. What will be emphasized here are the issues that should be covered.

1. The family should be told that the goal of the therapist is to get the young person back to normal as quickly as possible. The therapy should be defined as brief and practical—to achieve a return to school or work.

2. The therapy will focus on the present situation rather than on the past. There will not be an exploration of how the young person was raised, but rather, an emphasis on the issue of what is to be done now.

These two points, the emphasis on getting quickly back to normal, and not exploring the past will save misunderstandings. Many families assume that therapy must be lengthy, meaning years of interviews, and that it must explore all past miseries and faults. Much resistance of families, particularly those who have had previous therapy, is avoided if the type of therapy approach is defined in this way. Often the family will test the therapist by bringing up a past issue, and he must behave consistently with his statement.

3. The therapist should say that he would like this to be the last institutionalization of the young person (assuming the therapy begins in the custody situation; otherwise it can be stated that he wishes to avoid institutionalization). He should say that the goal of the therapy is to help the family solve its problems without having to put the young person into custody. Sometimes it is necessary to say that a cycle can occur where custody is used again and again, and the custody itself prevents the problems from being resolved. From this point on, therefore, the family,with the therapist's help, is to solve the problems.

4. The therapist should emphasize that the best therapists for the young person are his parents. In this way the problem is defined as a family one rather than one for the experts to solve. The parents know the young person best and if they pull together they can get him back to normal.

5. If the problem young person is of the troublemaking variety, at some point during the interview the father should be asked if he can physically restrain the child: "Can you whip him?" If the father expresses doubt, then can father and mother do it? If not, can father, mother, and sibling do it? If not, what about a neighbor to help? Such an inquiry should not be made immediately, but later in the interview when the parents are feeling more at ease with the therapist. (Occasionally there are abusive parents, and the issue of violence must be handled differently.) The inquiry emphasizes that this problem will be dealt with in the home, not by agents of social control and custody. It also helps the parents realize that the therapist knows the seriousness of the situation and is not minimizing the difficult behavior of the problem person.

6. If the young person is of the apathetic variety, the parents must be told that waiting for him to do something will not do. He must be pushed to school or work, even if he objects, because nothing will happen until the parents take action. (When the parents insist, the young person knows they are ready for him to resume a normal life and can tolerate that.) He

cannot be forced to get a job, but he can be forced out of the house at eight o'clock in the morning to look for one.

7. Suicide, or threat of it, is a special problem. In the orientation statement, the therapist might take the position that the family is to be responsible for the young person's life. They are to take turns watching him or her, or are to do whatever is necessary as part of their responsibility. The family structure is changed in the process of supervising the suicidal young person.

8. The parents should be advised that it is very important for them to reach agreement about what the young person is to do. If they pull together, the young person will straighten out. It isn't a question of which one is right, but of doing it together.

Correcting the Hierarchy

Often parents join with the therapist and do what he or she suggests without offering difficulties. The therapist should expect that. At times there is a reaction against what he suggests. As the therapist attempts to put the parents in charge of their problem offspring, there are at least six ways they can attempt to decline. The beginning of the therapy might center on this issue.

1. The parents may decline to accept the therapist as an authority. Sometimes they decline to bring to the interview the people the therapist wishes to have there, or they will not come themselves at the time necessary. Or they simply object to the therapist's plan. It is important that the therapist take charge at this time. (As Carl Whitaker emphasizes, the therapist must win the struggle at the beginning of the therapy, or failure is likely.[1]) If the hierarchical relationship with the therapist is not accepted by the parents, the children will not accept the hierarchical relationship with the parents.

2. If the parents are not behaving correctly in relation to their children, the grandparents are usually not behaving correctly in relation to the parents. Sometimes the parents decline authority and hand it to the grandparents. Often the grandparents intrude and prevent the parents from exerting authority, usually thinking they must rescue the grandchild from the parents. When this happens, the therapist must move the grandparents to an advisory position in relation to the parents and put the parents in charge of the problem child, without helpful interference by the grandparents.

3. When the therapist attempts to put the parents in charge, they decline

[1] See "The Growing Edge" in J. Haley and L. Hoffman, *Techniques of Family Therapy*, Basic Books, New York, 1967.

and offer outside experts as authorities instead. When the parents say they are only following the advice of other experts, the therapist must assure them that no other experts are authorities in the case, and that they must take charge as he asks. For example:

FATHER: I don't know what the doctors *(in the hospital)* will allow her to do.

THERAPIST: I think what's important—let me try to support you. I think what is important is what *you two* decide now.

(Later in the interview.)

MOTHER: *(After difficulty among family members has occurred in the interview.)* Does the hospital give us a recommendation about what would be the best after they've studied it? What would be the best situation?

THERAPIST: No. At one important level they've made one of the recommendations, and that's why everybody is here today. This is their basic referral. I've talked to her doctor and the social worker several times last week. We've been in very close contact. So the basic idea in terms of follow-up and all of that is made.

Having established himself as the one who has been referred the case, the therapist goes on to the issues of return to school, and so on.

4. Another variation is the parents' declining to take charge by turning to the child to make the decision, despite the young person's evident incapacity.

It is a typical pattern of the parents to turn to the problem young person when they are uncertain; that is what gives the offspring more authority in the hierarchy than the parents. It is as improper as parents asking a child how he should be disciplined or asking an adolescent daughter's advice about how they should conduct their sex lives.

Even when a problem young person is older and would normally be included in many life decisions, if not make them entirely himself or herself, that does not apply in this abnormal situation, where the offspring is incarcerated because of not taking responsibility for making sensible decisions.

If the parents do not turn to the young person, often the young person intrudes and insists on taking charge and making decisions instead of the parents. For example:

THERAPIST: One of the things is that Annabelle is going to be coming home pretty soon, and I guess you all have to make plans about what she's going to be doing, and things like that.

ANNABELLE: *(To parents.)* Are you guys going to make my plans?
FATHER: Isn't that strange.
ANNABELLE: Why can't I make my own plans?
FATHER: I think when he said *we*, he meant including you.

In this approach, the father is being inappropriately egalitariarian. The therapist will correct him and suggest that the parents will make plans for the daughter's immediate future, since she got herself hospitalized by behaving in an irresponsible way and forcing others to take charge. Often young people in this situation object, and the therapist must find a way to keep them from exerting authority without antagonizing them. Sometimes the problem is more extreme if the offspring is older. A drug addict said to his parents, "Nobody is going to make no rules for no twenty-six," which can be translated as no parents are to make rules for a young man twenty-six years old. In other cases the move to take charge by the young person is more subtle, as in the following example, when the therapist makes a brief opening statement and the young person responds. The parents and the young man and his wife are in the room.

THERAPIST: I want to meet like this on about a once weekly basis. I'll also be giving you the medication, and with you we'll work out the various dosages. I'll be in contact with the people at the day hospital in terms of how long you're going to stay. We'll work that out. What I see my role as— I want to help you get back to normal, get back to your normal life.
SON: O.K., I can understand that.
THERAPIST: We can all work together toward that goal.
SON: I don't think it will take, frankly—I think it will take less time than perhaps my father and mother are thinking.
THERAPIST: We'll work that out as the therapy goes . . .

Another way the problem young person can be put in charge is by the therapist. When nervous and uncertain facing the parents, a therapist can turn to the problem young person and ask how he feels about discharge or other issues. The young person can then take charge, and the therapist will have failed by placing someone who should be lower in the hierarchy in charge of a parental decision. In fact, at times the therapist will let the young person take charge of the therapy by letting him or her free-associate and "ventilate" and thus determine what happens in the interview. The nervous therapist and nervous parents can then be relieved of responsibility and also have someone to blame for the difficulties of the therapy.

5. A sibling steps in and takes charge, putting parents aside. This usually occurs later in the therapy, rather than in the first interview, at a time

when the problem young person is becoming more normal because the parents are asserting their executive position more successfully. At that point the sibling protests to the parents that they are handling the situation all wrong, that they do not understand the modern generation, and so on.

When the sibling attempts to take charge in the first interview, or later, the therapist must prevent this and say that the parents are in charge of the family and will make the decisions.

6. When placed in charge, the parents can turn on each other and begin a quarrel that prevents them from exerting joint authority. The therapist must prevent this and require them to agree and decide.

In other families, the mother and father can behave in such an extremely negative or violent way that the therapist is persuaded that they simply are not capable of taking charge of their child; they seem too incapacitated and incapable of parenting. Even so, the therapist must simply insist that they take charge and agree with each other, and set aside other issues until the problem child is on his or her feet.

These six ways that parents avoid authority occur in many different variations during the opening stages. As the therapist puts the parents in charge, they offer the authority to him or her, to other experts, to the problem young person, or to a sibling; or they collapse or attack one another in such a way that their inability to take charge seems evident. The therapist must require authority from them by patiently and repetitiously clarifying the responsibility in the situation. He must particularly emphasize that ultimately the problem will come back to them, because other people, including the experts, will only exert authority temporarily. The parents face a lifetime of being parents of this offspring.

Sometimes the disruption caused by the offspring makes it seem easier for the parents simply to throw up their hands and say they can do nothing. A typical example is in a first interview with a young woman experiencing anorexia nervosa. The parents must be told that they are to take responsibility to see that she gains weight. This can be done in a lunch session where they force the daughter to eat during the interview, as in Dr. Salvador Minuchin's original procedure, [2] or a plan can be made for what is to happen at home from that point on. As the parents express hesitation about whether they can make their daughter gain weight, the daughter will often begin to yell and protest, threatening to leave the interview, and thereby encourage the parents to say it is really too much for them. There must then be talk of dying, or the alternate plan of hospitalization can be

[2] S. Minuchin, B. L. Rosman, and L. Baker, *Psychosomatic Families: Anorexia Nervosa in Context*, Harvard University Press, Cambridge, 1978.

described as only a temporary solution, because the daughter will be back with them in this situation when she stops eating after coming out of the hospital. The fact that they must ultimately do something (so why not now?) is repetitiously emphasized. Out of such an interview will come a plan of how much she is to gain each week, who is to weigh her, who is to work out her diet with her, and so on.

The therapist can put the parents in charge and resolve their disagreements with each other by being firm and persistent but also reassuring. The fact that he is confident that they can do the job impels them to try and absolves them of guilt about the past.

Organizing Communication

In order to give the orientation statement and to arrange the response to it, the therapist must organize the interview so that business can be done. Besides declining their correct positions in the hierarchy, the family can respond to the orientation statement, or prevent the statement, by behaving in a chaotic way, with so many interruptions that nothing can be said. The therapist must organize the family so that everyone takes turns, no subconversations develop, and everyone stays in the room. Sometimes the family is chaotic because they do not have experience in talking together one at a time. Many find this experience a unique one. It can be a matter of training or requiring them to do that.

A common problem in the first interview is the way the mad young person saves the parents by misbehaving and disrupting the interview. I recall an impressive example of that kind of behavior many years ago. On a research project on mad families, we were visited by a Japanese woman psychiatrist, who described the families of hospitalized patients she was dealing with in Japan. They sounded so similar to American families that we included in our sample a Japanese-American family. The parents could hardly speak English, and the three teenage boys could hardly speak Japanese. The woman psychiatrist who dealt with the family had the language problem to make the interviews difficult, but also the disruption of the problem son. He was eighteen, occasionally hospitalized, and six feet tall, which is rather large for a Japanese. When tension developed between the parents, this son would lie down on the floor of the interview room. It was difficult to carry on a conversation with the parents while the large son was on the floor. The parents would both try to talk to the therapist while covertly urging the son to get up. The therapist would try to talk about a sensitive issue between the parents while trying to ignore the son, who would occasionally groan so that he would not be ignored.

In such situations, the therapist needs to be patient and firm and help the parents organize the family to conduct their business of planning the next step for their offspring. This organization of the communication is more important than what is said. It is the process in the room that is typical in the life of the family and needs to be changed. The therapist should make it clear not only that family members should speak one at a time, with the parents in charge, but also that young people should treat their parents with respect. This is not always easy to arrange when the parents do not insist on respect.

I recall an experience of Salvador Minuchin's with a father and three teenage children who were rude and insulting to him. (The father said the problem was their mother, who was in a mental hospital.) Dr. Minuchin said to the young people that they were not allowed to be disrespectful to their father in that interview room; that was not permitted. Whether they were disrespectful at home or not was another matter, but in the therapy room they must be respectful. The young people began to talk to their father with more respect. At one point when the daughter was rude, the father said, "That's not allowed in this room!"

There are several important factors which help the parents take charge. One is the authority which can be passed to them by the therapist, the expert who has power in the situation because social control has been activated. When he listens to the parents with respect and offers them authority, the young people follow that lead. Power is passed from an expert to others. The presence of siblings increases that effect. The children tend to impose restraint on each other when they see that it is expected. A large family can often prove less difficult for a therapist than merely parents and problem child. Another way power is passed to the parents is by putting the discharge decision in their hands; if the problem person is to get out of the institution, the parents must be persuaded to let him out and accept him back. The child will begin to orient correctly in the hierarchy of that authority.

One of the main ways a problem young person is persuaded to cooperate in the interview is by seeing that the therapist knows the parents are in difficulty and will do something about that. As the young person is dealt with competently by the therapist, he or she knows the therapist will deal well with the parents. Therefore it is important that the therapist let the young person know that he will be helpful to the parents without making that explicit, and that he will deal with them respectfully and not upset them irresponsibly. As that happens, the young person will not only be cooperative but will have no reason not to be.

The ability of a therapist to deal skillfully with the parents as well as with the young person is illustrated in interviews conducted by Don Jackson many years ago. In one of them an eighteen-year-old daughter had begun to act strangely when in college and had been brought home and hospitalized. She was violent enough to hit a nurse on the ward, so could be expected to be obstreperous. In the interview with the young woman and her parents, Dr. Jackson let the girl state that she and her parents were in the "eternal triangle" and that they had a block in communication. Then Dr. Jackson turned to the father.

JACKSON: What do you think of this idea that there is some block in communication?
DAUGHTER: There is.
FATHER: (Simultaneously.) You're speaking to me now?
JACKSON: Mm-hmm (Pause.)
DAUGHTER: I can tell you what it is.
JACKSON: No, you give your dad a chance now. (Laughs.)
FATHER: I don't know of any block in communication. Ah, I have always, for many years, felt that, ah, Sue was a pretty good girl and, ah, I was very liberal with her and, ah . . .
DAUGHTER: Mmm, yeah.
FATHER: . . . her mother, to offset my liberalness, ah, would, ah, be extremely strict with her.
DAUGHTER: Oh, Daddy, now wait a minute . . .
FATHER: . . . and, ah, then . . .
DAUGHTER: Wait a minute.
FATHER: . . . there were some times you . . .
DAUGHTER: I needed discipline . . .
JACKSON: (Interrupting, he speaks to Sue, with a gesture that indicates a confidence between them.) You do get your chance (laughs) to rebuttle, but we're getting what we're looking for.
FATHER: Two at once here.
DAUGHTER: (Overlapping.) Go on.

The conversation continues, with the daughter listening to the father and not disrupting the conversation, even though he is discussing a disagreement with his wife. When the father ends, the girl starts to speak, but Dr. Jackson quiets her and turns to the mother for her opinion. Jackson had a skillful way of getting the problem young person not to interfere, but instead to join him in dealing with the parents in such a way that something could be done about the parental problems.

An Example of Getting Started

To illustrate some of the problems in a first interview, excerpts can be given of a family with a twenty-five-year-old heroin and amphetamine addict. He had been an addict for five years and had been detoxified a number of times. The longest time he had been off drugs in those five years was two months. Present at the interview were his parents and two younger brothers. The therapist was Sam Kirschner, Ph.D.

This therapy was done as part of a research project; the therapist had met with the family at a research interview and had persuaded them to come in as a family for therapy. At this first therapy interview, he assumed that he had a contract with them for therapy, and he was taken by surprise when the mother began by saying she was not coming back again.

The therapist did not make an opening statement about the agenda of the interview and the goal of the therapy because he had done that in the research interview. He did not think he needed to repeat it. As the family sat down the father mentioned that the family was a sad group, and the therapist explored that. The result was confusion, which required the therapist ultimately to reorient the interview and essentially start over.

KIRSCHNER: So—what's doing?

FATHER: We got a sad group here.

KIRSCHNER: A sad group, huh?

FATHER: A very sad group.

MOTHER: Yeah, because, uh—I'm not coming back anymore.

KIRSCHNER: *(Startled.)* You're not coming back anymore?

FATHER: I didn't say it because of that. I'm just saying it's a sad group.

SON: We all have things to do tonight.

MOTHER: I don't have anything to do.

SON: I did.

KIRSCHNER: *(To father.)* What's the sadness about?

FATHER: In plain words, it's a screwed-up family. In plain words, a real screwed-up family.

KIRSCHNER: *(To mother.)* And you're not coming back anymore.

MOTHER: No, I don't think it's necessary. First of all, I'm moving. He *(second son)* is going on his own. He leads a life of his own. He *(third son)* comes with me. He *(problem son)* can do whatever he wants. He'll be twenty-six years old, and if he ain't gonna start now—that's it. He's already made a mistake since we left here.

KIRSCHNER: He's taken dope, you mean?

SON: Yeah, once. Cause I made more money than the boss of the shop. And he let me go. *(Laughs.)*

MOTHER: I mean it's not—it's not necessary for these—these two *(the other sons)* to tolerate this.

SON: Right.

MOTHER: I mean, I mean I'm . . .

SON: *(Overlapping.)* *I'm* not bothering them, *you're* bothering them. Explain to the doctor that. I'm not bothering these boys at all.

MOTHER: Well, where do you think this is all coming from?

SON: Me. It's been, for five years, you know.

(The son is willing to take the blame for the problem, but he also likes to protest that he is doing his best.)

SON: I try, you know how hard it is?

MOTHER: You do not try hard enough.

SON: Why don't you think about trying? Think about how hard it is.

MOTHER: You don't even try. Sleep in bed all day.

SON: Bullshit, man. Why don't you think about what I'm going through and how hard it is to go through it?

MOTHER: I can't imagine, I can't imagine.

SON: That's right, you goddamn can't imagine, can you?

MOTHER: No, I can't imagine that I would do such a thing to my parents. I can't imagine it.

SON: Oh, I'm doing it to you. You think I'm doing it to you?

MOTHER: How long have you been in school?

SON: Two weeks.

MOTHER: And you didn't go to school yesterday either.

SON: I went to school.

MOTHER: And you didn't go today.

SON: It was snowing out.

KIRSCHNER: Somebody fill me in on what has happened since I last saw you. *(To father.)* Why don't you fill me in.

FATHER: That's it. I just gave it to you all in a few words. This is a screwed-up family.

SON: *(Interrupting.)* I had a job, I lost my job, and I did dope.

FATHER: *(Continuing.)* She should go with him, or he should go with me, she should go her way, I should go my way. This kid *(second son)* I think he's the most—I pray to God he stays with it.

KIRSCHNER: You two want to separate, is that what's happening?

FATHER: Well, I—I don't know. I think it's the best thing for us.

SON: You think so. You're full of shit.

FATHER: I mean it.

SON: You're separating cause—cause of me.

FATHER: No.

SON: Oh yeah?

The first thing the therapist must do is take charge of the interview. He cannot let everyone speak freely, or the family will go on in the same helpless way and the therapy will fail. At this stage the therapist must organize who is to speak and, as much as possible, what is to be said. To correct the hierarchy, he must put down the son and quiet him.

It is assumed that the parents communicate through the son, staying together because of him. When the son begins to leave home and the parents face each other without him, they threaten to separate. At that point the son takes drugs and fails in life so that he remains tied to them. From this view, the son has improved by registering in the methadone program and starting school. The parents threaten separation, and the young man takes drugs and misses school.

KIRSCHNER: George, shut up.

SON: That's the whole thing, man.

KIRSCHNER: George, shut up.

FATHER: No, it isn't because of you.

SON: I'm not shutting up. When—when I want to say something, I'm gonna say it.

KIRSCHNER: You—everybody in this room has a chance to talk. I'm talking to your father now, man.

FATHER: *(To son.)* Why are you so incoherent?

SON: Because you're just doing this, cause you're saying—you—you . . .

FATHER: No.

SON: You should go your way, she should go hers—because I'm a dope addict . . .

MOTHER: Well, how have we been getting along?

SON: *(Continuing.)* . . . trying to make it, you know . . .

FATHER: Listen . . .

SON: *(Continuing.)* . . . and you know how hard it is to make it? It's like trying to pull an elephant.

The therapist has the goal of moving the young man out from between the parents in their marriage. A first step is to move the young man out from between the parents in the room and to place himself there, so he asks the son to change seats with him. The son is reluctant.

SON: I'm twenty-five years old and I can sit where I want.

KIRSCHNER: I'm asking you, I'd like you to sit *here*.

SON: All right, relax. *(They change seats.)*

KIRSCHNER: Thank you.

SON: Sit and be happy.

KIRSCHNER: O.K.

SON: They think I shoot dope cause I hate them. I want them to suffer.

KIRSCHNER: Right.

SON: They're all mixed up. They're very mixed up.

KIRSCHNER: O.K. Let—let me find out—let me find out what—what the fight is all about here. What's been happening in the last, uh—

FATHER: It's been a constant—constant turmoil between her and him (*son and mother*).

SON   Me?:

FATHER: Between her and him.

MOTHER: Not really.

FATHER: She can't cope, and he can't cope.

SON: Do you realize that I'm a drug addict?

That brief sequence illustrates the triangle in the family. As the father says the mother cannot cope, thereby criticizing her and implying a disagreement between them, the son draws them away from each other by making himself the problem. That sequence occurs in many forms in the life of the family. A typical form is one where the son starts an argument with the father at the moment a conflict develops between the parents, so the issue between the parents does not get out of hand and also does not get resolved.

KIRSCHNER: Hold it, we'll get to you. Hold on.

FATHER: (*To son.*) We're not talking about drug addicts. You made the mistake . . .

SON: I made a big mistake, man.

FATHER: We made—you made the mistake that time. I mean, it was stupid for you to do it, very stupid.

SON: And I'm still using dope.

FATHER: Your reason was—first, you wanted an excuse, and you got the cheapest excuse that you could have gotten.

SON: I didn't want an excuse.

FATHER: Well, you got an excuse.

SON: I had fun.

FATHER: O.K.

SON: That was my—I didn't believe—I didn't say . . .

FATHER: There you go, you're gonna keep having fun all your life.

SON: I didn't say I'm gonna—because I want my mother and father to break up.

FATHER: You have nothing to do with this.

SON: Or that I want them to drop dead—and die of a heart attack.

FATHER: You have nothing to do with this.

KIRSCHNER: George, your father is telling you that you have nothing to do with them breaking up.

SON: No? Oh, then how come it was mentioned in the beginning?

FATHER: You know, our life isn't much . . .

SON: (*Interrupting.*) She's making them crazy (*the other two sons*) cause she yells because of me.

FATHER: No.

SON: I got her a nervous wreck.

FATHER: She yells because of everything.

KIRSCHNER: Hold on.

FATHER: There's no reason why she shouldn't, cause you don't do a damn thing.

THERAPIST: Hold on.

FATHER: You understand?

KIRSCHNER: Hold on. Uh—I'd like to talk to the two of you alone. George, could you take your two brothers out into the waiting room?

The therapist now takes charge by essentially starting the interview over. He sees the parents alone and establishes a contract and an agenda with them.

FATHER: If he's gonna keep looking for excuses like this, little excuses. Now like this incident here, now he'll go out and shoot. Now this is wrong. I know it, it's a hundred percent wrong. We are not helping him.

KIRSCHNER: That's what we got to try doing.

FATHER: The boy is trying to help himself, but we need as much help as him, maybe more. Now this is not your affair. You know what I mean. I mean you've got problems with him.

When the father says that the problems of the husband and wife are not the therapist's affair, that is a decision point, and how the therapist responds determines the therapeutic approach. He could ask what kind of help the father needs. He could offer to help them with whatever problems they have. He could define the therapy as for the whole family, not just for the son. In the approach presented here, it would be an error to offer to help the husband and wife with their problems. The goal of the therapy is to establish a correct hierarchy, with the parents in charge of the irresponsible son. Any emphasis on their problems would divide the parents at this time of crisis. Divided leadership will fail. The therapist must therefore agree that the problem is the son and keep the focus on the addiction. He can offer help for them at some future time, but he should agree that their problems are not his focus at this time.

KIRSCHNER: Right, and that's what we're here for.

FATHER: Right.

KIRSCHNER: O.K. Now that's what I'm trying to say. You—the three of us have got to work together so we can help him to help himself, that's all. Now are you willing? The point is that the three of us as adults have got to straighten him out, and we can do it if we work together. I have worked with more difficult problems with success, and I'm telling you that if the three of us work together we will lick this problem. Then whatever else comes up between the two of you is another issue.

The therapist has now stated his agenda. He gets an agreement with the parents that they will continue to work with him to try to cure the son's addiction problem. When he brings the boys back in, he has begun to establish the parents as joint authorities over their son rather than as husband and wife in conflict and struggling helplessly with the problem. He is accomplishing the first interview task: clarifying the agenda of the therapy and correcting a malfunctioning hierarchy.

Finding Out Who Else Is Involved

A task in a first interview is to gather certain information, because the therapeutic strategy may depend on it, or failure may be avoided if the information is known. An important question is, Who else is involved with the family who is not present in the first interview? It is argued by some that one person alone cannot drive another person mad. It is even argued that one other generation cannot do it, and so the parental generation alone is not enough to drive a child mad; there must be another generation or level of power above the parents that is confusing the hierarchy. Of course, this is partly a question of how many people the therapist includes in his map of the territory. We have shifted from the idea that one person—the problem person—is sufficient when making a description. Next we included the mother, and after that a triangle including the father. By the end of the 1950s there was an awareness of the influence of the extended family. The issue is not how many people to include in the room during an interview but how many people to include in a therapist's thinking. For example, if a therapist helps the parents take charge of a problem young person and, just as they are exerting authority, a grandmother in another state joins the young person against them, the therapist has overlooked a powerful person in the situation. The therapy might fail because of that oversight.

In the first interview it is best to find out who else in the family is significant. It can often be phrased in terms of "Who is there to help you with this young person?" rather than, "Who interferes with your authority?" One does not wish to antagonize anyone if that can be avoided. The interview should uncover whether maternal and paternal grandparents are alive, where they live, and how often they visit. If possible, one should look into what sort of financial support they provide. It is also important to know whether there is an uncle or aunt who carries weight in the family. If one parent is a stepparent, a crucial question is where the ex-husband or wife is living, and what involvement there is. Divorced parents can continue to war through an offspring. By the end of the first interview, the therapist should have enough information about the extended family to decide who is necessary at the next interview. If grandparents are a powerful influence, they need to be present, at least at the second interview, to approve the therapeutic plan. When one enters a primitive tribe to do something about an Indian, it is best to clear the plan with the chief if one wishes to succeed.

Besides the existence of significant relatives, it is even more important that the therapist find out what other professionals are involved in the case. In the first interview, it is necessary to ask if anyone in the family is in therapy elsewhere if that inquiry is at all indicated. As with grandparents, expert professionals are higher in the hierarchy than the parents and can confuse the organization in the ways they intervene. There are cases in which all the family members are in therapy with different therapists, and something must be done about this. Usually it is best for the family therapist to be the only therapist during this period of recovery of the mad young person. A meeting of all the therapists to reach that agreement may be necessary. If the therapist finds that he cannot get rid of significant colleagues who will interfere with his approach, he is often wise to hand the problem to them and take up another family.

Usually one finds out about professional colleagues and their involvement before the first interview, but at other times that information does not come out until later on. I recall a family in which the parents were to require their son to look for a job. At about the fifth interview they were not doing it, and the therapist asked the mother why she did not insist that her husband carry the plan through. She said she could not insist, because he was not up to it; he was a mental patient himself. When the therapist explored this statement, he found out that the father had been depressed years before and had entered therapy. He was now seen once a month in "supportive" therapy and given medication. This was just enough "support" to define him in his family as incompetent. Although the psychiatrist involved undoubtedly thought he was being helpful, and was even helping the father draw some disability pay by his monthly interviews, it was actually a misfortune to the family. As in many such situations, the information did not come until there had been a therapeutic intervention—the pressure on the parents to take charge of their problem son. It was necessary to see the other therapist, to ask him to withdraw from the case, to give the father a clean bill of health, and to return to the problem of getting the parents to assume executive authority and a correct position in the hierarchy.

Sometimes there is a person involved who is neither a relative nor another therapist, and the weight that person carries in the family must be taken into account. For example, a close friend, or a boyfriend or girlfriend, can often have significance. At times there is a person who is both a friend and a professional. For example, I recall a family in which the mother's best friend was a family doctor. He insisted on seeing the problem son every day and even medicating him without the therapist's permission. When the therapist took on the case, he inquired about psychiatric involvement, but this doctor was not mentioned. Ultimately it proved impossible to get the doctor to come to the interviews or to get out of the case, and the therapy with the family failed.

INTERVIEW TASKS

By the end of the first interview, certain goals should be accomplished: the parents should be in charge, or defined as in charge; the problem young person should be showing them respect; other significant people should be known about and included in a therapeutic plan; a date should be set for seeking a job or for entering school; and normal activities should not merely be vaguely planned, but the date should be marked on the calendar. The therapy can then focus on having the normal activity achieved.

The parents should be setting down rules for the behavior of the young person if he or she is to live in their home. One way the parents achieve correct executive position in the family is by asserting the rules their children are to follow. Much of the first interview is devoted to the parents setting those rules in their discussion. It should be kept in mind that the issue is not the rules themselves, but the discussion and agreement between the parents that is achieved during that communication.

A variety of reassurances should be given to the problem young person and parents during the interview. It should be made clear that the therapist will not accuse or blame the parents. He also will not explore the unsavory past or allow free association and the wild expression of feelings in the present. The therapist should indicate that he expects the child to become normal, and that whatever medication is involved will be reduced and ended. He also needs to reassure the problem child that he is aware of the problems of the parents, that he will take care of them, and that he will not bring out sensitive issues in an irresponsible way.

By the end of the first interview, the parents should begin to suspect, as the therapist knows, that they are going to go through a hard struggle. The therapist needs to have a personal involvement with the parents rather than a merely professional one, so that they know he will stay on their side through the struggle ahead with their mad offspring and with each other.

Chapter 7

The Second Stage:
Apathy

Young people are institutionalized when they make trouble or when they are apathetic and do nothing. The apathetic youth can be a more difficult problem than the troublemaker. The parents must be organized to do something in both cases, but troublemakers usually force people to organize to deal with them, while the apathetic do not. Many of these young people live at home and do nothing while the parents helplessly wish that something could be done. Yet parents have total power over a young person if they wish to exert it; they can refuse to feed him or give him clothes; they can lock him in a room or out of the house; when the child resists them physically, they can call the police if there is real trouble. When parents do not exert authority it is usually because they are in conflict with each other and therefore are divided. They disagree about taking action, and each incapacitates the other when they start to act. They also benefit from the situation since it becomes the center of their lives and they need not deal with other problems. They go on financially supporting the young person while protesting helplessly that he must do something.

When dealing with the problem of apathy, there are several procedures which can be followed. A primary problem is motivating the parents to transform their benevolent concern from pity for the young person into a willingness to take action. Usually the parents wait, hoping the son or daughter will voluntarily change. The therapist needs to persuade them that such an event will not happen. Until they take responsibility and act, their child will continue to fail. Sometimes it is helpful to advise the parents that this problem can continue for five, ten, or twenty years, as it has with other parents. The future will be a continuation of the present unless something is done. Often they will accept the idea of taking one step at a time, the first step being their decision that ultimately they will have to do something.

The apathy of the young person can range from total inactivity and mutism to helpless protests that he or she will eventually do something about getting a job or going to school. The routine of the young person is typically one of sitting up most of the night watching television and then sleeping all day. The parents helplessly protest this regime while permitting it. Often the reason the offspring gives for not acting is transparently inadequate, for example, that an employer should come and offer a job. One young man reported to his parents that he had been out looking for a job, and he went into a store that had a "help wanted" sign in the window. When his parents asked him what the store owner had said to him about the job, the young man replied that he had not asked anyone about a job. He had just gone in and looked around the store. His father said he could hardly expect to get a job without asking. The young man indignantly said that his father should appreciate the fact that he went out looking and even went into a store where there was a "help wanted" sign. The more implausible the reason for inaction, the more obvious the fact that other problems, such as difficulties between the parents, are the real issue.

When a therapist begins with an apathetic family, there are several stages to follow as he joins the parents in the task of getting the young person on his or her feet.

1. The parents need to define a goal for the young person. They must be persuaded to say that they would like to see their offspring at work or in school, and behaving appropriately for his age. Parents will usually agree on this goal if it is not yet clear to them that they will be expected to take action to achieve it. Once they have said that this is what they wish, the therapist can refer back to their goal when having difficulty in getting the offspring active.

2. When the general goal is agreed on, the therapist must have the parents set a time when the first major step is to be taken. It is important that the step be one which can be achieved. To say that on such and such a date the offspring will go to work might not be possible, since a job might not be available. The parents can agree that on a certain date he will be up at eight o'clock in the morning and out looking for a job, however. Similarly, school might not start on that date, but leaving for school to register can occur on that date. It is important that the date be set and written down so that there will be no ambiguity. The therapy will focus on the preparation for that date.

When setting the date, the therapist should arrange that the parents set it at a time which seems reasonable. One can use a Milton Erickson approach to limit the range of choice and say, for example, that the parents can set the date a week from now "or as long as a month from now."[1] If they choose a date too far in the future, the therapist needs to negotiate a more satisfactory one. The goal of this stage is to have the parents agree, for example, that on Monday, April 12, the young person will be out looking for a job leaving the house at eight o'clock.

3. After the date is set, the interviews will begin to prepare the family for what is to be done on that date. There are necessary steps to be taken before the date arrives, and there are consequences if the young person does not take appropriate action on that date.

The preparation can include the young person learning how to look for a job by learning how to dress properly, how to talk to people correctly, and even how to work at home in preparation for learning how to work on a job. Mother and father can take him to the store for proper clothes, and take him out to restaurants and other public places to check his behavior. Tasks can be set for him at home so that he learns how to work under direction. He can immediately, or gradually, begin to get up in the morning to do some work in the home to prepare himself for future early rising. Part of the goal of this stage is to have him busy enough at home so that he might as well go out to work.

Of course, all of these preparations require the parents to take action; that is where the focus of the therapy must be. When the parents protest that nothing can be done to get the young person up in the morning, the therapist can discuss which one of them will throw the cold water on him if he does not get up. The preparation for the young person to go to work on a certain date includes preparation of the parents to survive when he or she does that. As they deal with him, they will argue with each other about what he does and who is to make him do what. The therapist needs to keep the parents focused on the offspring rather than on their relationship with each other, and on today and the future rather than on past failures.

The preparation can also include the parents preparing themselves to be less worried and concerned about their child. They can rehearse how relieved they will be when he is self-supporting by going out for an evening together now. Mother and father (or mother and grandmother or whoever is involved) must do more for each other to get through these difficult times.

4. As part of preparing for the action on the date set, the parents and

1. J. Haley, *Uncommon Therapy: The Psychiatric Techniques of Milton H. Erickson, M.D.*, Norton, New York, 1973.

offspring must discuss what is going to be done if the young person does not do what he is expected to do on that date. If he does not get up and go out and look for a job, what will the parents do? Consequences must be decided in advance. These consequences can range from removing all television sets so that he (and the parents) cannot watch at night and thus lose sleep to forcibly putting him out of the house on the date set. If force is to be used, it must be planned. Can father get him up and put him out? Can father and mother do it? Can siblings or neighbors help? If properly motivated, parents will not only throw water, they will change the lock on a door and lock a young person out during working hours. They will do this even when it is snowing if the therapist is properly persuasive.

One should keep in mind that the problem is not primarily getting the young person to act. The problem is working out the relationship between the parents so that they cooperate in a joint endeavor. The dissension between them comes up within a context of doing something positive for their child. As they negotiate with each other on the issue of getting action from the offspring, they are also negotiating issues between them that have been communicated *through* the offspring. These can include such issues as whether father is too apathetic and passive, whether mother does not do the work she should, and so on. Expecting more from the problem child, they will expect more from each other, and conflict can arise and be resolved. As the parents begin to get along better with each other, the offspring is free to act and no longer has to sacrifice himself.

5. The difficulties which might interfere with action on the date set must also be anticipated. Suppose the young person says he is sick: what should the parents do? Common decisions are to accept only a temperature higher than normal or a written statement from a doctor that he cannot go outside. What if he weeps and is afraid and miserable? Out he must go in any case, with the parents supporting each other in the task. Often it is helpful to ask the young person how he might try to get out of the task or to ask the parents how they might find ways to give up so that those ways can be brought out and blocked off.

When the day for action comes, several possibilities can occur: the young person can go off and look for a job; or he can decline in his apathetic way, and the parents can take the planned actions; or the parents can fall down on the task and not do what they planned during the interviews. When this last possibility happens, the therapist must have the attitude that they have failed their problem child—not that they have failed the therapist.

When a parental failure occurs, the first step is to find out what happened. Sometimes there is a legitimate excuse for the parents not taking action. If that is so, the action can simply be moved to the following day or to a short time later.

If the parents failed without an adequate excuse, the therapist needs to sympathize with them and with their problem young person. The sympathy should take the form of an expression of regret that the son or daughter will not have the chance in life that other young people have. The therapist should commiserate with the parents. He should not let them blame each other. Generally the therapist's tone should be benevolent so that the family cannot become angry at him.

In some cases, it is best to make the issue dramatic. For example, with an anorectic daughter, a failure by the parents to carry through a plan to make her gain weight can be dealt with by discussing the daughter's funeral: have they chosen the grave site? Other issues of a practical nature, such as who will be present at the funeral, can be discussed in a matter-of-fact way. This is reasonable when death by malnutrition or lack of resistance to disease is imminent. The problem is how the therapist can discuss this while remaining on the side of the parents. The hierarchy must be respected by not criticizing the parents or putting them down in front of the children. Again, sympathy—the ultimate weapon—can be used.

When the problem is simply not going for a job, the same kind of mourning session can be done. The therapist can sympathize with the parents about their problem son's or daughter's failure in life. The goal in such situations is to have the family mobilize itself and try again. When the sympathy and mourning are over, the therapist can indicate a confident assurance that they really can do this if they try. If the parents wish to try again immediately, it is sometimes best if the therapist delays action until the family has suffered for not following through with the original plan.

One of the special problems a therapist and family must deal with is the threat of suicide. Troublesome behavior to the point of threats of violence can be less of a problem. The threat of suicide can lead to rehospitalization for the young person's protection, thus giving the offspring the power to determine what happens and therefore to defeat the therapy plan. With suicide threats one must consider several issues. One is the fact that hospitalization does not necessarily prevent suicide; often it even seems to increase the probability. People who are hospitalized can lose their jobs or get set back in school where the stigma of being a mental patient is added to their other reasons for being depressed. Hospitalization can be said to delay suicide but not to prevent it, since a determined person will go ahead with the act after the hospitalization, or even inside the hospital. The therapist, however, not only does not want the tragedy of a suicide, but is also vulnerable in the professional community if he does not take the accepted steps to prevent it. Therefore, for professional protection as well as for the life of the patient, he might have to hospitalize even if he does not consider the threat a serious one. Yet to do so can mean having the young person succeed as a failure just by idly saying he has been thinking of killing himself.

In these circumstances an alternative to hospitalizing the young person is to ask the family, particularly the parents, to take responsibility for the young person's life. This means that they must set up a suicide watch, where someone is constantly with the young person, and must be certain that a suicide opportunity does not occur as long as there is any threat of it. The whole family can organize itself for the suicide watch with the parents in charge. In that way the threat of suicide leads not to a setback but rather to a therapeutic opportunity for reorganizing the family.

Persistence

The therapist must be willing to go to the mat with a family until either the offspring is functioning normally or the therapist is eighty-five years old, whichever comes first. This persistence should be evident to the family in a single interview. Often there is an interview that sharply focuses on a single issue and makes it clear to the family that there is no alternative— something must be done. The requirements of the *persistent intervention* are that it be simple and clear. If the family does not act at the time agreed on, the therapist must focus them on this one issue while they offer their repertoire of behavior.

As an example, there was a twenty-three-year-old man who went mad and was hospitalized just before his graduation from college. He had been living separately from his parents for four years because he had left home to attend college in another state. He had married and was living with his wife. He began to behave strangely, returned to the city where his parents lived, and was hospitalized. His wife moved in with his parents. After two months in the hospital, he was about to be discharged, and the therapist began with the family. In the first interview, the question of future plans was raised. The young man and his wife, as well as his parents, said that ultimately the young couple would move out to a place of their own. The therapist asked them to set a date for their move into their own apartment. They all agreed on a date, which was written down. The therapy was oriented toward that goal. The young man and his wife were to live in their own place while he went back to the local college to finish the one or two classes he needed to graduate. The therapy plan was that the young man return as rapidly as possible to a position of disengagement from his family, which was his position before therapy, when he was living with his wife and attending college. It was unclear whether the young man had collapsed in relation to his wife, to his parents, or to both. The move out of his parents' home would clarify that issue.

Two months later the young man and his wife were supposed to move into an apartment that was all prepared. On the day set they did not move. The young man simply did not get out of bed on that day until quite late. The wife was upset, and the therapist arranged an appointment that evening for the young couple. The interview focused on the young man's explanations of why they did not move. As part of the strategic plan, the therapist was to say, "Why didn't you move?" He was to say nothing else. The interview lasted for almost three hours. Nothing was talked about except the young man's repertoire of excuses, including his symptoms and helpless behavior. His wife, angry and disappointed with his excuses, expressed her ideas about his difficulty in leaving his parents and committing himself to her. After that interview, the couple returned to the parents' house, and the mother asked the young man what they had talked about in the interview for so long. He said that that was a private matter between himself and his wife, drawing that boundary for the first time. He also stopped behaving as if incapacitated, and the couple moved to their apartment that week.

In this approach a crucial issue is chosen, and nothing else is discussed except as it relates to that issue. The interaction becomes intense for everyone. All relevant matters come out around the crucial issue, like spokes turning on the hub of a wheel.

LOOKING FOR A JOB

A lengthy example will be given here of an interview focused on the common problem of arranging for an apathetic young person to look for a job. This family is different from some apathetic families in that they are talkative; to present a family which hardly talks at all is to offer a tedious interview. Some families talk little and do little. Others talk a lot but do nothing, as in the case of this family. In this interview the young man and his parents discussed nothing else except the date the son would look for a job. The therapist simply and persistently pursued that one issue. In this case the persistence almost led to a violent explosion. The father was a man who typically fled discussions at home when he became angry at his wife and son. No plan of action could be followed through by the father and mother because the father would not plan and, at the first sign of opposition, would angrily leave the house. In this therapy interview he was confined in the room and had to continue the discussion. Like many helpless fathers, he would get angry, loud, and threatening, but had a problem exerting influence on the family.

In this approach, the family finds it difficult to become angry at the therapist for carrying on a topic at tedious length because the discussion is for their sake. Since the therapist's benevolence forces them to pursue the issue, the benevolence must be particularly emphasized when using this intervention.

The twenty-two-year-old son was a handsome youth who was hospitalized because of bizarre behavior during his first year in college. He came out of the hospital and returned home. At college he had been rooming with a girlfriend. She was interviewed, indicated her desire to leave the young man, and did so. The family included a seventeen-year-old brother who was typically sullen and silent, and a twenty-three-year-old sister who was away in college in another state.

The problem son was heavily medicated when he came out of the hospital. The goal of the therapy was to have him return to college, but he could not attend until the next semester, which was a few months away. The family agreed that he should go to work in the meantime. He was agreeable to working, but he was also apathetic about it and did nothing. The first few weeks of therapy, as he came down off the medication, a job was encouraged, but none was obtained. When the young man was almost off the medication and able to function normally, the therapist focused an interview on the request that the parents set a date for the young man to go to work. Excerpts of the interview will be offered here to show the therapist's persistence and the range of issues related to the self-support issue.

The family was black and exhibited a pattern typical of an upwardly mobile family. The working-class father was a succussful and hard-working contractor. The mother had a more intellectual job in a university. The mother's ambition was to have their two sons and daughter go to college and become professionals. The father wanted the children to go to work; he was not an enthusiast for education, although he was more agreeable about the daughter going to college than the sons. The daughter attended college. The seventeen-year-old son was having difficulty getting passing grades in high school. The twenty-two-year-old problem son went to college but while there went mad and was hospitalized. He was in a context where he could either become a working man and please his father while antagonizing his mother (because she did not wish him to be uneducated like father) or become educated and please his mother while being defined as "not manly" by his father (since that was how the father looked on educated youths who did not do physical work). The solution of the son was to do nothing: he neither went to school nor worked, because he was "unable to."

In this interview the therapist, David Heard, Ph.D., forces the issue of looking for a job, which is obviously a crucial issue in this family. Present in the room are Dr. Heard, the parents, and the problem son. The younger son did not come.

HEARD: Albert, you look really good.

ALBERT: Thanks a lot, I feel good.

HEARD: Yeah?

ALBERT: Yeah, all I need now is a job. That's about it.

HEARD: Well, what have you been doing about that?

ALBERT: Well, I filled out an application from a cousin of mine's job, that's about it. That's only—I haven't been looking for none really.

HEARD: What kind of application you filled?

ALBERT: I don't know what it's for—some type of place that makes hamburgers like MacDonalds.

FATHER: (*Overlapping.*) It's working in a—what is it—hamburger?

ALBERT: A hamburger or meat place, or something like that.

HEARD: How's it you filled out the application, and you don't know what it is?

ALBERT: No, see I don't know what—what's the name of the place. I'd rather do clerical work, myself, to tell you the truth. But I'd take anything right now, it doesn't make any difference.

HEARD: How about the carpentry thing with your uncle?

ALBERT: Well, he works when he feels like it. Next time he works, I don't know if he use me or not, you know.

HEARD: Have you been doing any work at all in the last two weeks, since I saw you last?

ALBERT: (*Shakes his head.*) Mm-mm.

HEARD: How do you spend your time?

ALBERT: Around my grandparents' house, watching TV, 'cause somebody always there, you know, that's about it. Just wasting time, you know.

FATHER: Complaining.

ALBERT: Complaining, complaining.

This is a typical interchange of an apathetic young man talking about getting a job. He is casual about it, he says he is considering this or that, but he makes it clear that he is not about to go to work. He also anticipates any objection by saying he's just wasting time. The therapist begins to bring up with the parents, as he has before, what they expect the young man to do in relation to a job.

HEARD: (*To mother.*) So what do you think about him having nothing to do.

MOTHER: I tell him I think he ought to go and look for jobs. I look in the paper for him, every Sunday. And I tell him where to go. So, I mean, I don't know, he should do something, I know. He has to find a job first of all, but he's not that aggressive enough for me. He thinks he has to have a car before he can look for a job, he can't ride the bus. That's his words.

HEARD: What about that Al?

ALBERT: I'll get a job—I just—really, I don't know. I don't like riding the bus 'cause it's a waste of time. I go down and they tell me, "Fill out an application and we'll call you." *(Inaudible phrase.)* I did that once before, and it's a waste of carfare. So the only place I go is the sure place, like someone tells me, "Yeah, my job is hiring, come on down." Then I may go down there, or something.

HEARD: What kind of job do you want?

ALBERT: Anything. I'm about to do dishes now. I think I'm going to get a dishwashing job. I can always get a dishwashing job, you know. So I'll probably go ahead and get a dishwashing job.

HEARD: Are you sure about that?

ALBERT: Yeah, I can get a job.

HEARD: Now, are you sure you can always get a dishwashing job?

ALBERT: Sure, there are a lot—I'm, I'm, I'm,—I had a dishwashing job, I was a clerk, I was at—what was I at? I was at Gino's.

HEARD: I'm not talking about the past, I'm talking about tomorrow.

ALBERT: Tomorrow. You mean tomorrow? *(He smiles.)*

HEARD: Tomorrow.

ALBERT: Tomorrow. I don't know what I'm going to do tomorrow, I may get up and go somewhere, I don't know. I'll just go down and look in the paper and see where the nearest dishwashing job is. The sure one you can always get. I'll go ahead and get that. I did dishwashing before. That's about the easiest thing I can get, and I'll keep that for a while till I get tired and get another one.

MOTHER: It's the same old thing—'cause he gets tired and quits. He has the wrong attitude.

(The telephone rings, and therapist goes to it and talks to supervisor, who suggests that the therapist include the father in the discussion and focus more on the date to look for a job.)

ALBERT: I need some money, I'm going to do some dishes for a while.

MOTHER: All you do is *talk* about it and you don't *do* nothing.

ALBERT: I'll probably do it tomorrow.

MOTHER: You say the same things every day. *(To father.)* Don't he?

FATHER: That's right.

ALBERT: I don't talk about a job every day.

MOTHER: Yeah, you do.

HEARD: *(Returns and sits down.)* Speaking of jobs and breadwinners, you say that really your husband is the main breadwinner. How, ah—how long, Mr. Nelson, do you think, you know, how long do you think you should have able-bodied sons living at home, and feeding them steak, and whatnot?

FATHER: No longer than tomorrow.

HEARD: *(Laughs.)* No longer than tomorrow.

MOTHER: He means it too. He tells them all the time. He's getting tired of it. He tells them he's getting tired of all three of them. He wants them to get out and go to work.

FATHER: They should work.

HEARD: All three of them?

MOTHER: Yeah. John and Marlene *(their daughter in college).*

FATHER: They should—not for me because, you know, we don t have any problem. But just for their self. I mean laying around, laying around all the time is not right, you know. No one should just lay around, walk up and down the street, don't have anything to do. Should always have some activity. And you know, working is—well, relieves some of the tension.

HEARD: Good hard work is good for you.

FATHER: Well, it doesn't have to be necessarily hard work.

HEARD: No.

FATHER: But just have a job, something to go to every day.

HEARD: What did you do when you were Albert's age?

FATHER: Worked! I drove a truck. I drove a coal truck, I worked on a coal truck, for two and a half years.

HEARD: Did you like it?

FATHER: I liked every job I ever had.

HEARD: Really?

FATHER: Yeah.

HEARD: So how long do you plan to support your kids?

FATHER: Till they get a job.

HEARD: All right, let's say, you know, next week—next month?

FATHER: They don't have a job, I'll support them next year.

HEARD: Next year?

FATHER: If they don't have a job, what else can I do? Now I can't put them out on the street, much as I'd like to, to go get a job.

The therapist has a problem when the father says he will support the sons as long as necessary, even next year. He cannot put them out on the street. Such an attitude prevents taking any immediate action, which is what must be done. The therapist might argue that the parents could put the problem son out on the street, but that could lead to objections. Instead, the therapist wisely shifts the issue to the future. He talks about the years to come and even includes the possibility of the parents supporting the son when he is married. This suggestion provokes the correct reaction from the parents.

HEARD: What if, you know, what if three or four years from now, Albert gets married, has kids, no job?

FATHER: Well, that's an entirely different situation.

MOTHER: I'll move to California *(laughs)* if that happens.

FATHER: I'll have to back up a little bit on that.

HEARD: That's what you said.

FATHER: First of all, if he doesn't have a job, he's certainly not going to get married if I have anything to do with it.

HEARD: But you might not.

FATHER: I might not.

HEARD: No, he just might end up . . .

FATHER: Let me try to explain something—if he gets married, you know, well his wife can support him, because I won't be supporting him.

HEARD: Ahh!

FATHER: Because I don't think it's right.

HEARD: O.K., because you were saying that it would be just until he gets a job.

FATHER: Right.

HEARD: It could be a long time.

FATHER: Well, that is definitely out, there's no question about that. Unless he has a job.

HEARD: Yeah, it's uh . . .

FATHER: I wouldn't want him to take the responsibility of some lady and not be able to take care of her. It really wouldn't be fair to her.

HEARD: My point is it's a—jobs right now, especially, are hard to get.

FATHER: They're hard to get.

HEARD: But I'm wondering are you—are you satisfied with the kind of efforts Albert is making?

FATHER: No! He knows it.

ALBERT: I haven't been doing anything.

FATHER: All three of them know it.

ALBERT: I'll get a job when I want to get a job, when I get ready to get a job. A job ain't no problem, it ain't no problem.

HEARD: All-right.

ALBERT: I'm not even worried about it.

HEARD: He's laid the cards on the table. He's laid the cards on the table. He'll get a job—

FATHER: *(Interrupting.)*—When he gets ready to get a job.

HEARD: When he gets ready to get a job.

FATHER: Yeah, I heard exactly what he said.

MOTHER: Right.

This is an important statement by the son. He is not saying that he is unable to take a job, or is too sick, and thereby is behaving in a mad and eccentric way. He is simply refusing, which means he is behaving like a defiant son. This statement helps the therapist define the problem as a disciplinary one. Once that statement is out, the father can bring out the division between himself and his wife on the issue of work.

FATHER: That's why I stay on him. That's certainly why I stay on him. Because, see, they know, see they don't come to me for anything. They go to their mother. If they need money, they go to their mother, and they get it from her. They don't come to me and ask for money. I mean, occasionally he comes, once in a while, "I need a dollar," or something like that, and John says, "I need a dollar." I give them a dollar. If they want money for whatever they want, I say, "Look man, you gotta get a job." But they will go to her and she'll give them some. 'Cause she has it.

The structure of the situation is clear, and typical in a family with a problem son. Father cannot insist that the son work and deprive him of money until he does, because the mother will not cooperate with him, and since she works she has money of her own. In such cases one finds, however, that if the mother becomes firm about money, the father will change his position and give it. The parents are in basic disagreement with each other in their marriage on the issues of work, money and education: the son is a vehicle for expressing that disagreement.

If one examines the father's statements, it is evident that he does not take a clear position that the son should go to work: he says the son should go to work, but only for his health—to relieve his tension. He also says that the children don't come to him for money but go to the mother, and then he adds that they come to him for money and he gives it (with a lecture about getting a job).

The strong feelings of the father about the situation become more evident as the interview progresses. As mentioned in other interviews, he rises early. When he comes home during the day, he finds two able-bodied sons playing pool on the table he bought them, and drinking beer that he bought them with their friends. Though he protests that they should work, nothing happens and all he can do is rush off and work hard again, angry that his wife does not do more.

A skillful, apathetic son sometimes raises a problem for parents by asking for so little that they cannot deprive him of anything as a punishment or to encourage work. By not asking for any money, and by wearing old clothes and eating minimally, such a son gains an advantage in the parents' struggle with him.

ALBERT: I don't even ask my mom for money most of the time, really, last time—I haven't even asked for my allowance.

FATHER: The fact remains is, they need a job. There's no question about this. They do need something to keep them active.

HEARD: Everyone agrees with that!

FATHER: Well, of course.

ALBERT: I ain't going down there on no bus, looking every day for no job.

FATHER: See what happens is—I don't know what happened in the course of events—but what happened with me is different. If I needed a job, I would be out there beating the bricks every day. If my mother left me a dollar-and-a-half or two dollars, something like that, to go look for a job, let me tell you something, I would save the dollar and a half or two dollars and jump on the bicycle and go look for a job. Or either hitchhike to go look for a job. Or get on the corner and stand out there with some of the guys who are gonna look for a job, but see they aren't like I am. They don't aggressively do the things I do.

ALBERT: (Laughs.) Oh boy.

FATHER: If I was out of work tomorrow, I'd get a job tomorrow.

HEARD: Well, it's sounds to me like both of you have been very, very generous parents.

FATHER: We've always taken good care of them, there's no question about that. But the fact remains is, how long, you know—look, he's sick, right? He's not sick, but I think he's doing fine. The other one—

HEARD: (Interrupting.) Are you sick, Albert?

ALBERT: I'm fine.

The therapist must define the problem either as a disciplinary one or as laziness, but not as a sickness. This is difficult because of the young man's hospitalization and medication (now being eliminated), which define him as sick. When he is no longer considered sick, the parents can insist that he behave normally. That point is now arriving. The father's confusion over whether he should think of him as sick or not is evident at this transition point.

FATHER: He's doing fine now. But there's still something going on in there, because any time he can sit down and tell me that "I'll get a job when I get ready to get one." Knowing he needs a job.

MOTHER: Well, he means it too.

FATHER: He means what he's saying.

MOTHER: Sure he does.

FATHER: And that's what gets me a little disgusted.

MOTHER: If he don't get a car, he's not going to get a job. That's what he means.

FATHER: I don't think he needs a car to look for a job.

MOTHER: He said he's not going to get on the bus and go get a job.

HEARD: Let's back up. He's not going to get a job until he gets a car.

MOTHER: That's right.

FATHER: Now he didn't say that.

MOTHER: Oh yes, that's what he's implying.

ALBERT: I want to get a job 'cause I want to get a car. I want to get this car by September.

HEARD: O.K., wait a second, now you don't want to ride the bus around?

ALBERT: No, it's a waste of time.

HEARD: That's a waste of time, so . . .

ALBERT: A waste of time. Unless I know it's a definite job I can go to, I get on the bus and go get it. I'm not going to get out there every morning and catch no bus and look for no job.

(Telephone rings and therapist answers it.)

ALBERT: I'm going to get a dishwashing job, a job I know I can get.

MOTHER: Well get on the bus and get it.

ALBERT: Well, I wouldn't mind.

FATHER: First you got to fill out an application.

MOTHER: I don't know why you want a dishwashing job.

ALBERT: Just 'cause they hire.

MOTHER: They do not, where?

ALBERT: Wherever it say "Dishwashing" you get a job.

MOTHER: There's some in the paper too, but it don't mean you're going to get it. Don't tell me you're going to walk in and get it?

ALBERT: I might get it.

The following speech by the father is typical of the way an issue about a son is used to communicate between the parents about disagreement. Ostensibly the father is discussing the son's becoming more active and getting up in the morning to look for work. Actually he objects to the mother letting the son sleep and not taking enough interest in pushing him out to get a job. The speech is therefore put in terms of the son but is directed to the mother.

FATHER: You can't rely on what's in the paper. *(Talking to mother.)* Ten chances to one whatever is in the paper, the people that—when they put an ad in the paper for a job—let me try and explain something to you—when they put an ad in the paper for a job, and that paper is put out on Sunday, you can bet your bottom dollar that there's somebody standing out in front of that man's office at four o'clock in the morning trying to get that job. He's not getting up at ten or eleven o'clock in the afternoon, he is on that corner, if it takes him to get up three o'clock in the morning, he is the first one in line, or he's either the second. If there are one or two, he's there. But I keep trying to tell him, I don't want him laying in the bed till eleven o'clock in—you can't go out and look for a job eleven o'clock in the afternoon. You have to get up early in the morning.

MOTHER: *(Pointing to son.)* Tell him, don't tell me.

FATHER: I told him *(inaudible phrase)*.

ALBERT: *(Interrupting.)* I know how to look for a job. I'm twenty-two years old, I know how to look for a job.

FATHER: You do? Well unfortunately you're not doing it. But anyway, I don't even worry about that right now. *(To mother.)* What I'm trying to say is, you can't sit around and say, "I need a job, I need a job." You have to get out there and hustle for a job. Because of the present situation out there now, everybody needs the same thing you're looking for, and that is a job, there's no question about it. I told John the same thing.

ALBERT: If I had known that me getting a job was this important, I would have got one when I got out of the hospital.

FATHER: You couldn't possibly get a job when you got out of the hospital.

ALBERT: I'll go out tomorrow and look for a job every day, then.

FATHER: You should have been doing it. I've been trying to tell you this.

MOTHER: *(To son.)* Why you getting mad about it, why are you getting mad?

ALBERT: Because I didn't know it was such a big thing about me getting a job. I felt when I got ready to go ahead and just . . .

FATHER: It's not a big thing for us, you know, it's for you. I don't worry about you getting a job, but you need one.

ALBERT: I want to talk about something else, I'll go ahead and get a job tomorrow. I, I, I don't mind working, you know, 'cause I want to get out and get an apartment of my own. Because I don't like staying home no way. So I'm going to go ahead and get me a job, that's all.

(The young man makes the typical threat of abandoning the parents if they insist on pushing him.)

FATHER: Well that sounds fine.

HEARD: *(Gesturing to parents.)* These are the two people you need to talk to.

ALBERT: I don't like staying home.

MOTHER: I know that.

FATHER: We've always known that.

HEARD: Albert, I'd like you to switch seats with your mom. *(Son moves next to therapist, and mother sits next to father.)* I want you to come over here and sit next to me. *(To mother.)* I want you to pull the chair over closer to your husband.

ALBERT: I'll go out and get me a job tomorrow.

HEARD: These are the two people that you need to talk to about this.

ALBERT: I don't have to talk. When I work, I work. It's as simple as that.

HEARD: *(Pulling his chair back.)* You need to talk to your parents about that.

MOTHER: *(To son.)* But he always—you always get mad—every time somebody tells you to do the right thing, something we think you should do, then right away you get angry.

ALBERT: If you wanted me to get a job, you should say, "Al, I want you to get a job."

MOTHER: I don't have to say that to you.

ALBERT: That's all you should of said.

FATHER: You know what makes me angry about the whole thing?

ALBERT: Nobody mentioned to me about getting a job, that's why I come here tonight, you know, that's horrible.

FATHER: What did you say?

ALBERT: I didn't know you was pressing me to get a job.

FATHER: We've always said this, all the time.

ALBERT: You've been pressing John, you haven't been pressing me about a job.

FATHER: As soon as you come out of the hospital—"Albert, when you're better"—we told you when you come out, you should go out and try to find something to do and stay active. I've told you before, I told you here a couple of weeks ago, that rather than you go around to your grandmother's all day long, and sit around there talking to them bums that are sitting over there. I don't like the idea of them.

ALBERT: They're working.

FATHER: It's unfortunate it took them so long to get a job. 'Cause they needed one thirty-five years ago. They're thirty-five years old and older. They should of had a job, they just started working there what I would consider yesterday. They haven't been working for almost three months. So they got a job luckily. And if they hadn't, someone would have to give it to them. And pushed it at them, or they wouldn't have that. They just offered them a job or they would be laying up there now and drawing a check and doing nothing. I know them, they can't be relied upon. You can converse with them, and things of that sort, that's all well and good, but I don't like you being around them, 'cause evidently you're probably going to get in that same pattern. That's what I don't like about it.

ALBERT: I'm going to get me a job.

FATHER: 'Cause they don't want to do nothing.

ALBERT: I'm going to get me a job, a job . . .

FATHER: We asked you to get a job a long time ago. We're not forcing you to get a job. We told you before that you should have had a job years ago. You get a job and then you quit the job. "I don't feel like working." My wife said to me one day she had a job with the—doing something up at the—what's it called, the, the Internal Revenue Service. Well he lay in bed one day, "I don't want to go to work, I don't want to go to work." You can't have a job like that. I wish I could lay in bed every day until eleven, twelve o'clock in the afternoon.

MOTHER: (To son.) Why do you think I look in the paper every week?

ALBERT: If it's a problem now, I'm going to get me a job.

MOTHER: It's not a problem, Albert, it isn't a problem.

ALBERT: Yes it is. It must be a problem.

MOTHER: It's not a problem.

ALBERT: I'm gonna get me a job. I want a job and have some money in my pocket. I just haven't looked for no job. There ain't no jobs out there anyway.

HEARD: Al, I'm not, you know, I'm not disputing the fact that jobs are hard to get right now, so I'm not saying, you know, tomorrow morning, you know, by eleven, it's reasonable to expect you to have a job, but what is a reasonable, a reasonable expectation as to when Albert should have a job?

FATHER: Well, I can't really say—the only thing I can say is, if he's putting any effort into going and looking for a job, I would be satisfied with that. But he's not doing that. You know—I don't know what time he gets up, 'cause I'm out of the house very early in the morning.

MOTHER: He gets up early.

FATHER: Sometimes a quarter to seven. I mean, if there was, if he would say to me, "I been out here today, " or say to his mother, "I went out here today." Then I would be satisfied with that, at least I know he's looking for a job. But then when he come home in the evening, and he complains to her about, "Oh, I guess I gotta go get a job, I guess I gotta go get a job." Well, we know this, you know. But you can't get a job sitting up watching TV all day long. And running around spending the carfare that you give him for steak. Then he come home at night complaining that he got a pain in his stomach.

ALBERT: I'll get me a job. I don't know what's bugging you. I'll get me a job.

FATHER: It's not bugging us.

ALBERT: It's over. I'm going to get a job. Now talk about something else. Tomorrow morning I'll be up at eight o'clock looking for a job.

FATHER: Seven-thirty.

MOTHER: You have to go . . .

ALBERT: I know what time to look for a job.

MOTHER: I told you where to go several times.

HEARD: What's—what's a reasonable period of time for you to expect . . .

FATHER: To look for a job?

ALBERT: You don't have to set no standards or no rules for me to look for no job, man, I know how to look for a job, simple as that. You don't have to set no standards for me to do nothing. I know how to look for a job.

MOTHER: Now you're going to get angry, 'cause sometimes I talk to you—like I told him, if he wants a job and he doesn't find a job and he wants to go to school, fine, go to school. He can start back to school.

As the focus on the job continues, the mother brings up her own preference, college. The father never brings this up as an alternative. At this point the therapist drops the son out of the discussion and asks the parents to talk to each other.

The parents' conversation with each other is the stage of the interview that parallels the stages of the therapy. First there is a general family discussion about the young man getting a job. Then the therapist seats the young man beside him and stays out of it himself while he has the parents together talk to the son about getting a job. Next, the therapist has the parents talk to each other about the son working and prevents the young man from interrupting, so the parents communicate directly. As the parents attempt to communicate with each other, tension develops between them and the young man intervenes, indicating that they are not yet ready to communicate without the child rescuing them.

HEARD: When does school start?

MOTHER: I think it starts sometime in May. The summer course starts. So I told him, you know, if you don't have a job by then, go to school in the day. Or if you have something, a job, maybe you can work part-time and you can go to school part-time.

HEARD: Now Albert, I'd like this to be a discussion between your mother and your father. And so, you know, I'd like you to stay out of it. Just for the two of you to discuss for a minute what's a reasonable expectation, a reasonable period of time.

FATHER: You can't very well say that.

HEARD: Well, he may not have a job per se, but the effort is—I very much agree with you.

FATHER: What you're probably asking is, Are you going to put in the effort into going looking for a job?

HEARD: That's, that's the first thing.

MOTHER: Yeah.

FATHER: Fine.

HEARD: And how much of an effort, how would you be . . .?

FATHER: I think that would be the question.

HEARD: What a—what will satisfy the two of you?

FATHER: Well any time he can ask for carfare to go look for a job, which would be almost any day, if he wants to.

MOTHER: Yeah.

FATHER: You know, almost any time.

HEARD: (After a pause.) You think he should be looking in the paper himself, you think he should be, be going out for a job interview once or twice a day, or the morning.

FATHER: Well there's no need going out late in the afternoon to go look for a job. Unless maybe someone gives you a lead.

HEARD: That's . . .

FATHER: I rather prefer him being up early in the morning. And maybe looking at a paper or two. And say, well maybe I might try this one today. And get on the bus and—regardless whether you like the public transportation or not, you know.

HEARD: I'd like the two of you to talk about that.

(Therapist stands up to leave. He wishes to consult with the supervisor behind the mirror. Moreover, the parents are not talking to each other and he believes they might be encouraged to do so if he leaves the room.)

FATHER: Well, I—I've already said all that I'm gonna say. In regards to this.

HEARD: Have you talked this—you know, have, have you. . . .?

FATHER: We talk about this all the time. I tell him, "Leave when I get up in the morning." I'd like to get him up in the morning when I leave.

(Therapist leaves the room.)

MOTHER: You don't—you don't tell *them*.

FATHER: I tell *you*.

MOTHER: Yeah.

FATHER: You're the last one to leave.

MOTHER: You tell me and I don't relay all this stuff to them. Albert is up every morning. I don't need all this stuff. I don't really like hearing it my own self.

ALBERT: I'm going to get a job, so it's over, meanwhile.

FATHER: *(To mother.)* I don't want to hear it either, but I would like to see them getting up in the morning and going to work.

MOTHER: I feel like . . .

ALBERT: I'm going out to get a job, so what's this talking . . .

FATHER: I'm not talking to you now.

MOTHER: I'm talking to *him (meaning father)*.

ALBERT: I'm talking—I don't care if you're talking to me or not.

FATHER: Let me tell you something, Mister.

ALBERT: *(Rudely.)* What do you want to tell me, Mister?

MOTHER: Hmm-mm. *(Raising her eyebrows.)*

FATHER: Your getting to be—you know—I'm—what did you say?

ALBERT: What are you going to do to me, knock me out? *(He stands up.)*

FATHER: Wouldn't be any problem.

ALBERT: I've had enough of that shit, man.

FATHER: You had—you got . . .

ALBERT: You want me to get a job. *(Standing over father and looking down at him.)* Why didn't you say, "Al, get a job"?

FATHER: Sit down before I knock you down.

ALBERT: I wish you would knock me down.

FATHER: Don't you ever come up in my face.

ALBERT: I wish you would knock me down. I wish you would knock me down.

FATHER: You just sit down, 'cause you're about to get in trouble.

ALBERT: You'll be in trouble too.

FATHER: Let me tell you something . . .

ALBERT: *(Interrupting.)* I never talked back to you in my life. So all you had to say was for me to get a job.

The sequence here is the typical one which is emphasized often in this work. A disagreement between mother and father appears when mother says that it isn't father who tells the boys to get up. She says that father tells her, and then she is supposed to tell the boys. She says she is tired of being the one to relay all this stuff. The father begins to get angry at the mother and says he doesn't want to hear this stuff either. At that point the boy is rude to father. The father drops the issue with his wife and reacts against the son. What is typical about the sequence is the way the son engages the father at the moment the parents are in disagreement, with tension building up between them. It is a common sequence and the therapist often finds himself dealing with the action between father and son and forgetting what set the trouble off. The son succeeds in sacrificing himself either by acting strange or, as in this case, by provoking the father, with the risk of being "put through the wall."

FATHER: Now you swore at your mother before, you know you're about to get a whole lot of problems. She is taking care of you. You do what she—let me tell you—you know you make me angry, I'll come and knock you right through the wall.

ALBERT: I wish you would. *(Sits down.)*

FATHER: *(Beginning to shout louder.)* She can't even go out and buy herself a decent dress on account of you.

(Therapist returns to room and sits down.)

ALBERT: All you had to do was go out there and tell me to get a job.

FATHER: We've been telling you for years to get a job. You got another woman and went to live with her. You wouldn't listen to nobody *(inaudible phrase)* my wife *(inaudible phrase)*. *(He shouts.)* You don't listen to nobody. I'm getting disgusted. *(Standing up and leaning over son.)* I'm getting so tired of you and that other bum in my house. Now I'm gonna eventually . . .

ALBERT: Who do you mean?

FATHER: The both of you. You don't even listen to her. You're getting under my skin.

ALBERT: All this is coming out in the open now.

FATHER: *(Inaudible phrase as he argues with son, who shouts back. Mother sits without expression.)* You're twenty-two years old. *(Sits down.)*

ALBERT: I'll go out tomorrow and get a job.

FATHER: We've been telling you for years to go and try to do something. *(Inaudible phrase.)* You don't want to get dirty: "Go clean the yard up"— "I don't want to get dirty."

ALBERT: It's a joke.

FATHER: It's a joke? But you didn't go do it. You do what she says to do. You don't want to get dirty, you don't want to get dirty.

ALBERT: I been dirty for years, it don't bother me.

FATHER: And you tell me John don't do anything. You don't worry about what John does. Look, let me tell you something, Mister, you ain't— you're getting under my skin. Now . . .

(The therapist gets up to answer the wall telephone; the supervisor tells him he should stop this quarrel or it may lead to violence.)

ALBERT: I been *(inaudible phrase)*.

FATHER: *(Inaudible phrase.)* I don't care how old you are, we gotta take care of you. You can't take care of yourself, you're not qualified to take care of yourself.

One of the tragedies of hospitalizing a young person, particularly one from a working-class family, is that on the surface he might be called "ill," but the family often believes that he is weak. To be hospitalized can indicate that he is not manly, which is a special stigma.

ALBERT: I can do it tomorrow, I prove to you I can take care of myself.

FATHER: See what happens even now, you were out there before, you couldn't stand up under the pressure.

ALBERT: Oh, I couldn't stand up under the pressure, huh?

FATHER: She *(the wife)* took care of you all the time you was living with that damn woman up there.

HEARD: *(Making a gesture to stop.)* Time. *(He moves his chair in.)*

ALBERT: Where do you get off *(inaudible phrase)*.

MOTHER: Well, stop being so . . .

FATHER: Don't tell him nothing, don't tell him a thing.

HEARD: This is really the issue we started on. And it is a serious issue.

FATHER: It's a serious issue! *(Inaudible phrase which may be "He's been a fool.")* All his life. Now we tried to straighten him out. *(Shaking his finger at therapist.)* Let me tell you something right now. When anything happens to these kids, they don't come to you, they come home to us. But we don't sit there and say, well, you're wrong, I'm not going to do for you. We still got to take care of them, 'cause they are going to be children all their life. If I only—any time that one of my kids jump up and say something to me, I tell them something, and they don't like the idea, I feel this way: if you don't like what I tell you to do, then you make other arrangements. He did this at one time. Which he wasn't qualified to do, he thinks he's a man, he's just a child at heart. He can't hold a man's position, we try to steer him in the right direction. I told him before, I'm going to tell him one more time, you go out, you try to find a job, don't come in and complain to her about what you have been—what you have to have. We know you need a job.

ALBERT: I'll get a job . . .

FATHER: And watch your attitude with me, 'cause I don't—I don't—I don't play with anybody.

ALBERT: I ain't playing with you either.

FATHER: I'll get too angry, I'll do something to you.

ALBERT: I wish you would knock me—I wish you would . . .

HEARD: No, no what—it's true Albert will always be a child of yours, but he is at an adult age.

FATHER: Absolutely right. But he doesn't—let me tell you something, none of my kids talk back to me. You know, 'cause I don't like it. I'm not one of them kind of men who say, "You can say anything you want to say to me." You know, 'cause right away I'll do something to you, you know, 'cause I don't have to take it from anybody. I never once talked back to my parents. And I was one of the worst kids in the world. But I'm one of the best of them now.

HEARD: *(Pause.)* When we started, we were talking about, you know, how much time, what's a reasonable expectation . . .

FATHER: I told you before, I can't say. All I want is them to put some effort in it. That's all I'm asking.

HEARD: Fine, that's what I'm saying . . .

FATHER: Don't tell me (*imitating him*) "I gotta get me a job." We know you got to get a job, but put some effort in it.

HEARD: What's reasonable effort? What do the two of you agree on?

FATHER: We feel as though he should get up in the morning and go look for a job.

(*Gesturing between them to indicate that they should speak to each other.*)

HEARD: If the two of you . . .

MOTHER: Yeah.

FATHER: That's what—we've always thought this.

HEARD: O.K., that's not—that hasn't been happening?

Despite the tension and discomfort in the room, the therapist persists with his emphasis on the parents talking to each other and setting a date for the young man to look for a job. Not letting the issue between the father and son distract him, he again asks father and mother to agree on when the son should look for work.

FATHER: No, it hasn't. The other day she went to one of her nieces who was talking to her about the job. And I took him over in my car and signed the application. This was Sunday. I try, I tell my own son, look—I just get to the point and say nothing, you know. I'm working, and as long as they've got enough to eat in the house, I got something to do, I'm satisfied. But I get so disgusted. Eventually I say something, it's either, well—you know, I get angry myself. But rather than go through the hassle, I say, well look, just let them do what they want to. 'Cause I'm getting tired of it.

HEARD: But the problem is still there.

FATHER: It still exists.

HEARD: And that's what a—that's what I'm trying to get at. Saying, you know, what would you be satisfied with?

FATHER: I would be satisfied with him getting up in the morning and go to look for a job. That's all. If he doesn't get a job, at least he went out and he tried to get a job, that's all. I know jobs are hard to get.

HEARD: Mm-hmm. Mrs. Nelson, what's your point on this?

MOTHER: I think that he should, I'm not saying he should go out every day, just to go out, just to go any place. He has to have something definite. You have to look in the paper, or I suggest to him, go down to one of these pay jobs that he went to once before. And buy a job, 'cause he did it once before. And maybe he'd get something that way. I told him that just the other day. He said, "Well I might do that," but he didn't go. So, if he just goes there, or I told him just to go there to the electric company, they usually hire.

FATHER: Then what did he say to you when you told him?

MOTHER: He didn't want to ride the bus. *(Pause)* But you're going to ride the bus from now on, right?

ALBERT: I'll get on a bus and get a job.

This time as mother and father begin to talk about their expectations, it is the mother who turns to the son and engages him instead of the father, thereby not talking with the father.

MOTHER: Look, you're not—you're not doing it to spite anybody, you're going to help yourself.

ALBERT: I know that, Ma.

MOTHER: You don't do it in anger, you do it because you want to do it. I don't want you to go with the attitude, "I am going to get a job 'cause you people want me to work." You should want to work yourself. Do something. *(Inaudible phrase.)*

HEARD: It's really, I guess a . . .

ALBERT: Now I been, I—I didn't look for a job for a week, about a week. You know and all of sudden, me, he starts telling me, "You get a job." John hasn't had a job in three months. At least he give him three months. He don't give me more than two or three weeks. How do you know I ain't gonna get a job next week somewhere?

FATHER: What do you mean, two or three weeks? I haven't—it's very seldom I mention to you, go get a job.

HEARD: I think it's important . . .

FATHER: I haven't said anything to you about going to get no job.

ALBERT: That's what gets me, man, 'cause—

FATHER: I never said a word to you about going and getting a job.

ALBERT: —they would look for a job for one week, one or two weeks.

HEARD: Albert, I think . . .

ALBERT: It's a big thing now.

FATHER: When have I told you to go look for a job?

The father, as is typical, now defines himself as never having asked the young man to get a job. The therapist had best not bring up this inconsistency because the problem is to maintain the status of the father, and that would not be achieved by criticizing him. The younger son, John, is discussed, and the father insists that he wants him to work too.

FATHER: Every day I'm on John, every day I'm on John.

HEARD: On the same issue about a job.

FATHER: About getting a job, get something to do. All the day long. How would you like to see your son walking down the street all day doing nothing? He's eventually going to get in trouble. I'm not there to watch him, my wife works every day, she can't watch him. We don't know what they're doing in the house. But if we know he got something to keep him active, we know at least from the time that we leave till the time that we get back, till dinner time, that they're doing something. They're doing something constructive for their self.

MOTHER: John claims he goes out and—downtown. I give him carfare to go two or three times a week . . .

FATHER: I have doubt that he does.

MOTHER: He says he goes out—puts in half a day looking for a job, that's what he told me he does anyway during the day. He goes to town, different stores, grocery stores.

FATHER: And he rides around with a couple of his friends of his sometimes. He might be out there, who knows, he might smoke a little reefer, but he's out there moving around a little bit anyway. I don't like to see anybody being in the bed until ten in the afternoon. I want you up when I get up, you know, you get up, 'cause it makes you lazy.

MOTHER: Albert doesn't do that. Albert is often up before I go to work.

FATHER: I didn't say he wasn't. I don't know whether he was or not. You tell me this, right? I don't get him up.

MOTHER: John is the one who don't get up.

HEARD: That's why I say it's unfortunate that John wasn't here too. Because this is something that relates to both.

The pattern of coalitions seems to be that mother defends the problem son, who is interested in college. Father defends John, who, like him, is not interested in an academic career. The therapist continues with the job issue, applying it to both sons later in the interview.

HEARD: You know, it seems like to me, it's really very important you've got two young men, two sons in your house, and dealing with some issues that uh—I think are normal with growing sons. I think the two of you have been generous parents.

FATHER: We don't bother our children.

HEARD: And—

FATHER: We just like them to work, that's all.

HEARD: —It's very normal, the kind of problems you know, getting—

ALBERT: What makes you think anybody got problems?

HEARD: I think it's important that you don't let the kinds of—this issue that you're dealing with right now, divide the two of you.

FATHER: Listen, we've been married for twenty-some years, and you know what? We're gonna stay married.

HEARD: Yeah.

FATHER: We don't have any problem there. But all I insist upon is, for some reason or other, you know, that I don't want anybody sitting around making a bum of themselves.

ALBERT: That's all you . . .

FATHER: This is eventually what it will lead to.

ALBERT: That's all you—I'm gonna get a job.

FATHER: We've been telling you to get a job.

ALBERT: Why, man, you ain't been telling me nothing.

FATHER: When you walked out of the hospital—

ALBERT: *(Interrupting.)* You didn't say anything.

FATHER: Are you finished? *(Pause.)* When you walked out of the hospital and walked down here that night, I said, "You know, Al," I says, "if you go out and get a job, maybe you might get"—*(to mother)* didn't I tell him? I said, "Get a little active and you might get back on your feet again. It might help you a little. Something to do." The day I walked into this clinic, and I haven't said anything to you about a job, except for the time we come down and we talk about the job. I don't tell you to get up in the morning and look for a job. But I do tell John.

HEARD: O.K., you know—I—I understand your point, Mr. Nelson, you aren't saying Albert has to have a job, John has to have a job, you're saying . . .

FATHER: He doesn't have a job, he's home.

HEARD: He should be making the effort.

FATHER: He should be making the effort to get a job. He keeps putting up to me, "I'm twenty-two years old." Well let me see how old you are.

ALBERT: I ain't got to show you nothing.

FATHER: You can tell me that you're a man, but you can't prove to me that you're a man.

HEARD: O.K.

ALBERT: You always worry about if somebody's a man, shit.

FATHER: That's all I hear from you, is you're twenty-two years old.

HEARD: Albert . . .

FATHER: I don't like your bad language either, I don't use it.

HEARD: Can you sit here, please? *(The son is pacing.)*

ALBERT: I don't feel like sitting there.

MOTHER: Sit down anyway. *(He sits down.)*

HEARD: What—um . . .*(pause).*

ALBERT: All that "man" talk.

HEARD: We don't have much more time, really, the one thing . . .

FATHER: I don't need too very much more time.

HEARD: O.K. The one thing I'd like to finish this evening is to get a kind of clear agreement. *(To father.)* I've heard you say this evening that, you know, you think it's important on an everyday basis that Albert be looking, and I'm not sure what your position exactly is with John, whether he should be looking on an everyday basis. Mrs. Nelson, I heard you say that "Well, maybe every day, but not necessarily." And I think the two of you need to be together on this, so you're not divided.

FATHER: *(To mother.)* Well, I think he should look for a job every day.

MOTHER: I don't think so, unless it's some definite place that they have to go.

FATHER: I'm not saying to go out in the street every . . .

MOTHER: You can cover, you can cover—in a day you can cover three or four jobs in the city.

FATHER: Of course you can, probably by then you might have one.

MOTHER: Right. From nine to three, so therefore it's not necessary to go every day unless it's something you see in a paper that comes up, or somebody put you on a lead. So maybe you go out like three times a week, four times. I'm not saying go out every single day.

FATHER: Not enough . . .

ALBERT: I—I have me a job tomorrow. I'll get me a job tomorrow.

HEARD: What . . .

FATHER: I say, "Go look for a job every day."

MOTHER: Well, this is . . .

HEARD: What does—what does looking mean, does it mean going and actually finding . . .?

FATHER: It could be looking in the paper for it, you can read the paper. Neither one of them will pick up a paper. And look at it and say, "Well here's the unemployment, well maybe I'll try this tomorrow." I know 'cause I have the paper.

HEARD: So, maybe the two of you are really talking about the same thing. Because you're saying, Mrs. Nelson, that looking . . .

MOTHER: *(To father; they talk together.)* Yeah, I'm not saying going about and just looking every day, but someday you may pick up the paper and they may be nothing there, you've been out Monday and Tuesday and Wednesday and you have applications in, right? So, you pick up the paper, there's nothing there for that Thursday, well if you don't have any place definite to go to, why just go downtown and stand and—where you gonna go? Or anyway, if you have nothing definite to go to . . .

FATHER: Well, there's a lot of industry downtown. Tailor shops, baker shops and—

MOTHER: You have to have experience for tailor shops, baker shops—

FATHER: Who knows, I mean, just to do some—

MOTHER: I know.

FATHER: —just to do something to get in, you can always work your way up.

MOTHER: He has the wrong—you have the wrong attitude—

FATHER: I don't expect anybody to go in and work for nineteen dollars an hour when they go into an establishment. It's impossible. I worked for a company and when I went in I was making two thousand, one hundred dollars a year. I didn't start making fifteen thousand dollars a year until years later.

MOTHER: This is a different time.

FATHER: Well, I'm saying you have to start someplace and maybe you might get in there and have some interests and you might move yourself up the ladder. You have to start somewhere. You know he don't have any experience at doing anything . . .

HEARD: What will it be so that both of you can be together on this and both be satisfied so that the—

FATHER: All I want him doing is looking for a job, that's all. I don't give a darn if its every day, just go out and look.

HEARD: O.K.

FATHER: I'm not saying no two or three—I'm saying every day go look for a job.

HEARD: Mrs. Nelson?

MOTHER: If he gives them the carfare, they can go every day. I'm not going to give him carfare every day.

FATHER: You think because they probably won't go.

MOTHER: No, because you need more than one carfare, you know, jobs aren't right next to one another. And it takes carfare to go different places lots of times, it all depends on where you go.

FATHER: Look, anyone that sits down and says, "I need a job, I need a job, I need a job," you let me tell you something, they'll go through plain ordinary hell, pardon the expression, to try to find a job. And if it takes even going downtown and walking ten or fifteen miles a day, you know, or walking around the area and just putting an application in. All right, so there's nothing there. At least you have the application—you don't know what is going to transpire.

HEARD: O.K., see this is—my point is I think it's an important issue. I don't want it to divide the two of you. And I'm not . . .

FATHER: I like them up when I get up in the mornings! When I holler up the steps, I says "Get up and go to work." Occasionally she might say, "Well leave them stay in," you know.

MOTHER: I never say, "Let them stay in bed."

FATHER: Why get them up early in the morning? I say, "All right, I won't say nothing." I don't say nothing. I want them to get up when I leave. I leave the house at seven o'clock, quarter to seven. Get up, be dressed, be downstairs, be out looking for a job, but you can't get no job . . .

Father and mother have talked for quite a long time, with disagreements, and the son has not saved them. The sacrifice within the interview no longer occurs.

MOTHER: That don't mean anything. When you go, you called up there many a morning, and you said, "Get out of bed, you bum."

FATHER: Long as he gets up.

MOTHER: O.K. He gets up, and when you leave, he's right back in bed.

FATHER: Well I don't know that.

MOTHER: I know it, because I'm there.

FATHER: I don't know that, maybe I may think, well maybe he's out there doing something, I don't—

MOTHER: No he's not.

FATHER: I'd rather see him up and out doing something, if I got to get him up and take him out to the street and park him on the corner to go and look. They don't need to complain to me, we know you need a job. I know it's hard to get a job. But you're certainly not going to talk one on yourself.

HEARD: O.K. Can I . . .?

ALBERT: I want to leave. Let us get out of here.

To increase the direct communication between parents, it is often helpful to give them the task of talking for a short time each evening at home about the son. Here the therapist makes an attempt to have the whole family talk at home, but, the idea is not received with enthusiasm. Mother describes how difficult it is to have father discuss an issue.

HEARD: Do the two of you eat supper together regularly every evening?

MOTHER: Mm-hmm.

FATHER: Yeah.

HEARD: I was going to say, as a way of suggesting—maybe at the end of each day, could it be possible for you, Albert, do you eat supper with your parents, you and John together?

ALBERT: No, man I eat—yeah, I eat something with my people.

HEARD: I was just wondering whether you eat supper.

FATHER: At dinner time, he's in.

HEARD: Could it be, Albert, could it be a topic, could it be a topic of discussion at the supper table?

FATHER: Not for me it wouldn't, I don't want to discuss the issue.

HEARD: You don't want to talk about it?

FATHER: No.

ALBERT: He don't talk about too much of nothing.

MOTHER: He's telling you right, he don't. He just sit there and he does most of the complaining to me. Like I told him, "Tell Albert you want him to get a job, don't tell me." So I know every day what he says to Albert. I think he should do it himself. 'Cause I tell him what I want. I'm not going to tell him, he knows I tell him all the time. You don't tell me to do it, do it yourself. And he doesn't know how to even talk to them, not in no civil tone. (*Pause.*) And like he said, he's not going to discuss it. He's right, he's not going to discuss anything with anybody. Once he said it, that's the end of it, he'll probably start yelling at Albert in the car, and yelling at me.

HEARD: Well. It is a very real concern of mine that, you know, this not divide the two of you. That the two of you need to give your children one unified message.

FATHER: You know what makes me angry about the whole thing, What I do is, I tell them once. I shouldn't have to tell you every day to go look for a job. If I tell you one time, that should be sufficient. That's all.

ALBERT: You told me, so everybody go home, I'll get a job tomorrow, it ain't no big thing.

FATHER: So what is there to discuss? If I say, "John, go look for a job," if he happens to go out once and look for a job, the minute I see he's not doing anything, I jump on him again. Have—did you go anywhere today? No? Then you get your body down there and go somewhere today. And he might—I don't know what he's doing out there.

MOTHER: Nothing.

FATHER: Well I don't know, but I want to see him out there. I got to work every day.

HEARD: Do you think it's enough to be told once?

The interview continued for a short time, but was essentially over. The father merited an apology because he was allowed to get upset enough to threaten to hit his son. He needed to be reassured that the therapy did not require an angry emotional scene and that the situation had inadvertently gotten out of control. The father could be expected to feel ashamed at losing control of himself and shouting. If the therapist apologized, the father would be reassured that when he came again, he would not be expected to become angry and upset in that extreme way.

To review, this interview occurred in stages: first, parents and son were encouraged to talk together. The therapist was a central participant and organized the discussion, motivating them all to deal with the job issue. Next, the therapist moved to the periphery and arranged that the parents talk with the son. To make this more possible he changed the seating: he placed the son beside him, facing the parents, and then moved himself to the edge of the group. Finally, he asked the parents to discuss the issue with each other and intervened to block the son out of their discussion.

As the parents were required to talk directly with each other, tension developed between them. The son began a quarrel with the father, distracting him from the issue with his wife. The therapist, who had briefly left the room, returned and again set up a discussion between father and mother, blocking the son out of it. This time the son did not rescue the parents despite the tension and disagreement between them. As they communicated more directly, rather than through the son, the son was detriangulated.

This interview, tedious because it focused on a single issue, accomplished its goals. The parents were able to discuss a sensitive issue directly rather than through the son. The interview also accomplished the goal of allowing the young man to get a job. He obtained a part-time job and later began classes at the university.

Ultimately the youth solved the problem of satisfying the conflicting parental wishes about school versus work. He joined the army, which satisfied the father's desire to see him as manly. In the army he received advanced training, which satisfied the mother's desire to see him educated.

Chapter 8

The Second Stage:
Troublemaking

When a young person has been put in custody because of troublesome behavior, it can be assumed that there is a social cause in the family and community. To institutionalize and medicate someone means putting them on "hold" until they go back into the community to deal with the same issues again. In a certain percentage of cases, the crisis brought about by custody, and the shock and embarrassment of such a situation cause the family to reorganize. Sometimes the young person chooses a different form of adaptive behavior because of the trauma of custody. But in most cases, it can be expected that after a first institutionalization the trouble will recur, often just when the problem person seems to be doing well.

The young person who comes home from custody is typically on probation and is treated like someone who is handicapped. The use of medication reminds the family daily that the person is "ill." While the young person is defined as abnormal, the family can avoid dealing with its usual problems because it still has this crisis problem. At a certain point, however, the convalescence must end, the social situation that led to the problem behavior may then be reactivated. The family again faces whatever was happening when the problem offspring erupted; it again begins to malfunction and threatens to dissolve. The young person offers a second episode of the problem which was presented before. If mad behavior was used, it recurs. If anorectic before, the young person stops eating again. If he was apathetic and did nothing, he stops looking for a job and again sits at home. If he was violent, he is now violent. If he was on drugs or drank too much, he will again take drugs or drink. Usually no new problem is presented, but the behavior which led to custody before is repeated. That is why it is possible at the first stage of therapy to anticipate with the family what they are going to do if the behavior recurs. What is important is that the relapse of the second stage be handled without custody to prevent the family from going back and starting over as if nothing had been done. Otherwise institutionalization can simply repeat itself again and again.

Sometimes there is an attempt to extend the convalescence after a first hospitalization in the hope that the problem will somehow resolve itself in time. Medication is prescribed for a set period of time, like six months, no matter how the person behaves, so that he is defined as handicapped for that length of time. In most cases this effort does not succeed. The family gets in difficulty, the young person relapses, and the family says he needs a different drug because the current one isn't working or reports that he has stopped taking his pills. The pill becomes part of the social struggle, and if there is positive change the credit is given not to people but to a chemical. Until drugging the problem person is stopped, the family does not know if it can deal with normality.

Another attempt to extend convalescence is to put the young person in a halfway house or day hospital. He is thus defined as halfway back to normal. Often it is hoped that the situation will help him halfway out of his family. In that approach, the young person continues to be defined as abnormal and the family continues to be stable during that period. Usually nothing is done for the family, since most professionals who inhabit halfway houses are antifamily. They are trying to save the young person from his parents, while the young person is trying to save his parents and will escalate his behavior if necessary, no matter what is happening in the halfway house.

The Causal Situation

To review what has been said earlier, one can grant that there are many reasons why a young person goes wrong. There can be unfortunate involvement with gangs, with friends on drugs, with crises in school, with tragic love affairs, with friends who have harmed themselves, and so on. The peer culture has a powerful influence on young people and presumably can generate enough social conflict to lead to behavior problems. However, for severe problems, and for purposes of therapy, it is best to assume a simple explanation based on family relationships. One should assume that the young person is caught in a family triangle and that his abnormal behavior represents a reaction to a crisis among these intimates. Typically he is under pressure to disengage and leave that triangle, while also being threatened by unpleasant consequences if he does. His solution is either to collapse or to misbehave in such a way that the triangle stabilizes as a way of dealing with him.

In this therapy the first stage is primarily designed to prepare for this second episode so that the problem is contained in the family, which reorganizes to move the young person toward independence. How to disengage the young person so that problem behavior is not necessary to stabilize the family can be explained simply but achieved with difficulty. It is necessary to (1) correct the hierarchy so that the young person is in a lower position than the parents, and (2) have the parents communicate directly with each other rather than metaphorically through the problem young person. Sometimes these two steps occur at once. Usually it is necessary to put the parents in charge of the young person first, and then, step by step, to resolve the issues between the parents.

If the first stage of the therapy is successful, when the young person comes home from the institution the parents are in charge. They are also communicating with each other more directly, first about the rules for the young person and then about other issues. The therapist has immediately pushed for normal activities, such as school or work, and the family is faced with the basic issue—the possibility that the young person will become self-sufficient and leave home, thus dissolving the triangle. At that point the parents malfunction: they have difficulty in agreeing on leadership over the problem young person and in communicating with each other directly. If they reach the point of threatening to separate, the young person will escalate his behavior and relapse. The therapy has then entered the second stage, and the therapist's task is to use the relapse to help the family solve their problems in some other way than making one member an invalid. The therapist requires the parents to take charge of the relapsing young person, thereby pulling the pair together in more direct communication with each other. The parents oscillate between encouraging their child to be normal and being concerned about the consequences.

Two factors help the parents at this stage. One is a personal relationship with the therapist. If the therapist is personally involved rather than merely professional, the parents will turn to him in their difficulty and also be motivated to extend themselves. It is often helpful, for example, for the therapist to visit the home early in the therapy. An invitation to dinner is usually easily arranged. The willingness of the therapist to extend himself, as well as the personal aspect of the visit, make the parents more willing to turn to him and not to someone else when trouble comes. A home visit in these circumstances is best defined as a social call to see what the family home is like, and the dinner should be a social one. Discussions of problems should be reserved for the office; in the home only positive aspects of the family should be emphasized, and enjoyed.

Another factor that motivates the parents at the second stage is the amount of effort they have invested in the first stage. If they have struggled with each other and with their child to straighten things out, they react to the child's subsequent failure like people who have an investment in success. An example is with drug addicts. When addicts detoxify in a hospital without family involvement, the parents are only bystanders. If the young person shoots up again, they are disappointed that he has relapsed again, as he has so many times before, but the problem is essentially one for the experts in drug abuse. If detoxification is arranged in the home, however, with the parents taking care of the young person, as I have encouraged in an addict therapy program, quite a different result is possible. Having gone through the distress and pain of the detoxification, the parents are indignant about all their wasted effort if the young person shoots heroin again. They are therefore more likely to insist on the straight life because of their previous investment.

Errors

It is easier to suggest what a therapist should avoid in this situation than what he should do, because unpredicted situations arise. A few common errors—in the sense that they tend to lead to difficulty rather than to success—can be described.

1. Any treatment which defines the person as abnormal tends to perpetuate the problem. The family crystallizes at this stage of life: the offspring stays at home, and the parents do not move on to the next stage of their marriage.

2. It is an error to explain or interpret to the parents what the therapist thinks is happening. It is better to assume that they know what is occurring and cannot help what they are doing. If one points out to parents that they are holding on to a child because of problems in their marriage, they usually defend against such an accusation by protesting that it is really the child who is the problem. As the parents become upset at the accusation, the child erupts into misbehavior to stabilize them. Everyone can then point out that obviously the young person, not the parents, is the problem.

It is sometimes helpful to make explicit that the young person is misbehaving for fear that the parents will separate, but the therapist should do so only when he has such a good relationship with the parents that they can acknowledge the correctness of this idea and deal with it. (The interview in this chapter illustrates that procedure.) The purpose of such a comment is not to help them understand what is happening but to force them to deal with the issue more directly.

3. It is usually an error to leave tasks undefined and issues unclear. The

therapist needs to focus on concrete "bits" of behavior to keep the therapy focused. To discuss child rearing, or contemporary young people's problems, or other general issues, perpetuates an abnormally stable situation. Change comes with acts defined, dates set for them to happen, and specific consequences if certain things are not done.

4. The average therapist should not attempt to be clever, give an ingenious directive, or attempt a paradoxical intervention. The odds for success remain with his simple, clear emphasis on the young person's going to work or school and on the parents being in charge of someone who lives in their home.

5. The young person's leaving home should not be used as a threat against the parents, but at the same time the prospect must be mentioned—preferably in passing—during the early interveiws, so that everyone knows that event must ultimately be accepted. However, if the young person threatens to leave home, or if the parents say he really ought to, the therapist should immediately say that there is no hurry and that the offspring's departure must be arranged in an organized way.

Generally, the way to proceed is to push the parents to take charge, and then back off and see if they take charge spontaneously. If they do not, the therapist must push them again. One of the goals is to have them spontaneously define their marriage as their business and not their offspring's. When they say that, they are drawing a generation line, correcting the hierarchy, and freeing the young person from the triangle with them.

A SECOND-STAGE INTERVIEW

In the following case, the second stage of therapy occurs in a single interview rather than over several interviews. The family is the one discussed at the first stage (see Chapter 5). It is now about nine weeks after discharge, and up to this point Annabelle has been doing well. She has been going to school, working, and following the parental rules. The parents have threatened separation but have been asked to stay together for the few months until June, when the daughter graduates from high school. They have agreed to do that and are themselves having sessions as a couple with the therapist for their marital difficulties.

At this point a problem arises, ushering in the second stage. Supervisor and therapist meet before an emergency session with the family to discuss what to do. The girl has been difficult and rehospitalization is threatened.

LANDE: After we saw them Monday night, the next day I got a call from the mother that Annabelle hadn't slept the whole night, and had kept them up. And her general hostility that she showed towards me was kind of diffused to everybody to the point that she told a couple of her teachers to "fuck off" and got thrown out of school. She was really basically hostile to everybody, including her boyfriend, and it did not seem to be a particular response to something going on in therapy. The parents were very, very concerned. She was really acting pretty wild—she hit her mother at one point. The whole family centered around her all week. Since I couldn't get hold of you Tuesday, I decided I would put her back on a low dose of medication, partly because she was keeping them up all night. I thought their tolerance for it was about to break. And that night she slept through the night, and with her sleeping, they seemed more able to take care of her. They really weathered the crisis very well, at least when I talked to them over the weekend. The mother made some very positive comments about her husband, and how strong he had been, and supportive.

HALEY: And you didn't go through with the dinner?

(The therapist had arranged to visit the home and have a social dinner with the family.)

LANDE: I didn't go through with the dinner because of a combination of things. I wasn't sure during the crisis, I guess I should have. The mother called me and said she wasn't really cooking, she was devoting full time to Annabelle. And I was sick last week, so I took the opportunity to get out of it. I probably should have gone through with it.

HALEY: Yes, you should go through with whatever your plans are during a crisis, if you can. Because it makes it more—it makes it stabilized. As I remember, around the medication you tried to be somewhat tricky with them. What I suggest is that you be absolutely straight with these people on what you want done. As simple and clear and straight as you possibly can, in as complex a situation as it is.

LANDE: Yeah.

HALEY: What are you going to do when they come in now?

LANDE: O.K. There are several agendas that developed kind of by themselves. One is the real issue of the mother wanting to engage me on the phone about Annabelle going back to school. She said Annabelle was very upset about school, and I said she should be. And I want her to take that as a realistic concern about graduating with her class and feeling that she didn't want to be left behind. So I would like to go with that as something to really be concerned about.

HALEY: I would agree with you that she should be upset about accomplishing what needs to be accomplished in school. But the question of her misbehavior in school I would put in terms of the parents being embarrassed. It is the same as having them making a rule about what they will put up with at home so they won't be uncomfortable. That they shouldn't have to have a daughter in school who is embarrassing them. So if she is going to embarrass them, she can stay home. Then it's not for *her* sake. It's because why should they have to be embarrassed by a daughter who is telling teachers to "fuck off." And I think the more you can put it on what is good for them and what they should have to put up with, and the less on how upset is the girl, the better you'll be.

The rationale for this is as follows: if the decision to return to school is based on the daughter's behavior and state of mind, the daughter has the power, since the parents can only wait for her state of mind to improve and are incapacitated. If the issue is put in terms of the possibility of the parents being embarrassed, then they are the ones to decide when she returns to school and so have the authority.

LANDE: What about—we talked about going back and exploring what happened that set this off.

HALEY: I think you have got to begin to explore this some, and I think you've got to begin to go into some of the marriage problems with Annabelle present. What I would hope is that you could openly discuss their discussion of separation in Annabelle's presence, because it may have not been done. You may decide at a certain point to send the kids downstairs. I would be tempted to send the boys down, after you've settled whatever that is, and keep Annabelle, if you go into the marital problems. Even though you want to draw a generation line, you also want to define her as older. And I think she is in the middle of it.

Present at the interview are therapist, parents, daughter, and two siblings. The therapist had asked the parents to bring in two of the older boys in the family, since he preferred working with a larger family group. Instead, the parents brought a fifteen-year-old son and an eight-year-old daughter. These children were hardly of an appropriate age for a crisis interview, but it was decided to include them, with the possibility of moving them out to the waiting room if necessary.

LANDE: How have things been going at home?

MOTHER: Really good today. We had a nice day.

ANNA: You know what? I think that all the questions you ask are too personal. (*Family laughs.*)

LANDE: Too personal?

ANNA: Yeah.

LANDE: What kind of questions shouldn't be asked?

ANNA: Basic questions. "None-of-your-business" questions. (*Laughs.*)

MOTHER: Like "it" questions.

ANNA: Right. Like "it" questions.

FATHER: Well, we are trying to get you some personal help here, so I hope he asks personal questions.

ANNA: I don't want his personal help.

FATHER: Well, I want—you need it anyway.

MOTHER: We need his personal help.

ANNA: You guys need his personal help. I don't need his personal help.

MOTHER: I need it.

ANNA: Well then, you guys can have it, 'cause I don't want it no more.

FATHER: O.K.

LANDE: Is asking about going back to school personal?

ANNA: No.

LANDE: Have you started back?

ANNA: No.

LANDE: What's—what is going to be happening with that?

ANNA: Nothing.

FATHER: I think the situation is, the school wants something from you before she goes back.

ANNA: A report on—uh—my actions.

FATHER: Or some kind of analysis of Anna.

LANDE: An analysis?

MOTHER: An evaluation.

FATHER: Yeah, an evaluation.

LANDE: A personal one or impersonal?

ANNA: I guess they want a personal one, I don't know. I don't even care what they want. I hate that school. It stinks. It smells like trash.

LANDE: Well I'm—so you're trying to say that going back to school is up to me?

MOTHER: It is. (Therapist laughs.) The school would rather not have her there until they get an evaluation from you that she is able to go to school in a normal school situation, and they would also like some kind of an evaluation about what would be best for her as far as her education is concerned. I mean, whether it is best for her to be in a normal school situation, or if it's best for her to have a tutoring—a home tutoring situation.

FATHER: Or a combination.

LANDE: Have you all talked together about this—the three of you?

FATHER: Yes, we have.

ANNA: Have we?

FATHER: We haven't gotten very far, Anna.

ANNA: I just said that I hated school. That's all I said.

FATHER: I remember the other day you said you didn't want tutoring.

ANNA: I didn't want anything from that school.

FATHER: Yeah but, I think, and we really haven't gotten back to it, and probably should have.

ANNA: Gotten back to school, or gotten back to what—the discussions.

FATHER: Just talking to you some more about it.

ANNA: Well, if they could tutor me at home, I would take that. Otherwise I'm going to quit.

LANDE: O.K. I'm really confused.

ANNA: You usually are confused.

LANDE: I get confused pretty easily.

ANNA: I know this.

LANDE: Especially about this, because I thought you were very concerned about finishing school this year.

ANNA: How can I finish school when I'm taking medication?

LANDE: How do you mean?

ANNA: How can I finish school when I'm taking medication?

LANDE: Does it interfere with your going to school?

ANNA: Yes, it interferes very much. It interferes with my eyesight, and it interferes with my emotions, it interferes with everything. And I can't stand that school.

MOTHER: Well, if you go into the normal school situation, you can't any longer become a discipline problem for the school.

ANNA: Who's a discipline problem? They're the ones that are the problem.

MOTHER: When you don't obey the school rules.

ANNA: Then I ain't going back to school at all and that's final.

LANDE: You know what I'm concerned—because I think I share both your thinking—is that . . .

ANNA: Question. Why is Stuart and Sarah here?

LANDE: Excuse me one second, Anna. —Is that this must have been a kind of an embarrassing thing for both of you—what happened to Annabelle.

ANNA: It certainly was.

MOTHER: Well, let me say . . .

ANNA: I spoke my mind and I embarrassed you . . .

MOTHER: It is embarrassing, yes, it's very definitely embarrassing, but her welfare is more important than that, you know.

LANDE: Well, what I'm thinking is that you, for your own sakes—because I think your feelings are very important, should be assured in your own mind that you won't be embarrassed again if Annabelle goes back to school. I share with you completely that a normal school and Annabelle acting normally is a goal.

MOTHER: Right. We do have to be assured of that.

ANNA: *(Interrupting.)* I was acting definitely normal in that office. I just sat there and I told them what I thought of them, what I thought of their rules, what I think they should do. And you know what they said. Well, you can go to school without going to this one. I said, "No man, if I'm going to graduate, I'm going to graduate from this school."

FATHER: O.K. Annabelle, we don't need a repeat of everything that happened.

ANNA: Yes we do. What do think we're here for?

FATHER: Well we are here to kind of talk about how we feel about it, not what happened. But that's part of it, yeah.

MOTHER: Honey, do you feel that you could go back to school without creating a big . . .

(The daughter turns her finger by her temple, mocking her father as mad.)

ANNA: That's for the people behind the mirror.

MOTHER: Hey, Anna? Do you think you could go back to school without some embarrassing situation arising again?

ANNA: Embarrassing for who?

MOTHER: For us.

ANNA: I doubt it.

The special problem of the therapist can be put in this way: it is assumed that the daughter's crazy behavior is a result of a crisis in the parents' marriage which has brought instability to the family. If the therapist confronts the parents with that idea, it is possible that they will deny it and blame the daughter, saying that she is the problem. That is a typical response when a therapist joins an adolescent against parents. When that happens the family triangle cannot be resolved, and the girl is likely to be rehospitalized. Therapy then has to begin again. If the therapist does not bring up the marital issue, however, but instead tries to have the parents spontaneously bring it up, they may not do so. The girl too will make herself the issue to prevent the marital conflict from being explored. The more unstable the marriage, the more trouble the girl will make both in her life and in the interview. She will distract the therapist, and if he is provoked by her or attempts to confront her, he will find himself dealing only with her rather than with the marital issue. The task of the therapist is to have the parents bring up the marital crisis without letting the daughter prevent that happening. The supervisor suggests on the telephone that the therapist weaken the girl's central position by talking with the siblings.

ANNA: I can't control myself when I'm under the medication. That day

I had smoked a cigarette, and I was pissed off at being suspended for it, because I smoke cigarettes normally, and I don't see why I can't smoke them in school if I can smoke them at home.

FATHER: Well, Anna, the reason you can't is because you are one of the student body and you must follow the rules—

ANNA: *(Interrupting.)* Then I ain't going to be one of the student body and—all right, I'm not following the rules.

FATHER: —That's applicable to everybody there—

ANNA: All right, too bad then. I ain't going back to that shitty school.

LAUDE: What grade are you in, Stuart? *(The fifteen-year-old son.)*

STUART: Tenth grade.

LANDE: Do you go to the same school as Anna?

ANNA: He certainly does. What do you think about school, Stuart?

STUART: Just about the same. It's run pretty—they don't have buses.

ANNA: They don't even have buses and people pay for those buses.

STUART: It's all right. It's better than—I think it's the best school, but it still is not very good.

ANNA: It's better than Galmore, it's better than . . .

FATHER: *(To son.)* Well, what don't you like about it?

LANDE: Well, let me, maybe I can help . . .

ANNA: The way it's run.

STUART: It's just minor things. They don't really matter, but you know.

LANDE: Stu, let me help your dad out with the questioning, because you are kind of an expert on that high school this year since you're in it. What do you think—your sister is in the twelfth grade, your opinion?

STUART: On what?

LANDE: We're talking about going back to school—the pro's and con's.

ANNA: I ain't going back to school if that's the way it has to be.

LANDE: Do you have any ideas about it?

ANNA: If I have to follow those stinky rules, I ain't going back.

MOTHER: What do you think it would be best for her to do?

STUART: I don't know. Probably get back to school.

MOTHER: You think it's important that she graduate?

STUART: Sort of.

ANNA: It has to be. I need a diploma to get any kind of decent job. And I want a job when I get out of high school.

MOTHER: So you do think it's important.

ANNA: I will not be able to hang in the house all day because—

(The telephone rings and the therapist answers it.)

ANNA: I wish you would stay off that phone, it annoys me.

The daughter continues to dominate the session, provoking the therapist against his will. The supervisor suggests that the therapist place the father in charge of the girl. This places a parent in charge, which is a goal, and it also involves the daughter in the family struggle rather than with the therapist.

LANDE: Maybe one of the reasons it's hard to use everybody's wisdom is because Anna keeps on, kind of . . .

ANNA: Barging in.

LANDE: Yeah. *(To father.)* Maybe you can help Anna just kind of, for a second, because there are a lot of people who have experience in school and know Anna pretty well. I'm still having—I'm still not clear about what you thought, Stu, because you know the school and what they demand and what not.

STUART: Well—uh—I don't know.

LANDE: Is it a pretty strict school?

STUART: Yeah, sort of. You know. you gotta be quiet and stay calm and everything. You can't run around and break the rules or anything. And then when they, you know, if you can't take the punishment they give you, if you break the rules . . .

ANNA: They give you detention.

FATHER: Stu has the floor now.

STUART: Right, then I guess you can't, you know, get along with the school.

MOTHER: Do you get along all right?

STUART: Yeah.

ANNA: It's hard though, ain't it?

STUART: Sort of.

ANNA: It's hard with the way the teachers treat you. Teachers treat you like babies, but then when you act like a grownup . . .

FATHER: Anna, let's let Stu speak now . . .

LANDE: It's hard to resolve the issues, because Anna's point of view, which is certainly an important one, is the only one that gets expressed.

ANNA: That's damn straight, 'cause I feel I'm the only one in here that can get myself out of here.

FATHER: I didn't understand.

LANDE: I said that one of the reasons that it is so hard to resolve this kind of issue is that Anna's point of view, which certainly is an important one, is the only one that gets expressed, because she kind of cuts everybody else off.

FATHER: Yeah, she dominates it.

ANNA: I dominate everything I do.

FATHER: No, you don't, honey.

ANNA: Yes, I do. I try and eat the dinner, I dominate the dinner table. I try and clean the house, I dominate the house.

FATHER: Relax.

ANNA: How can I relax when I'm under medication?

FATHER: I think you can if you just work at it.

ANNA: My eyes hurt.

LANDE: *(After a pause.)* Well this is very far from being a resolved issue, I guess, in everybody's mind.

FATHER: I think it's pretty well resolved in everybody's mind except Anna.

ANNA: Right. And I'm the one that has to do everything! Why do you have to make all of the decisions for me?

FATHER: And I think, you know, one of the things—you know—when she is ready to go back—that will be part it—her attitude of doing it. I don't think she is ready yet.

LANDE: Yes, as long as there is a danger to you two—that it will be an embarrassing thing.

MOTHER: On top of that, since I don't know how much school played an issue in . . .

ANNA: In my nervous breakdown.

MOTHER: In the way she was reacting last week, because she's really been very calm since she's known that she couldn't go back to school for a while.

ANNA: In other words, I enjoyed my suspension so much that I think maybe if I go back there I just might get myself suspended on purpose.

MOTHER: Did you get yourself suspended on purpose?

ANNA: No man, I was just doing what I was doing. I wanted to smoke a cigarette, and they came up and said, "You're smoking? Either you take detention or you're suspended." I said, "To hell with it, man, I ain't taking detention."

LANDE: *(To father.)* Maybe you can help us. Annabelle seems—maybe you could help her kind of give others a chance to talk in the family.

FATHER: Anna, now look, there's five of us here, now. We all have—

ANNA: O.K., then let Sarah talk, I want to hear what she says.

FATHER: Look, you are not moderating this meeting. Sit quietly and be quiet!

ANNA: Yes, sir!

FATHER: Defiant.

ANNA: Anything you say, sir.

FATHER: Start doing it.

ANNA: Sure, any time. It's called defiance.

FATHER: You know you have to have the last word, you're argumentative.

ANNA: I know this.

LANDE: The issue you raise seems to be kind of a central one, and I certainly don't know the answer. Maybe everybody here could help. What did happen—uh—last week . . . which would be important—thinking in terms of the future?

MOTHER: Well, on Sunday she got very upset. She was crying and got very hostile and belligerent . . .

LANDE: What . . .

MOTHER: And on Monday she didn't go to school.

LANDE: What I'm thinking, maybe I didn't make my question clear enough is—you were speculating—what set these things going in the first place?

MOTHER: Well, I was speculating that she demanded to go to school all last week, and it was quite—uh—we had to be quite insistent that she didn't go, because she couldn't go last week. She wasn't uh . . .

LANDE: Let me interrupt you. This is my fault, let me try one more time. What I'm interested in is—that something happened Sunday, or Saturday, or sometime last weekend—not this week, a week ago this weekend.

MOTHER: Well, she got herself suspended on Tuesday for insolent behavior.

LANDE: Yeah, but even before that—but even before that, something happened that got Annabelle all upset and anxious.

ANNA: You want to know what it was? I'll tell you what it was. I was in work, and I had my period, and I had cramps. And I didn't feel like staying at work any longer. So I called up my father and he said, "Well, listen, Ed has the car, so you can call Arnold *(her boyfriend)*, and I freaked out, and I said, "Well, if I would have called Arnold you would have yelled at me." So I called Arnold—

FATHER: It's something that came before that.

ANNA: Well would you let me tell him what happened so he can analyze it?

FATHER: O.K., honey, but I think you told him this earlier last week.

ANNA: But anyway, so then I got upset and I started crying, and crying, and crying. And I called up Arnold and Arnold wasn't there either. So then I asked Mrs. Henderson to come pick me up. So then, I told the old man he better think about something. Because I know what is wrong with me now. So then he said, "What are you going to think about, what should I . . . "

This interview illustrates a major point. The young person misbehaves and sacrifices herself to save the parents not only when they are in difficulty in life, but also in the moment-to-moment interactions of an interview. The therapist has indicated that he will pursue what upset the daughter. Presumably that upset was caused by a parental conflict, which Annabelle forced her parents to drop to deal with **her.** *In this interview, to keep the parental conflict from coming out, the daughter will make every attempt to distract therapist and parents so that they will deal with her rather than with the parental tension. Here she distracts them by acting crazy and rambling. Another technique is to start a fight with one of the parents. The fact that she "filibusters" indicates that there must be a parental conflict which she is concealing.*

LANDE: I'm getting confused.

FATHER: This is after she came home she told me.

ANNA: Yeah . . .

MOTHER: Can I say something about this?

ANNA: No.

MOTHER: Let me make a point.

ANNA: Make a point.

MOTHER: My point was pure speculation, but all last week you were very uptight over everything.

ANNA: I was missing all my subjects.

MOTHER: Until we imposed it upon you that you couldn't go to school. Now with school out of the way and with your job out of the way, you have been very calm.

ANNA: *(To therapist.)* I quit my job.

In this situation, the danger is just what the mother expressed—the fact that everything is fine at home after the daughter has quit school and work and is sitting at home, quieted by medication. The therapeutic problem is not how to quiet the girl but how to free her from an abnormal situation so that she can engage in normal activities.

MOTHER: So with your job and school gone, you've been very manageable around the house . . .

FATHER: Well, the way I'd like to . . .

ANNA: Around the house—I'm a domestic person.

MOTHER: You know, maybe she created the whole thing because she wanted to. . .

LANDE: Well, that's what I'm trying to find out from everybody here— what—something must have happened someplace that got Anna down.

ANNA: Ask Sarah a question, she ain't sitting here for nothing.

MOTHER: It was all very frightening anyway, wasn't it, Sarah?

ANNA: Oh, but you didn't know about the freaking-out part.

LANDE: I knew a little from talking to your mom.

ANNA: She tells everything so screwed up.

LANDE: I'm still—Sarah, Stu—does anybody have an idea about what happened that got Anna so anxious?

ANNA: Yes.

LANDE: Is it a mystery to you, Sarah?

ANNA: Man, it was the medication the whole time.

FATHER: I think there were a couple of things. One, I think we were trying, you know, on an experimental basis of taking her off the medicines, and we did that, and I think that didn't help, and second, we—uh—I'm not quite sure, but . . . *(Pause.)*

ANNA: He kept forcing the pill at me and he kept saying, "Take it, take it," and you know what he did to me one time?

One can assume from the father's hesitation and the daughter's rescue that the father was about to bring up a previous conflict with his wife. It is because the therapist has consistently sided with the parents that the father is able to decline the daughter's rescue operation and return to the marital issue.

ANNA: *(Continuing.)* I wanted to eat dinner, and him and his wife were having martinis. So I said, "Can I eat now?" and he said, "No, we're going to wait longer."

LANDE: *(To father.)* I think you are going to have to help Annabelle stay on the point, because we're talking—I think a couple of days before all of this.

FATHER: Yes, see this was just a couple of days . . .

ANNA: I'm telling you what happened, now would you listen?

FATHER: All right, Anna.

ANNA: I sat down to the table to eat, and Dad said, "Get up out of the table," and I said, "No." So you know what he did? He came over and he pulled my chair right out from under my seat. And I sat there on the floor and I cried and cried, and then he said Arnold couldn't come over, and I cried and cried. And then I called Arnold, and Arnold came over anyway, and as soon as Arnold came over, man, I stopped crying.

FATHER: Okay, well, look—uh—getting to what might have happened that created it all, I think it was, you know, a series of things, and I don't really know, this is just speculation on my part. But I think, one, you know, the fact that she had been taken clear off the medicines, and also—uh— some arguments that Jane (his wife) and I had had—probably that she heard.

(The daughter makes a gesture of exasperation, as if meaning that he was going right ahead no matter how she tried to stop him.)

LANDE: These are arguments that you two had?

FATHER: Yeah.

Finally the division between the parents has been brought out by one of them. The goal of the therapist is to reorganize the family, and if the parents are to take charge, they must concede and negotiate their difficulties with each other. If they deny their own problems and insist that the daughter is the whole problem, the family cannot be reorganized. If the parents attack each other, they cannot take charge, just as any leadership will fail if it is divided in an emotional battle. All the therapist's emphasis on the parents' needs and rights, even to the point of minimizing the daughter's rights, was preparation for the point when the parents could comfortably concede that the division between them was a problem in the family. The fact that they have had private sessions with the therapist to discuss their differences does not make it less important that they deal with them in the presence of their agitated daughter, who is trying to distract them from their marital problems. This does not mean that the therapist should immediately welcome and explore the marital fight, however. He still has the problem of what to do about it. He proceeds to normalize the fight by discussing it with everyone in a general way.

ANNA: I can't stand it when they fight. They fight, and it causes so much noise and hassle because he gets uptight and he takes it out on her and on him and on me *(sigh)* I can't stand it.

LANDE: Were all the kids aware of the argument happening?

FATHER: Well, the one that I had in mind was late at night, but I think, I don't know whether she heard it or not—she was in bed.

ANNA: I hear all your arguments.

LANDE: What about Stu, and Sarah?

MOTHER: *(To Stu.)* What about it?

STU: What about what?

The fifteen-year-old Stu's response to the parents' quarrel is a classic way for a child to remain within his own generation and outside a triangle with his parents. The disturbed daughter, of course, considers her sibling irresponsible, if not a cad, for not trying to save the parents' marriage. The difference in the sibling's situation and response clarifies how one child in a family can go mad while another does not.

MOTHER: How do you feel about the arguments?

STU: Whose arguments?

MOTHER; Your dad's and mine.

STU: I don't . . . *(Pause.)*

FATHER: Come straight, you can tell us.

MOTHER: What do you do? You withdraw from them, huh?

STU: Mm-hmm.

ANNA: You mean you don't even care?

STU: I don't.

ANNA: You don't even care if they argue?

STU: No.

ANNA: It figures.

MOTHER: Well, on Friday night we had—yeah—Friday and most of Saturday we had . . .

FATHER: This weekend, or the weekend before that?

MOTHER: The weekend—this weekend.

FATHER: (Irritated.) Well, we're talking about the weekend before that. What caused her to have problems at school?

MOTHER: I don't know about the weekend before that. I don't know what caused her . . .

ANNA: (Interrupting.) I do. I didn't take the medication.

LANDE: I was interested in what Stu was saying. It's interesting in the family when parents argue, which happens in a lot of families, how different kids react differently. You were saying, I didn't quite follow, you withdrew, or . . . ?

STU: I don't say anything, I don't get into it. I just be quiet.

MOTHER: Make yourself scarce.

STU: I wait until they end.

LANDE: How do you . . .

ANNA: He's called the hanger.

LANDE: The hanger?

ANNA: He just hangs. He don't even care nothing about the house.

LANDE: He hangs loose, you mean?

ANNA: He just hangs. He's told something to do and all he does is gripe about it, but he does it. And he gripes about it for about five hours, and you have to tell him to shut up.

LANDE: But do you kind of leave the room, I mean, or just—if Mom and Dad are having an argument?

STU: Yeah, like if I can—I just leave the room, you know.

MOTHER: You shut it out, don't you?

STU: No.

LANDE: Sarah, what do you do when Mom and Dad argue?

SARAH: Nothing.

LANDE: Nothing? Do you join in, or do you watch television, or you . . .

SARAH: I usually watch television.

LANDE: Is that what you do?

SARAH: I'm already doing it.

LANDE: You're already watching television. Do you make it any louder? Are you more like your brother or your sister? When your mom and dad fight?

SARAH: I don't know.

LANDE: You don't know? *(Pause.)* It's interesting—I guess with a lot of kids you have an opportunity to see . . . uh . . . they must react differently to a lot of different things.

MOTHER: They do.

FATHER: I think they are a little embarrassed to speak their minds right now. Both Sarah and Stuart. I get the feeling.

LANDE: They are embarrassed about the fact that . . .

FATHER: That they're there.

LANDE: That you two argue?

FATHER: Oh yeah, probably that, you know, but they probably have some feelings about it they are a little concerned about expressing.

LANDE: They don't want to hurt your feelings?

FATHER: Yeah, probably.

LANDE: Is it a secret that you argue?

FATHER: No, I don't think so. *(Family laughs.)*

MOTHER: I don't think so.

ANNA: We try to make it secret, but it don't work.

FATHER: How do we try to make it a secret?

ANNA: We try and close all the windows and close all the doors so none of the neighbors can hear.

MOTHER: *(Laughter.)* Yeah, right.

ANNA: Man, I've heard the neighbors fight so many times and I don't even care about the neighbors' fighting. All's I care about is if you and Mom fight.

FATHER: I know you do, honey—I think . . .

ANNA: I try and tell you to "shut up" all the time, but you just say, "Anna, you shut up, you sit down, and you shut up."

MOTHER: Anna, Anna, you are not responsible.

ANNA: But I feel responsible. God, what can I say to make you people listen to me?

MOTHER: Why do you feel responsible?

ANNA: What's that noise?

FATHER: That's your things down there. *(Annabelle is shaking her legs and she has pins in her cuffs that rattle against each other.)* You are really carrying a whole armor of those pins there.

ANNA: I just found those today. I just put them somewhere because I didn't know where they went.

FATHER: Anna has got an awful lot of—uh—anxieties that way, and it causes a lot of problems around the house.

LANDE: Anxieties, what way?

FATHER: Well, I don't know if that is the right word, but she . . .

ANNA: Anxieties *is* the right word.

FATHER: O.K., but she is very concerned, you know, about the way we get along. And she has a prescribed order of things that she wants to see. And if they don't happen the way she wants them to, she gets very hostile.

ANNA: No, not hostile.

FATHER: Oh, you just—if you really look at it, Anna, like, "You want to eat right now?"

ANNA: *(To therapist.)* You dropped your matches.

FATHER: And I said, "We'll eat in a few minutes," and you insisted we do it right away, and as things go along you'd almost manage the home if we would let you.

ANNA: I manage it perfectly.

FATHER: I'm sure you could manage your own home—in pretty good shape sometime. But I don't want you to manage mine.

ANNA: Man, I can't help it, because you don't manage it in the right way.

Father laughs. There is a knock at the door and the therapist exits to talk to the supervisor. While walking up and down the hall, they decide to make the threat of parental separation explicit as a way of reducing the daughter's power in the hierarchy. It is assumed that the family knows perfectly well what is behind the problem, and that the real problem is not being able to solve it. Therefore, the comment the therapist makes will not be an interpretation in the sense that it offers the family a discovery about itself. Everyone knows the girl is responding to the threat of parental separation. The purpose of the comment is not to educate the family but to block off the sequence in which a concealed parental conflict leads to disturbed behavior by the daughter. When the issue is brought out, the daughter continues her attempts to distract the therapist from it.

LANDE: The issue which everybody seems to be talking about—I'm not a hundred percent sure, but I'd like to make this a hypothesis—is something I think you all are saying in different ways, is that you two fighting has an effect on everybody, particularly on Annabelle.

ANNA: Definitely, especially with that medication.

LANDE: So I would—I'm pretty sure that of all the different things that are going on, Annabelle doesn't know how to do it as well as Stu—just to kind of leave, when she hears you two fighting very strongly that she is afraid that you two are going to separate. I don't know what goes on in her mind, but I would guess that is what gets a lot of this anxiety building up.

FATHER: Well, the one night that she was awake all night and very fearful, she kept saying that all the time—she didn't want us to leave one another and split up. So, I think she is very much concerned about that.

LANDE: That would kind of corroborate my hypothesis.

As it becomes evident that the girl became upset as a result of a threat of separation by the parents, she once again attempts to distract the therapist. She brings up something that might interest a young psychiatrist. He responds by staying with the issue.

ANNA: *(Interrupting.)* You want to know what I saw, Doctor?

LANDE: Well, I'd be—I'm more concerned about this issue about how your parents . . .

ANNA: You know what I saw? I saw ghosts in my room.

LANDE: You see, I was wondering if when you two fight, if Annabelle gets anxious and upset and sees things and imagines things—if that's not some way that she becomes very helpful to you by letting you unite and pull together. If she starts acting kind of nutty, it helps you two get together.

ANNA: No, it just makes them go farther apart. Except for today when we met at the restaurant. Dad didn't say one harsh word to Mom because I was pulling it all out of him, I said, "What time were you here? Were you waiting for us long? We're really sorry, man. We were hassling with that lady, we couldn't find the right shades."

FATHER: Annabelle, you didn't have to worry about that, I wasn't going to be harsh.

ANNA: You looked so mad.

FATHER: I wasn't looking mad.

ANNA: You said you didn't like being a something-or-other—ordering the food and waiting, because we were late.

FATHER: That's right, I didn't. That didn't mean I was mad, though.

ANNA: But you looked mad.

LANDE: I think this is all kind of saying that my idea is probably pretty straight on target. Annabelle is very afraid that your arguing means that you are going to break up, and she is really trying—not always consciously—trying her best to hold you two together. And the way she does it is in kind of an . . .

ANNA: Extreme.

LANDE: *(Continuing.)*—In an extreme way, yeah. Being kind of an extreme, but a creative person.

The girl attempts to say a word and has difficulty, perhaps because she is creating a neologism made up of "creative" and "curative."

ANNA: Being extreme and creative—curative.

LANDE: I think, you know, that Annabelle getting back to school, and [for] things to stabilize, she has to really have a sense that that's not going to happen right now. That you two are not going to separate now.

ANNA: They're not going to separate. They won't separate, because if they separate, you know what I'm going to do? I'm going to kill myself. I swear, if they separate, I will die by own hand.

MOTHER: Why?

ANNA: Because those little kids need you. Those little kids need the love—I swear, how can you show love—

FATHER: Honey, we won't separate.

ANNA: I'm not worried about it because I know that you won't, but it's just these stupid, petty little arguments that you have. Especially the ones over me. "Can Anna go out to the movies tonight?" "I don't know, let's talk about it. Uh, do you think Anna can go to the movies with Arnold?" "I don't know. Can Anna go to the movies with Arnold?"

LANDE: I think Anna has to hear from you two, probably in a louder voice than that, you know, that that's not going to happen right now— between the two of you. Because if not, her fantasies—every time you two have a little argument . . .

FATHER: I think that's a problem. Even when we are discussing something and don't agree about it, she considers that an argument.

LANDE: Well, I think that's why she has to hear from you two that right now that is not the reality of what's happening.

ANNA: Is it?

MOTHER: Well, I think one of the most important things is not necessarily—well I think that it is important that she knows that we're not going to separate, but I think it's more important, too, that we don't have to put up with intolerable behavior simply because we can't separate.

LANDE: Intolerable behavior . . .

MOTHER: Well, I mean there are limits to what people should have to tolerate to stay together, too.

LANDE: You mean from each other.

ANNA: Then how come you guys are trying to make me and Arnold separate?

FATHER: No, we're not, honey.

ANNA: Well it sure does seem like it with all these rules and restrictions that you are putting on me and him. It sounds like you don't trust him at all.

FATHER: Now, Arnold and I had a big talk the other day. He understands me. Did he talk to you about it?

ANNA: No, he didn't.

FATHER: Oh well . . .

This is a typical maneuver by a problem young person. When the parents bring up marital conflict, such as the "intolerable" behavior mentioned above, the girl picks an argument with one of them.

LANDE: *(Interrupting.)* You know, it's interesting that Annabelle, in being so helpful in the family—one of the ways she does it is to centralize everything on to her. It is very hard to even have a petty argument about a hamburger when—she's really an artist in kind of focusing and trying to hold everything together in her own way.

ANNA: That's what my mother used to call me all the time, an artist, and I couldn't understand why.

LANDE: *(To mother.)* We must be on the same wave length.

MOTHER: You are very talented, Annabelle.

LANDE: She is really working at like time-and-a-half—if she charged for her services, they'd be very expensive—to really help—you know she has some idea that you two need her help to, you know, keep your marriage together.

ANNA: That's because they think that I need their help. And I don't need your help, your time has expired. I'm a woman now—I'm an adult. And I don't need nothing from you—except for your food, and your house, and your TV, and your plants, and all your materialistic things.

MOTHER: *(Laughing.)* That's quite a bit.

FATHER: You know, you're probably right.

ANNA: If I could get out of it, you know, I would get out of it right now, and I would go and I would buy my own house and I would live in my own house.

(The telephone rings and the therapist answers it.)

The daughter has said that if the parents separate, she will kill herself. Something must be done about that statement. The parents should not use the daughter's suicide threat as an excuse for staying together. This keeps the daughter in the middle of their marriage, and she can become normal only if she is moved out of the parents' struggle into a life with her peers. The goal of the therapy is to reorganize the family, with the parents spontaneously drawing a generation line and preventing their daughter from being part of their marriage. The therapist will try to hold the parents together at this point, but their ultimate decision to separate or stay together should not be based on the daughter's health. An intervention to deal with this issue should be more than an intellectual comment. The therapist must become involved with the daughter if he is to exclude her from the parents' marriage. To put it another way, he must first lower the daughter in the family hierarchy, and then the parents will be able to follow his lead. Therefore the supervisor asks the therapist if he thinks he can get angry with the girl. He says that he thinks he can. The supervisor suggests that the therapist get angry at the girl for asking for her right to indepen- dence while unfairly depriving the parents of their rights to independence.

ANNA: Don't you want to talk about the medication?

FATHER: Not right now.

ANNA: I do.

MOTHER: We do have to talk about medication at some point.

ANNA: We've got ten minutes to talk about medication.

LANDE: I think there are some other things of pressing importance that are going on here.

ANNA: There is no other things, it's the medication that breaks my nerves . . .

FATHER: Dr. Lande is chairing here.

ANNA: Dr. Lande is stupid. He doesn't know one damn thing.

FATHER: Annabelle!

MOTHER: Would you be quiet, Annabelle?

ANNA: No.

MOTHER: I want to talk, I want to talk all the time. (*Laughs.*)

ANNA: All right, then talk. You got ten minutes.

FATHER: Damn it, Anna. Be quiet.

ANNA: Damn who?

FATHER: (*Whisper.*) It. Now be quiet.

ANNA: What is "it"?

LANDE: There are a couple of important things that kind of got brought up, and I'm not sure of the total—at least they impressed me—which is one, you (*to mother*) feeling that there are certain intolerable behaviors that you have to put up with . . .

MOTHER: Right.

ANNA: What happened today, Mom?

LANDE: The feeling—the feeling is—'cause Anna is bringing up some interesting points. Some of them are hard to understand, the way they are being brought out, but—which is, she has some kind of idea, which is really strange, that she should be independent, and grown-up, and have her own house, and be respected by you—which makes a lot of sense to me. In the same sense she says, if you two separate ever, she should com- mit—kill herself.

ANNA: Why should I live, if my parents are going to . . .

LANDE: (*Interrupting.*) That gets me really angry, because that's one of the stupidest things I have ever heard.

ANNA: Yes, it is very stupid.

LANDE: You want your parents to be—you want to be independent from your parents, which seems right, but you give them no room to be independent from you. I don't understand why, if they want to do something that they—

ANNA: 'Cause they are so worried about me and everything, that it's my business.

LANDE: Yeah, but if they want to do something—if they ever did decide to do something, that you make it your business that you should hurt yourself is one of the dumbest things I ever heard anybody say.

ANNA: All right, why should I live if my parents ain't going to live together?

FATHER: Your life don't depend on that, honey.

LANDE: I don't see— if you're going to have some privacy and independence, they have to be treated as adults also.

ANNA: They don't act like adults.

MOTHER: Well, you are probably right about that, but we still are trying to be adults, and we need to have—simply because we separated wouldn't mean that you wouldn't have us both.

LANDE: The point being that you are not separating now, but living with intolerable behavior on either—on anybody's part—the word "intolerable" means "not to be tolerated." But that Annabelle, somehow her health is connected to that, it seems.

ANNA: My eye hurts.

LANDE: So there are some ideas around here, you know, that really need to get straightened out pretty soon.

MOTHER: Yes.

LANDE: Which is partly people feeling that certain things need to be changed so they can live together, which kind of seems to be a basic rule of living in a family. And also people knowing who those things are about. I mean *(to parents)*, this seems like this is business between you two, not the children.

MOTHER: I think it is.

LANDE: And somehow, Annabelle got caught in it—she feels caught in there.

The ability of the therapist to keep his cool and side with the daughter as well as the parents is well illustrated here. Even though the therapist is under pressure, with the family in crisis, a supervisor intruding on him, and a daughter being rude and provocative, he manages not to attack the girl, but rather to describe her as caught in the situation just as much as the parents are caught in it.

ANNA: Caught in the middle.

MOTHER: Can I tell you some things that . . . ?

LANDE: Sure.

MOTHER: Well for several years Annabelle kept asking me, "Why don't you divorce Dad?" This went on for several years. Then I went into marriage counseling, and we've been trying to work out our relationship, and things have been improving from Annabelle's viewpoint because she has told me they have improved. So now I think she has a sense of guilt over the years before. Now she feels that I may have taken her ideas too strongly, which isn't the case. I'm going to make up my own mind, you know.

LANDE: I think she has to hear that from you. I think Annabelle has to hear that message.

ANNA: I hear it, I hear it.

LANDE: I don't think you really do.

MOTHER: What you tell me to do, whether you tell me to live with your dad, or whether you tell me to separate from him, I'm not necessarily going to do either one.

ANNA: I know.

MOTHER: I'm going to make up my own mind about what's best for me and for the family.

Mother's statement can be taken as the turning point in the interview and the therapy. The goal was to have the parents take charge and keep the daughter out of their marital issues. When the mother defines her rights, she reduces the daughter's power in the family. The girl acts swiftly to intrude in the marriage by bringing up something that may divide mother and father, thus increasing her own power. The therapist moves equally swiftly to lower the girl to her correct position in the organizational hierarchy. From that point on the girl begins to behave more like a normal daughter, and the family stabilizes.

ANNA: Then how come you have to ask Dad every time you want something?

MOTHER: Well, I try to show consideration for your dad.

LANDE: *(Interrupting.)* Let me—you're sitting here justifying what you do with your husband to your eighteen-year-old daughter. I don't like to see that, for your sake.

MOTHER: That's a good point.

LANDE: I don't think—I think there are some things that are your business—

ANNA: *(Interrupting.)* Doctor, who really cares on what you think?

FATHER: I do.

MOTHER: I care.

LANDE: Hopefully some people who do . . .

ANNA: Well, I don't.

LANDE: I wish you did.

FATHER: Yeah, well I do.

ANNA: You do?

FATHER: You're damn right. Now be quiet.

ANNA: Yes, sir. *(She laughs for the first time in the interview.)*

LANDE: *(To Sarah.)* Your sister is a comedian? Is she the funny one in the family?

SARAH: No.

MOTHER: She throws a lot of weight in the family, though, doesn't she, Sarah?

LANDE: I'll bet she does. You have at least three parents, I bet.

ANNA: She sure does.

LANDE: Everybody is trying to be the adult—the parents in this family.

MOTHER: We've got too many parents, that's for sure. *(Laughs.)*

ANNA: I'm called the motherly type.

LANDE: Yeah, you are, but I think . . .

MOTHER: More motherly than Mother, I think. *(Laughs.)*

ANNA: I wanted Mom to get up and do exercises with me. You know what she did instead? Slept and let me fix her a cup of coffee.

MOTHER: *(Laughs.)* Yes, I really got service today.

LANDE: I think you have to decide *(laughs)* you can retire and take up her job.

ANNA: You know what she did? Forty-five minutes later? Exercises. *(Laughter.)*

LANDE: I don't know what they are going to do without you if you go off and start your own family.

ANNA: Neither do I. They are just going to have to break up if they want to.

(Later in the interview.)

ANNA: In other words, I don't like people from New York because I am prejudiced.

MOTHER: You are?

FATHER: You are, that's the case.

ANNA: Right. That is the case, I'm a prejudiced, uptight, stubborn, stupid, immature little girl. Trying to act like an adult. But can't do it because there are too many rules . . .

FATHER: O.K. Anna, let's get on to something else for a bit.

ANNA: We've only got three more minutes. What else can we talk about?

FATHER: BE QUIET! *(Daughter laughs.)*

LANDE: I think this is an area that's not going to be—

ANNA: I can't wait until you come to our dinner table. *(She is referring to the invitation to dinner of the therapist.)*

LANDE: —settled tonight. *(Laughs.)* I can't wait either.

(Everyone laughs.)

MOTHER: I'll have to taste all your food.

LANDE: Are you going to take me on on your own turf, Annabelle?

ANNA: What's that?

FATHER: You don't—don't you know what turf is? Your own area. Your own stamping grounds.

ANNA: Turf. Isn't that like a guy that's . . .

LANDE: This is going to be a good one.

ANNA: Isn't a turf a guy that works on other people's property?

(Therapist laughs.)

FATHER: No, that's a serf. Turf is like a football field, you know.

LANDE: I think Annabelle knew what she was saying.

FATHER: Mm-hmm.

LANDE: Annabelle is going to have to end the session having the final put-down. We'll see what happens at your house.

ANNA: We sure will, won't we?

LANDE: *(Making a deep voice.)* Yes we will, young lady.

ANNA: You sound like him *(meaning father).*

LANDE: I do? *(To the parents.)* This issue of whose marriage it is, and who gets involved in it is going to take—is not going to get solved now, but I think—at least the lines have been drawn out. The thing about going to school is something that I think you two are going to have to decide when you feel comfortable and don't feel there's a chance of being embarrassed. At which point, one of you, after you have decided together, can get in touch with me. And we'll talk about it, and I will do what I have to do with the school. But I think the decision—you get in touch with me when you feel comfortable, because you know Annabelle and you live with her. And I think what you're comfortable with is what's going to have to be.

After this interview the daughter went back to school and back to work at her part-time job. She graduated from high school in June. All was going well with the family and therapy was recessed.

In August the mother separated from the father. She went to another state with the three smallest children and went to work. The couple attempted reconciliation and then separated again. In this period the therapist saw the father and children for a few interviews to help the father organize the household. It was also considered important to see that Annabelle did not replace her mother. She did not do so, but instead shared the household work with her brothers, had a busy social life, and worked. The therapist talked with the mother on the telephone in this period. She said she did not wish to return to her husband, but was having difficulty working while taking care of the children.

A year after therapy, the mother became depressed and spent a short period on a psychiatric ward. At this time she discussed her history, reporting that she had grown up in an "uptight" household, gone to an "uptight" school, worked at a restricted job, and then married and had eight children, one right after the other—not out of choice but because of religious beliefs. At the time Annabelle had her episode, the mother was wondering if she had not wasted her life so far and was seeking something different for the rest of it. She later moved to another state by herself and worked as a teacher.

Annabelle's episode expressed the family problem in that she created the delusion of being pregnant with multiple children—twins—and was concerned about an abortion. She expressed the idea that she would sacrifice herself by killing herself if the parents should separate and abandon the children. Her upset forced the mother to stay with her husband and children to help deal with Annabelle. When Annabelle was moved out of the marital problem, the mother left. When the mother found she could not work and also take care of the small children, she returned to her husband but became depressed, and finally moved far away from the family to work and live alone. She later divorced her husband.

In a four-year follow-up, it was learned that Annabelle was doing well and had not had any psychiatric problems, even though she had been in a serious accident and had a physical injury that made it difficult for her to find work. Two years after therapy ended she had moved to an apartment of her own and was self-supporting.

Father and mother were still separated. All the children were doing well in school and college.

Chapter 9

The Process of Therapy: A Heroin Problem

One way to begin therapy with the family of a problem young person is to have the parents reach agreements by discussing the problem young person with each other. The emphasis is on the parents jointly becoming executives in the family. Their communication about the offspring can resolve the division between them as they jointly head the family hierarchy. Another way to begin is to have the parents take turns being in charge. Conflict between them is avoided if each is in charge of the problem young person for a set period of time. When one is in charge, the other is simply to stay out of it. Such an approach makes it more difficult for the young person to be caught between them, or to turn them against each other. The hierarchy is assumed to have one person at the head, but not a particular person, since the parents can take turns.

Another way to begin therapy is for the therapist to decide which parent is more involved with the problem young person and which is more peripheral, and then to put the peripheral parent in charge of the problem person (the first stage). The more involved parent will object and even attack, bringing out the marital issues (the second stage). This approach is commonly used with children's problems and with many families of young adults.[1] It works best with families which seem to lack subtlety in interpersonal skills, such as the families of drug addicts.

A social approach for schizophrenics was once considered inappropriate

1. The stages of this approach are described in J. Haley, *Problem Solving Therapy*, Jossey-Bass, San Francisco, 1976.

194

because such patients were "withdrawn from reality" and "in another world." Yet family therapy was found to be the best approach quite soon after the importance of families was recognized. Narcotic addicts too were thought to be unsuitable for family therapy because they were in a peer-oriented street world. For years the treatment was one in which fellow addicts, rather than families, were brought together in groups. The addiction seemed so clearly an individual problem, and the addict was so frequently part of the street world, that the family was not considered relevant. Only in recent years has it been realized that the heroin addict is far more involved with his family than was previously acknowledged and that, in fact, a family-oriented therapy is the most effective one. The originators of one of the more successful family therapy research projects reported the following figures from a survey they conducted in 1972 of eighty-five heroin addicts at the Philadelphia Veterans Administration Drug Dependence Treatment Center. They report that of addicts "with living parents 82% saw their mothers and 59% saw their fathers at least weekly; 66% either lived with their parents or saw their mothers daily".[2] These men averaged twenty-eight years old, and all had been previously away from home in military service. Similar findings were made by others who examined the family contacts of heroin addicts.[3] Once one realizes that heroin addicts are enmeshed in their families, it is apparent that the therapeutic approach should systematically involve those families.

In the following case, the intervention placed the father in charge of the son at the first stage of therapy, thereby beginning to disengage mother and son. The problem son had been a heroin addict for five years and had recently begun a methadone program. The family interview was described and quoted earlier (Chapter 6). After the interview began, the therapist moved the young people out and saw the parents alone to renegotiate an agreement that they would continue to come to therapy to help their son. Sam Kirschner, Ph.D. was the therapist. This case report is based on the film script of selections from the therapy which we edited together.[4]

After seeing the parents alone, the therapist brought the problem son and two younger siblings back into the interview room. The addict was still

2. M. D. Stanton and T. C. Todd, "Structural Family Therapy with Heroin Addicts, " in E. Kaufman and P. Kaufmann (eds.), *The Family Therapy of Drug and Alcohol Abusers*, Halsted, New York, 1979.

3. G. F. Vaillant, "A Twelve-Year Follow-up of New York Narcotic Addicts: I. The Relation of Treatment to Outcome," *Amer. J. Psychiat.*, 122:727–737, 1966.

4. This therapy was part of a research project directed by M. D. Stanton with T. C. Todd, consultant. The long-term therapy results with this case are reported in M. D. Stanton and G. Zug, "Case History of a Male Addict and His Family," a report to the Services Research Branch of the National Institute on Drug Abuse, 1978.

making an issue of his parents' threat to separate when he came back into the room with the therapist.

KIRSCHNER: *(To son.)* Well, I told you what I have to say in the hall, that any kind of stuff that's going on between your folks has little to do with you.

SON: Right.

KIRSCHNER: All right?

SON: Right. I got that down pat. They don't like each other.

MOTHER: That's not true.

SON: Well, I don't know what's true. You know? What is true?

KIRSCHNER: Let's say this. When they don't get along with each other, it's not necessarily because of you. Is that a fair statement?

FATHER: Definitely.

KIRSCHNER: O.K., that's a fair statement.

SON: Oh, no, it's only ninety percent me, how's that?

MOTHER: No, you're wrong.

SON: Fifty?

MOTHER: You're wrong.

SON: Oh, bullshit, you don't know what it is, man. Be realistic with me at least. Have I caused you—

FATHER: Oh, yeah.

SON: —heartbreak?

FATHER: Oh, yeah, well certainly you have.

SON: Well, your boy never got arrested, you—the fast, quick, little, jackass, queer, jerkoff never got arrested, but he was a junkie, turned into a junkie, can you understand? How could you understand it, my own father. Understand all that *(weeping)*. Do you know what hell I'm going through? Hate each other, I don't give a shit, I'm trying to do *my* thing. Trying to do it, and it's hard, man.

KIRSCHNER: O.K., tell—tell—why don't you explain to your parents what you're going through?

SON: They don't want to hear shit.

KIRSCHNER: They're listening now.

SON: They want to see me high, everytime, check my arms.

KIRSCHNER: They're listening.

SON: They want to do what they want to do.

KIRSCHNER: They're listening, they're listening now. Tell your folks what you're going through.

It could be considered an error for the therapist to encourage the young man to express his feelings if he does so with the idea that the expression of feelings is curative. Any addict has been through group therapy experiences which include the expression of emotions and so the addict will do it well, but it is irrelevant to therapy. It makes a session more exciting but things can be said which may make it difficult to organize the family to change. This therapist encourages the addict to express his despair because it will help bridge the gulf between addict and parents. He argues that most addicts simply do not believe that parents can understand the struggle with addiction.

KIRSCHNER: Tell your folks what you're going through.

SON: Hell man, hell!

KIRSCHNER: O.K. What's going on?

SON: Just—you know, I'll be straight, and as soon as the word "dope"— everything just stops. I don't think of nobody, you—her—nobody. Just Miss Heroin.

KIRSCHNER: You were straight—you were straight—

SON: Miss—when I'm high—

KIRSCHNER: Hey, you were straight for how long?

SON: Two months.

KIRSCHNER: O.K.

SON: And for free I got it, not even from Tommy or Marion. They get high, but they know how to control it, I'm a glutton.

(Later in the interview.)

KIRSCHNER: As soon as you get a job, you mean. So the plan is for you to get a job, make some money, and then move out, is that the idea?

SON: I don't want to move out.

KIRSCHNER: You don't want to move out?

SON: 'Cause I think he *(the father)* needs help too. They both need help, like I need help.

KIRSCHNER: That's a different problem. We've already talked about that when you were gone.

SON: No, he could drop dead right now. You know, I think that. More than I think of my own problems. That's how I escape myself, thinking of how I can help my father and mother—from being nervous. But yet I'm crazy. That's crazy that I'm high and I'm thinking how am I helping them.

The son expresses the situation nicely. When he's high on drugs, he's thinking of how he is helping the parents. The therapist does just what he should at this point: rather than discussing whether the father needs help (something the son understands better than the therapist), he offers to take on the father's problems himself. This must be done to free the son. The expert who is paid to do the job must help the father, while the son is freed to lead his own life.

KIRSCHNER: Hey, George, could you do me a favor? Do me one favor. Will you turn that job over to me? I'll worry about your father's health.

SON: *(Weeping.)* Yeah, but he made me. He didn't make you, man.

KIRSCHNER: That's all right, so what?

SON: Do I make any sense coming there with that sentence?

KIRSCHNER: I hear you.

SON: *He* made me.

KIRSCHNER: So. So what do you have to . . .?

SON: I care.

KIRSCHNER: I know you care. O.K. I . . .

SON: More than anybody else cares.

KIRSCHNER: I want to make an agreement with you. If you care about your father's health, right, which I know you do, turn it over to me. And you worry about your own business.

SON: As soon as they move, everything will be cool. Like a happy home. I come in, I want to go and stay with a chick, she has three kids. If I'm having fun, I want to stay. I'm twenty-five. *(To mother.)* I feel like I have to report in to the army, but I want to call you, 'cause I know you're worried, you don't sleep, you're nervous. You understand, Ma, why I call my Ma. "Mommy, I'm at so-and-so's house, and I had a good time last night, and I'm all right." What does that sound like to a twenty-six-year-old girl? That I'm—it sounds like I'm checking in with my sergeant.

The therapist must take charge and organize action if change is to take place. The goal of the therapy is to draw a generation line where the parents hold together in relation to the son without either one shifting and joining the son against the other. A first step in achieving this end is to ask the parent who seems more peripheral to take charge of the son. The therapist directs the father to be in charge of the son, and he asks the mother to communicate with the son through the father. The father is thus put in the middle of the intense relationship between the son and the mother. Even though this move is defined as for the mother's benefit, she will probably respond by activating her previous involvement with the son. The therapist must block that off. If the therapist can hold the father in the position between mother and son, it is the first step in the ultimate joining of mother and father.

KIRSCHNER: I would like to try something. O.K., since George is so upset, I would like to try something.

SON: I ain't upset, I'm having fun now. I really feel like a nut.

KIRSCHNER: I would, I would like, uh—(*Long pause.*) Yes, this is what I'd like to try—for one week. Just for a week as an experiment, O.K., in the house. (*To mother.*) If you have any complaints, or you want to check up on George, or whatever you want to do, you know—tell your husband to do it.

SON: Everybody's checking up on me, Sam.

KIRSCHNER: Hold on. Hold on.

MOTHER: Well, that's no problem, because whatever I ask him, he tells me.

FATHER: You gave us permission to tell—

SON: I tell—

KIRSCHNER: (*Overlapping.*) No, no, no, no.

SON: You know, the last time I got high—

KIRSCHNER: (*To mother.*) But I don't want you to do it.

SON: (*Continuing.*)—and how I jumped on—tell him, tell him I'm getting high. I want to tell you, 'cause you don't understand.

KIRSCHNER: (*Continuing to talk to mother while son talks to father.*) I want to give you a rest. Seriously. I want to give you a rest. I mean that. You got a lot of things on your mind, you got a lot—

MOTHER: He offers that, he tells me. He (*the father*) says to me, "Please be quiet. When something is wrong, tell me, let me talk to him." But I just can't seem to keep quiet.

KIRSCHNER: O.K. Hold on—

MOTHER: I feel like I'm the only one that's gonna make him better, and I feel like I'm making him worse.

KIRSCHNER: Hold on. O.K. O.K., so let's try it different—

SON: (*Overlapping.*) You got to do it, I know that, Mom, you know how much it hurts me when I do dope, huh?

KIRSCHNER: George, hold on, we're trying something.

MOTHER: I don't feel like him (*father*), him (*second son*), or him (*third son*) is capable of helping him.

KIRSCHNER: Well, right now what you're trying is evidently not working. O.K.? Let's look at the facts—it's not working. You're concerned, but the way you're going about it, it's not working. That's all. You've got a lot of things on your mind, maybe that's why it's not working. You've got a lot of things on your mind now anyway, O.K.?

When parents perpetuate a problem with their child, the therapist must change what they are doing. Sometimes he must object to the way they are doing something. If this is done by implying that something is wrong with the parents' character, a great deal of therapeutic time can be wasted by the parents proving their innocence or proving the therapist wrong. If the ther-

apist objects to the **operations** *of the parents in a matter-of-fact way, they will accept his objection. In this comment to the mother, the therapist managed to correct her without being offensive.*

MOTHER: Mm-hmm.

KIRSCHNER: So I'd like to have you worry about your own things, and if you have something that you're concerned about with George, tell your husband and let him tell George. O.K.? Is that fair enough?

MOTHER: Yeah.

SON: He's been telling me in a pretty good way, too.

KIRSCHNER: OK, hold on.

SON: And I been telling him. We been getting along, haven't we been getting along better, Dad, than ever?

KIRSCHNER: Hold on. Hold on, George. *(To father.)* Are you willing to do that?

FATHER: *(Puzzled.)* Say that again.

KIRSCHNER: If your wife has some kind of thing that she's concerned about with George, that she wants to ask some kind of question, some information, or whatever, would you be willing to do it instead of her?

FATHER: Certainly.

The father clearly agrees, and in his next statements begins to take charge of the son.

KIRSCHNER: You're willing.

SON: *(To mother.)* When are you moving to the South Side?

MOTHER: We looked at a house there.

FATHER: *(To son.)* Did you get your uh—did you get your medicine Monday?

SON: Nah, 'cause I was—hell, I can take my medicine, that I'm on now. You know that methadone makes me talk, makes me go nuts. As you say, I'm dopey.

FATHER: Did you go to the clinic?

SON: Methadone lasts for eighty hours, Dad. I can stay—I can go for four days without getting sick.

MOTHER: Well, how come you go every day, then?

SON: Why? 'Cause you have to, that's the law. It's the law.

MOTHER: Well, then why—

FATHER: But you didn't go—

KIRSCHNER: *(To mother.)* Hold on, there you go, you're asking him again. You were asking him again.

SON: No, I didn't—'cause I was . . . I just didn't go. I was with a girl. And I was—right, I should have been somewhere.

FATHER: You're not being honest with them, because you have to take—

SON: I lied to you.

FATHER: Will you let me talk a minute? They have to take the urine test, right? You didn't take it Monday? Are you having trouble urinating?

The directive that mother communicate to son only through father seems simple, yet it is a major intervention, and the outcome of the therapy will depend on the therapist's skill in enforcing it. In the interview room the therapist becomes a communication traffic cop, encouraging father and son to talk together and preventing mother from communicating with son about his problems. The therapist must persistently prevent the inertia of the system from causing a relapse to a mother-son intensity with father on the periphery. One can expect that all three family members will take some action to return to the previous system. That action can include threats to leave therapy.

SON: No, man. They didn't take it, they know I did heroin. I told Henry. I said, "I did heroin." I do so much that I did forget. But usually I don't forget, I shoot up—

FATHER: *(Interrupting.)* When did you do it, Sunday?

SON: *(Continuing.)* It hurts me more, when I get high. It makes sense? I can't figure it out either, Mom.

FATHER: *(Interrupting.)* When did you do it? This Sunday?

SON: No, Saturday.

FATHER: You did it this past Saturday?

MOTHER: Again.

KIRSCHNER: *(Restraining mother from talking.)* Hold on.

FATHER: Why?

SON: Why? Why and again? I don't know. It just was there. Nobody understands.

FATHER: *(To therapist.)* You figure it out.

(Later in the interview.)

SON: I ain't coming back, Sam. I'm telling you.

SON NO. 3: Well, I'm coming back.

SON: I'm asking Henry *(his drug counselor)* for medicine. You can come back, but I'm not.

The therapist responds simply and correctly to the young man's threat by making it personal.

KIRSCHNER: I want you to come back. I want you to come back. I want you to come back at least one more week, to see how this works for one week.

SON: 'Cause, as soon as—you know, I'm gonna make a loan and get away from them. After I'm away—

MOTHER: You couldn't make a loan from nobody.

SON: No? You want to bet?

MOTHER: The only way you're gonna make it is to sell heroin to your friends.

SON: Oh, there's ways, Mom, I'll hustle and bustle.

KIRSCHNER: (Interrupting.) Hey, George, (Whistles.) Hey, George, one more week. I want to see how this, how this works out.

SON: I don't want to come, Sam. You talk to them.

KIRSCHNER: I'll talk to you privately then.

SON: Yeah—uh, I'll do that.

KIRSCHNER: O.K., fine. I'll tell you what—

SON: Nobody understands me, I'm a nut. You know, I'm retarded. I'm a nut, I have a disease—

SON NO. 3: You want to be.

SON: Oh, yeah, I want to, sure.

SON NO. 3: (Crying.) Then what do you keep on saying it for, huh? How come? It's real funny, ain't it!

SON: Oh, see now—I knew you were gonna cry.

SON NO. 3: Ah jerk off, man, get off!

SON: See, he's right.

SON NO. 3: I'm right. (Runs from the room, crying.)

SON: He's right. (Standing up.) You're right, come on in and sit down.

KIRSCHNER: He's not going anywhere.

SON: I don't care where he goes. I don't care.

FATHER: You don't care for nothing.

SON: I don't care about nothing, I want—

FATHER: (Overlapping.) He just don't care.

SON: I've tortured these people so much, I don't want to care no more. That's why I want to leave.

FATHER: (Standing up, as son does.) Sam, we're holding up your time.

KIRSCHNER: You're not holding up my time. (To son as he goes out the door.) Where are you going now?

SON: I'm gonna thumb it home. I don't need a ride.

A therapist always has a problem when someone gets upset and leaves the interview room. When it is the problem young person, he must decide whether to bring him back and, if so, who should go and get him. Sometimes when a young person leaves, the therapist should merely continue with the *parents. He should take the young person's departure as an indication that the parents need to talk with the therapist. In this case, the therapist had already talked with the parents alone, and so this did not seem the way to respond. Typically it is best to send a parent after the problem young person. This defines the hierarichal issue as one within the family. Whoever the therapist is encouraging to take charge should be asked to go after the young person. In this case, it is unclear whether the father, if asked, would have been able to bring the young man back or whether he was there so tentatively himself that he would not himself have left. The therapist acts in what appears to have been the correct way: he goes and gets the young man himself. The problem son and the other two sons reenter to continue the interview. This determination to keep the young man involved could have influenced father to do as he did later, when he pursued his son.*

KIRSCHNER: *(Sitting down.)* We got some other shit to talk about here. O.K. *(To father.)* You got a cigarette?

FATHER: Yeah.

KIRSCHNER: *(To son.)* O.K., so you're upset, and that's why I don't want you to move out of the house.

SON: No.

FATHER: Did you go to the clinic Monday?

SON: What?

FATHER: Did you go to the clinic?

SON: No, I didn't go nowhere. I don't want to go nowhere.

KIRSCHNER: You been to the clinic this week?

SON: Huh? Since I got high that one time—oh, yeah, I was there tonight. Henry don't even—I'm gonna talk to him and ask him one more time if he'll bear with me—'cause all I'm doing is jive-assing. If I keep— I'm trying, but it seems like I'm not trying. I'm—I'm like double-talking right now. I am really trying, but it's impossible sometimes.

KIRSCHNER: I hear you.

SON: You understand?

KIRSCHNER: I understand.

SON: Nobody believes it, that how—all of a sudden, somebody says *(whispering)*, "I got some heavy shit." Everything stops! *(Sliding off his coat.)* My coat falls off, all my clothes, I'm nude, and that's all there is. "Baby, I'm gonna be nice." That's all there is, that's what this does to you.

MOTHER: *(To therapist.)* Is that a mental illness?

KIRSCHNER: *(To mother, overlapping.)* You understand that?

MOTHER: That's not a mental illness?

SON: That *is* a mental illness.

MOTHER: No, I don't understand.

SON: It's a sickness, it's a disease.

MOTHER: I don't understand.

KIRSCHNER: Hold on. You're saying your mother and father don't understand how hard it is.

SON: They don't.

KIRSCHNER: Do you understand how hard that is for him to resist that?

MOTHER: No.

SON: They don't. I love them, but—

MOTHER: *(Interrupting.)* Not when a boy says that he loves me, and he loves his father, and he wants—

SON: *(Interrupting, standing, and shouting.)* But I forget all about you when I see my baby "Heroin."

MOTHER: Well, then, you might as well pack your clothes and get out with your baby!

By the end of this first interview, the therapeutic plan has been set. The therapist has a contract with the family and a plan to follow. He will have father deal with son, and mother deal with father about the son's problems. Predictably this will lead to marital tension and threats of separation. When that happens, the son will relapse to save the parents. The therapist must help the parents to consolidate both their relationship with him and their relationship with each other. The focus should be on the problem that the family wishes to solve: the addiction.

(At the second interview, the therapist interviews the parents alone.)

KIRSCHNER: The next four weeks are gonna be tough.

MOTHER: For Georgie?

KIRSCHNER: And I wanted to prepare you in advance for that, to know what you're coming up against. It's gonna be a very tough period. And—depending upon what we decide today, in terms of how I can—of how you can use me in the best way, in terms of ensuring that this guy stays off drugs for the next—I would say the next four weeks is going to be critical. You know, how he's gonna react to the detox, and so on.

During the second week, the young man was detoxified and taken off a massive dose of methadone. As reported in the following interview, the parents had an argument in which the mother threw dishes around the house. This was followed by the son shooting heroin and the father getting into a physical fight with him. The expected sequence therefore took place within just a week: the young man improved; the parents had a fight; the young man relapsed. What was new was that the father got actively involved in stopping the young man from taking heroin.

(Therapist, parents, and son are present in the interview.)

KIRSCHNER: You're relaxed.

MOTHER: Yeah.

KIRSCHNER: How come you're relaxed?

MOTHER: When everything's fine, I'm fine.

KIRSCHNER: So you had a stormy evening the other evening.

MOTHER: Mm-hmm.

SON: Wasn't too stormy.

KIRSCHNER: *(To father.)* You know, I can see that you're making a real effort to get this guy to, uh—to be what he could be.

FATHER: It's either do or die for him.

KIRSCHNER: And you're gonna stick it out, right? You're gonna really . . .

FATHER: If he don't do something this time . . . I'm not coming . . .

KIRSCHNER: *(To mother.)* You must be proud of him, huh?

MOTHER: Mm-hmm.

FATHER: I don't know why.

KIRSCHNER: Were you proud of him?

SON: What were you proud of?

MOTHER: Well, I didn't stop it.

SON: You didn't stop what?

MOTHER: I mean, I knew neither one was really gonna hurt each other.

KIRSCHNER: *(Cutting off George, who is talking.)* Hold on George.

MOTHER: He would never hurt his father.

KIRSCHNER: Right.

MOTHER: And he could have.

KIRSCHNER: I know he could have.

MOTHER: He could have. He could have killed him.

FATHER: And I've been crippled since Monday or Tuesday. *(Everyone laughs.)*

SON: No, it ain't that. It's just that he followed me down the street, kept following me down the street. "Come on back, you bastard. Come on back. Are you scared? No? You want to get killed again?"

FATHER: I said, "I want to talk to you."

Just as the therapist pursued the son and brought him back after the first interview, so does the father pursue the son in this situation.

SON: Talk to you, yes, and to take another shot. *(Demonstrating a blow.)* Try another right? That made my head go like this. *(Laughs.)* Twice. You're getting over the hill, Pete. You taught me how to throw them lefts, Pete. You dropped—you dropped your right so easy that it come right across the chin. Does it hurt here?

KIRSCHNER: But how about, how about the fact that your father is making a real effort to keep you in line, and make sure that you're doing the best thing for yourself.

SON: I didn't really—I appreciate it, but I didn't do nothing the other night. I was just standing there. I walked in and all of a sudden lamps were thrown and everything.

FATHER: You know what it is. You know how happy we were—last time we spoke about him, we were so happy, he was doing good. And we were sweating out that there, uh—"atressin," whatever they call it. And then just like that he just gives up everything. So there was a little, uh—medical mistake.

KIRSCHNER: Mm-hmm.

It is important that a therapist reach agreement with his fellow professionals so that nothing medical is done without his permission. If custody or drugs are used without his permission, the therapist will fail. In this case, this medical arrangement was not made at the beginning of therapy. During the second week, the young man was detoxified and placed on a drug that would cause him to reject heroin. This experiment was done without considering the therapy, and it went badly. The young man shot up on heroin again, perhaps in relation to this drug treatment, perhaps in relation to his family.

The therapist should not condemn his fellow professionals but should find something positive in their actions, as the therapist does here when he returns to the subject.

FATHER: So it seemed like that little medical mistake gave him an excuse.

KIRSCHNER: Mm-hmm.

FATHER: Now I'm almost positive he must have shot after he got out of the hospital. Did you?

SON: Once.

FATHER: Once. There you go. He needed that excuse.

(Later in the interview.)

KIRSCHNER: Didn't I tell you it was gonna be a tough week?

MOTHER: Yeah, you said that, but I figured, you know, a week . . .

FATHER: When we come here, he had been discharged from the hospital, and that's what disappointed me. He put all that in there, all that effort, and then he just . . .

MOTHER: The third time *(referring to the detox)*. He looks great, doesn't he?

KIRSCHNER: A little tired, but good. Real good, yeah.

MOTHER: He looks good, and he says to me that—

KIRSCHNER: *(Interrupting and turning to father.)* Wait a minute. Hold on. You said that was a waste?

SON: That was not a waste.

MOTHER: It is a waste because he doesn't want to do nothing.

FATHER: Being in that hospital.

SON: I don't want to be on Notrexon.

KIRSCHNER: He detoxified, so it's not a waste.

MOTHER: Well, I mean, we thought, you know . . .

SON: I was on forty milligrams. To come down in six days, you know what it did? You know what it is—forty milligrams? If you and him *(meaning father)* split it, you'd die.

MOTHER: Well, that's what I'm saying . . .

KIRSCHNER: So first of all, it wasn't a waste, 'cause he detoxed. That's the first thing, so his system was clean, and that's important.

FATHER: And now his system is dirty again.

SON: No, it ain't. It's been since last week, last Friday.

The therapist attempts to shift the focus to the parents' marriage, wishing to bring about the second stage of the therapy.

KIRSCHNER: Now what—now let's get back to work. So, in other words, he was wedged between the two of you, and aggravating the two of you, in addition to anything else that was going on. O.K.?

MOTHER: It makes everything else worse.

KIRSCHNER: O.K., it makes everything else worse.

MOTHER: Right, it makes everything else bigger.

KIRSCHNER: O.K. Now the question is—the question is, how much longer are you going to let George do that to the two of you? Now you're moving into a new house, and I see that as a fresh beginning.

It is always good to refer to a "fresh start" in therapy as a turning point. Later in the interview the therapist tries another approach to the parents' marital problems.

KIRSCHNER: *(To mother.)* Now if your husband is taking over the job of helping his son straighten out, you know, in conjunction with me, is that gonna satisfy you? What more needs to be done in terms of you? I'm concerned because you've got a lot on your mind now. You're moving, and you're doing a lot of things, you got your job, you got a lot of responsibility there—I'm still concerned about your being overworried.

FATHER: She can't put him out, she can't stand the thought of him being on the street, and being like a derelict, or starting to steal, or—so that's her problem. She has to be strong. If he isn't gonna help himself—I don't intend to have an invalid in my house. I mean, if he didn't have arms or legs, I mean that's different.

MOTHER: And you know what I thought? I'd leave him *(the father)* and take him *(the son)*.

KIRSCHNER: Mm-hmm.

FATHER: And you know what I thought? I was gonna do that. I was gonna let—I was gonna leave her and have her take him.

The therapist has a particularly difficult problem here. Mother has stated the basic issue clearly: she is tempted to ignore the generation line and go live with her son. The father merely agrees. Instead of striving to draw a generational boundary between themselves and their son, the parents accept an absolutely confused hierarchy in a classical Oepidal triangle. The therapist's problem is that if he discusses this situation either as a practical matter or as a philosophical one, he is accepting the premise that this resolution is a tenable one. The therapist chooses an alternative that dismisses the mother's proposal.

KIRSCHNER: You know what I think? That's the shittiest idea I have ever heard.

MOTHER: I know it is. *(All laugh.)*

FATHER: That—that's the way I feel.

KIRSCHNER: What can your husband do for you that will ease the worry about your son?

MOTHER: He can't do it. He *(the son)* has to do it. He—it's what he—

KIRSCHNER: No, no, we're gonna work—I'm working with Georgie separately, and we're gonna meet together. But what can your husband do for you to make you less worried? Besides he's gonna help Georgie and talk to him and stuff, and check him out, and that kind of stuff. What can he do for you? What can your husband do for you?

MOTHER: He can't do nothing for me, because I feel that I'm the only one that can do it.

FATHER: *(To mother.)* I don't know, I'm stuck there. I don't get what you mean.

MOTHER: I feel that I can do a better job than you.

KIRSCHNER: Mm-hmm.

FATHER: Job with Georgie?

MOTHER: I feel like I can.

SON: Give in too easy.

KIRSCHNER: There we have it, you're saying that you're the one who can do the job, so you don't really want to give over charge to your husband. You're afraid that he's gonna blow it and kick Georgie out of the house, and then you're gonna get upset and leave with Georgie.

MOTHER: Well, it's—it's what I think I would do.

KIRSCHNER: Right, yeah, right.

MOTHER: But I don't know how I could ever manage it.

KIRSCHNER: Right, but I'm saying that's how your mind is running, right? That's the way your imagination goes.

MOTHER: Mm-hmm.

KIRSCHNER: And I'm telling you, and George—George senior has already said it, that because he's a man, he understands his son's problems, and what he needs to do in his life, better than you can, even though you're her—you're his mother.

Later in the interview, the therapist summarizes what he thinks the husband should be saying but has not said.

KIRSCHNER: Then what you're saying, what you're saying then is you would like to get your son straightened out so you can get closer to your wife, is that what you're saying?

The therapist assumes that he and the parents want the same results. He defines the parental job as interfering with conjugal pleasures. Mentioning this interference does not make the parents willing to shift from the parental issue to the conjugal issue. As the therapist states the goal of the parents becoming closer as husband and wife, there are significant pauses and other indications that they prefer to deal with each other through the problem son.

FATHER: If he was straightened out, I'd raise him again from the time he was a child, in this new house.

KIRSCHNER: If he was straightened out, then you would get closer to your wife, is that what you're saying?

FATHER: *(After a pause.)* Well, naturally. When there's—when there's contentment, peace and contentment in the house, uh—then definitely everything would be straightened out.

KIRSCHNER: *(To mother.)* And that's what you want?

MOTHER: *(After a pause.)* Yeah, I'd want that with him. But it ain't gonna be if he's *(the son)* not there—if—if he's not all right. 'Cause I just don't feel right, nothing else matters to me.

KIRSCHNER: I know. I know. O.K., so that's—that's where we want to go. We want to get him straightened out, and the two of you closer.

FATHER: *(After a pause.)* Definitely.

KIRSCHNER: And they are—and as you pointed out, they're wound up with each other. You know, the two of them—like they depend on each other.

It is better for the therapist to receive the parents' hesitations as indications to him that he has work to do to bring them together. These messages do not merely report how the parents feel, they are guides to the therapist and should be received that way. The therapist pursues this issue by projecting them into the future.

KIRSCHNER: O.K., let's say he gets the job, O.K., and he starts working for about a month. Things are going well. Then what do you want? I want you to tell George. What do you want George to do then?

FATHER: Save his money.

KIRSCHNER: Tell him, tell him.

FATHER: Save your money. Get what you want, the things you say that you want, which would be great—wonderful. You give your mother a little money for the food. And that's it.

KIRSCHNER: You want him to stay at home?

FATHER: *(Continuing.)* You got your room.

KIRSCHNER: You want him to stay at home?

FATHER: Yeah, as long as he's—

SON: I'd like to, Sam, to tell you the truth.

FATHER: He can be with us the rest of his life. I mean, we want to see him married, have children, and all.

SON: I mean they don't have nobody, you see.

KIRSCHNER: *(Noting wife shaking her head.)* Your wife—your wife disagrees.

FATHER: Oh, she just . . .

MOTHER: I don't want him married.

FATHER: She doesn't want him married. She wants him the rest of her life.

SON: She don't have nobody.

FATHER: *(To therapist.)* You—you misunderstood. She wants him the rest of his life. I do too, as long as he's straight.

SON: Straight?

KIRSCHNER: You want him to live with you for the rest of your life?

The therapist's values, which represent the wider culture, are contrary to those of the parents. To disengage the addict, the therapist asserts his values in a way that can lead to constructive change.

SON: Sure.

MOTHER: Why not?

SON: As long as I'm straight, Sam, I told you that.

KIRSCHNER: How about getting married and having a family, so you have grandchildren?

SON: They don't even care.

MOTHER: If it happens, I guess— I mean, what am I gonna do? But I prefer that he stay.

FATHER: Suppose if I become senile, I start becoming senile, I'll be coming to that age.

MOTHER: Especially to have children—I don't want any of my children to have children.

KIRSCHNER: Why not?

MOTHER: I just don't.

KIRSCHNER: Let me understand, you want to have him and have to take care of him the rest of your life?

FATHER: I'm not gonna take care of him.

SON: Naturally, naturally I want to . . .

KIRSCHNER: You'll have to feed him, and do all that stuff.

MOTHER: I got to feed myself and my husband, so what's one more?

FATHER: When he's ready to go.

SON: The only way.

MOTHER: Yeah, it's up to him. I don't—I'm not insisting.

KIRSCHNER: Wait, what, what you're saying though, is you would prefer to have him live with you for the rest of your life.

FATHER: No, she prefers him not to get married.

KIRSCHNER: Hold on, let's find out.

MOTHER: No, if he decides that he's—wants to go on his own, and you know everything's fine, that's good. I mean he could have a place of his own. He's got things he would want to do, and uh—that he wouldn't be able to do at my house.

KIRSCHNER: Would that be all right with you, if he moved out?

MOTHER: Yeah, if he wanted to, oh yeah.

KIRSCHNER: *(To father.)* How about you?

FATHER: Certainly.

SON: Is that a goal?

FATHER: That's a real, that's—that's his goal. That's our goal, that he straightens out, that's our goal.

The therapist, by persistence, is persuading the parents that they will have to give up their son and deal with each other even though, as the son says, they feel that they don't have anyone else. The persistence through the hour ultimately pays off, as will be shown. At this point the therapist physically separates the son from the parents.

KIRSCHNER: Sit next to me. *(He pulls over the chair and they sit and watch the parents talk.)*

SON: This is ridiculous.

KIRSCHNER: Hold on, we're gonna watch this now. Hold on. Hold on.

SON: I see it all the time, Sam.

KIRSCHNER: Hold on.

SON: I don't have to stare and watch.

KIRSCHNER: O.K. I want you out of it. Could the two of you as parents please discuss what you have in mind for your son and come to an agreement on it. About whether or not—specifically, what your idea as a goal for the future for Georgie is. I want you to tell—tell her, don't tell me.

FATHER: The only disagreement we have is she don't want him to get married. But she still feels, if he—if he was straight, then he'd go out and find a girl.

MOTHER: How can you say you don't want someone to get married when they don't even have a girl, there is no girl present, there was never any, anything of this, or close to this, how could I really know how I feel?

SON: How do you know I wasn't close to this?

KIRSCHNER: Hold on.

MOTHER: I know who it was close with, the one who started all the shit!

KIRSCHNER: You—you're talking to your son again, instead of to your husband.

(Later in the interview.)

KIRSCHNER: You want him in a good environment in his own apartment.

FATHER: Right.

KIRSCHNER: Once he's ready. Is that what you want?

MOTHER: That's all right with me.

KIRSCHNER: That's O.K.

MOTHER: Mm-hmm.

KIRSCHNER: And you're going to work towards that.

MOTHER: Towards what?

KIRSCHNER: Towards making sure that he's prepared, that he doesn't leave prematurely, that when he leaves—your husband has helped him prepare, you know, the finances, and you know, showing him, going over how much he needs. And then giving him your blessing.

Although some therapists think of the problem as one of the parents holding on to the child, it is best to keep aware that the child also holds on to the parents. When the parents sound as if they are willing to let the son leave, he responds with a certain reluctance.

SON: As much as they don't need me, they think they don't need me, they're gonna need me.

MOTHER: Why?

FATHER: Why?

SON: You'll need me.

MOTHER: For what?

FATHER: For what?

SON: You don't know yet.

MOTHER: Well, you must have some idea, George. I mean you're getting me scared, like maybe you know I got some kind of, uh, cancer or something, that I'm gonna die.

FATHER: You mean, I may drop dead, and your mother may need you.

MOTHER: Hey, you know how nice—I'd like to be *(laughs)* in my own, in my own apartment.

KIRSCHNER: Can you tell your son you don't need him?

MOTHER: I don't.

KIRSCHNER: O.K., you tell him that. Tell him that.

MOTHER: I don't think anybody needs anybody, if you have yourself.

KIRSCHNER: Tell George that you don't need him.

MOTHER: I told him that. I told him that coming up in the car.

KIRSCHNER: Tell him.

MOTHER: Right. I don't need you, George.

KIRSCHNER: *(Overlapping.)* Tell him in the straightest possible way that you do not need him, that when he is straight and together, you don't want him around because you don't need him.

FATHER: We love him but we don't need him. He needs himself.

SON: Now.

FATHER: Now? Later.

MOTHER: You need yourself all the time.

FATHER: We need each other.

KIRSCHNER: You want him to live with you and take care of you, is that what you want?

MOTHER: Not the rest of his life, no.

KIRSCHNER: You don't want that.

MOTHER: Not when we're two old people, how's he gonna benefit from two old people?

This third interview was a turning point in the therapy. Early in the interview, the mother said this about sons who lived with their mothers:

MOTHER: There's so many families where sons are still with them, and they're happy. These boys come and go as they please. Sometimes they don't come home for weekends. . . . I know a fellow who works with my other son, his aunt works in my place. This boy is about twenty-eight or thirty years old, and he lives with his mother and father. I guess 'cause they're old. He has older sisters who are married. There's no problem there.

Toward the end of the interview, after the therapist's persistent efforts, the mother said:

MOTHER: *(To son.)* Maybe you ought to talk to Edgar and see how miserable he is, being with his mother. That he wishes he could put his mother away. That's really how Edgar honestly feels. Not that he don't love her, it's just that he has no mind of his own. None at all. He would love to be married. And Edgar could have been married. And so could Robert. Robert don't even want to stay in that house where his mother was.

FATHER: Edgar had a miserable life in his house.

MOTHER: He's so unhappy, Edgar, it's pathetic. All that laughing and joking, it's all a front. Just talk to Edgar, and see how he feels.

The interviews continue to focus on a job, school, and disengagement from the parents. The parents are required to talk more to each other—first about the son and then about other aspects of their lives. Three weeks later, in the seventh interview, the progress continues.

KIRSCHNER: Your son had tremendous cravings for heroin. If he's not taking heroin, it means that big changes are taking place. That's what it means. And it means that what you're doing at home, and what we're doing here, is helping him to get on his feet.

FATHER: That's what I say too.

MOTHER: *(To son.)* Well, I tell you, I don't want you to be with this boy.

SON: I go with who I want to go with.

MOTHER: But then this upsets me, 'cause I don't like this boy. And you know what . . .

KIRSCHNER: But *you* don't have to go out with him.

MOTHER: No, but I—he's gonna entice him again, I know it. He has ways, you can't imagine how . . .

FATHER: When he entices him again, that's *his* problem.

MOTHER: He really is an evil person.

KIRSCHNER: Listen to what your husband is saying. Tell your wife again.

FATHER: That's his problem. That's all. When he don't come home one night, that's his problem.

SON: Right.

KIRSCHNER: What do you mean?

FATHER: What I mean, I don't like him staying out overnight, if he's gonna live with us, and he's under treatment, I don't want him staying out overnight.

KIRSCHNER: All right. So let's make—

FATHER: That's all.

KIRSCHNER: So make a rule about it.

MOTHER: I told him that.

SON: You're not making no rules for no twenty-six *(his age)*.

MOTHER: Well we got rules over here, me and your father have to come here, we have things we have to do to help you.

KIRSCHNER: *(To the son, who is looking in a mirror and combing his hair.)* Hey, George, could you stop grooming yourself for just a moment, for the heavy date that you got?

SON: I ain't got no date. I'm here to talk about myself.

KIRSCHNER: Your folks—your folks are saying that they don't want you to stay out all night.

SON: Yeah, so? That's one reason why I'll be getting my place sooner than I think. You know, they don't need me. You don't need me to do this work that I'm doing. You don't—you don't need me. You're just telling me you don't need me.

KIRSCHNER: How did you hear it that way?

SON: That's the way I heard it.

KIRSCHNER: How do you figure?

SON: 'Cause if I—if I do the work for them, I'm gonna go out.

KIRSCHNER: They're not saying that you can't go out, they're saying that they get, uh—

SON: Overnight.

KIRSCHNER: Yeah, that's what they're uptight about.

As the parents and the son face the issue of separation, it becomes more real to them. There is no relapse and the improvement continues. Three weeks later the young man is working and making plans to go to school and to move to his own apartment. One can predict that the parents will develop conflicts with each other as this time of separation from the son approaches. They talk of separating from each other or of substituting someone else for the son.

SON: I've had enough of that frigging area, it makes me sick. I'm moving up to the East, get me a nice little place somewhere up there. And I'll just go to work from there.

FATHER: O.K.

SON: Then you'll know where I'm at, there'll be a phone booth in the apartment building, or whatever I'm in, and you call me if you need any help or something.

KIRSCHNER: Right. So the first step then is for you to get a job.

FATHER: The second step is, she has to—she has to change her mind about not coming here anymore.

KIRSCHNER: O.K., George . . .

MOTHER: I'm not coming the next couple of weeks. You go.

KIRSCHNER: *(To son.)* George, could you excuse us for a few minutes? I'd appreciate it. Here, you can take your college bulletin. I'll meet with you alone, we can discuss some things, maybe I got pointers 'cause I worked in college.

SON: All right. *(He leaves.)*

KIRSCHNER: *(To mother.)* You don't have to—come all the time. Give you a breather. If you think that's the best thing. Because I think you've had a very—despite the fact that you and George agitate each other—I think you've had a big influence on his getting better. Believe it or not.

MOTHER: Well I can't take anymore, I got news for you.

KIRSCHNER: But what is it that you can't take anymore?

MOTHER: Anything. I'm tired. All I want to do is be left alone.

KIRSCHNER: How come you never went dancing to New Jersey to that place with your husband?

MOTHER: Where?

KIRSCHNER: What was that place you were telling us about?

FATHER: I don't know.

KIRSCHNER: You just want to be left alone, huh?

MOTHER: Hmmm.

KIRSCHNER: You and your husband are at your wits' end.

MOTHER: You just finding that out?

KIRSCHNER: No, I'm not finding it out. *(Pause.)* I told George something on the phone when I spoke to him the other day. That one of the problems that your son has is that he's constantly afraid that the two of you are going to break up.

MOTHER: Well, maybe that will bring him right out of it. That's what I've been thinking about.

KIRSCHNER: No. This is his greatest fear.

MOTHER: Why?

KIRSCHNER: 'Cause he feels he's responsible for it. And that is his greatest fear, that the guilt . . .

MOTHER: Well, he apparently would be responsible.

KIRSCHNER: I don't think so. Why would he be responsible?

MOTHER: You don't? Well I don't know, any time that this boy has been in the hospital, or he ain't been home, we've gotten along fine.

KIRSCHNER: You get along better when he's not there?

MOTHER: Yep.

KIRSCHNER: Is that true? George, is that true?

FATHER: *(After a pause.)* I'm a little confused.

MOTHER: Only when he's in the hospital, not when he's out anywhere else. 'Cause I'm still nervous worrying about where he is.

KIRSCHNER: Oh, oh, yeah, when he's in the hospital, yeah, well what about the rest of the time?

This is a typical reaction in the families of disturbed young people. When the problem person is in the hospital, the family triangle and the parental marriage are stable. Treatment by custody and restraint stabilizes the family by perpetuating the problem.

MOTHER: Well, that's different.

KIRSCHNER: So anyway, so that's why, his greatest fear is that, you know, when he's—he's not in the house, you know, and making sure that the two of you are living together. In some crazy way, you know, that's his greatest fear, that he's gonna be responsible for it—for you two breaking up. This is a tremendous fear that he lives with, you can't imagine how powerful this is.

FATHER: I don't know what she's gonna accomplish by even thinking of us breaking up.

KIRSCHNER: Well, find out. *(Suggesting father ask her.)*

MOTHER: It don't have nothing to do with you, it's me. I'm thinking about me. You have a fine time, you don't worry about nothing. You come and go as you please, do what you want. I just want an out. I'm going to my brother, I don't know where you think I'm going. I hope you don't think I'm running off with somebody.

FATHER: Oh, I wish you would. You need somebody.

MOTHER: Yeah, you wish I would.

FATHER: I swear to God in heaven.

MOTHER: There ain't anybody.

FATHER: I wish you would find somebody.

MOTHER: They're all the same.

FATHER: 'Cause you deserve a better life than you've had, believe me. You definitely do. My word of honor, you really deserve somebody.

MOTHER: *(To therapist.)* We feel sorry for one another.

FATHER: I don't feel sorry for you, I think it's stupid.

KIRSCHNER: *(After a pause.)* Tell her why it's stupid. I don't think she's—she made it clear. Why is it stupid for her to leave?

FATHER: I think it would be the greatest thing in the world if she would find somebody—have a love affair also.

KIRSCHNER: You want her to have a love affair?

MOTHER: Yeah, I could have a love affair with all this piled inside of me, right?

FATHER: Well, that's what you want.

MOTHER: I need some other jerk.

FATHER: Well, it would take some of it out of your body and your mind.

MOTHER: Would it? That's you, not me.

KIRSCHNER: I don't believe it. You're telling your wife to go have a love affair, and she's saying no. *(Laughs.)* This is a strange discussion.

MOTHER: Well, that's the easiest thing to do.

KIRSCHNER: What's the easiest thing?

MOTHER: To go out and find somebody. It's easy for a girl.

KIRSCHNER: But you haven't done it though.

MOTHER: Well, I don't care to do it. And he knows—if I find anybody, he'll be the first one to know about it. Because I would leave, I wouldn't make any fool out of him or out of myself.

KIRSCHNER: But you haven't done it.

MOTHER: No, I'm not interested.

One should never underestimate how involved a peripheral father actually is and how intense his reaction can be to the son's leaving. It is important that a father-son discussion take place, to lay old issues to rest and to allow the son to begin a new relationship with his father as he disengages. The therapist sees the father and son alone.

FATHER: I am so frigging fed up!

KIRSCHNER: Right.

FATHER: He's giving me hell. Who is he to give me hell?

KIRSCHNER: You're right.

SON: I'm giving nobody hell.

KIRSCHNER: Right, he's your son.

FATHER: You think you don't give me hell?

SON: Who is the one that told me, "I'm a jackass, and you'll be a jackass the rest of your life"?

FATHER: That's the only saying you've been saying all night!

SON: And that's all I dream about.

FATHER: That's all you—my goodness, that's all you've been dreaming about?

SON: Yes.

FATHER: What a terrible statement that is. "I'm a jackass, and he'll be a jackass the rest of his life too." In other words, I've been a stupid ass—I'll admit it.

KIRSCHNER: All right, so how do you think that makes your son feel?

FATHER: He says it.

KIRSCHNER: It makes him feel bad, right?

FATHER: Like a jackass, he's a jackass like me.

KIRSCHNER: No, it makes him feel bad that his father talks about himself that way. More than what you're saying about him, it makes him feel bad about you.

FATHER: You're twenty-five, I'm fifty, twenty-five years older than you.

SON: Right.

FATHER: What the hell have I got, but a few more laughs? You've got everything ahead of you.

SON: A few more laughs? You've got more than a few more laughs.

KIRSCHNER: He says you've got more than a few laughs.

FATHER: Bullshit.

The therapist skillfully lightens the tragic air of the interview.

KIRSCHNER: Ah, come on. You got a few good golf games.

FATHER: Yeah, I got a few good golf games.

KIRSCHNER: What do you shoot in golf, anyway?

FATHER: A woman beat me this Sunday. Twenty-one handicap, and I'm an eighteen, and she beat the shit out of me.

KIRSCHNER: You were off that day. Now look, I agree with you, you know, it's not good for anybody for him being there *(at home)*. I agree with that. And I think you're doing the right thing. But we have to plan it in such a way, you know, that he gets out financially okay.

SON: Tomorrow I can be out of there—packed up.

KIRSCHNER: No, I don't want it done that way, though. You see, when you do it that way—

SON: When you get out—when you feel you're going to get out, get out as fast as possible so there ain't no more complications.

KIRSCHNER: No, there's not—there's no more complications if you leave in two weeks. What's the complication?

SON: I'm not leaving in two weeks. He needs me two weeks more like he needs, uh—the black plague.

KIRSCHNER: *(To the father.)* George, do you think you could stand your son another two weeks? If we know that he's leaving, and he's got a room, and you see that he's got his money situation straightened out? Do you think you can live with him for two weeks? You know what I'm saying. I mean I want it to be done right.

FATHER: I definitely know what you're saying.

Although the family was interviewed once or twice more, the therapy was essentially over, having lasted only a few months of weekly interviews. The son moved out at the end of therapy. After a short time the parents separated. The son moved back home again, and the parents reunited.

In a two-year follow-up, the parents were still together. The young man was living at home. He had a responsible job at a managerial level and was doing well. He no longer took heroin and had not done so during the two-year period.

In a follow-up four years later, the son was still off heroin and was working; after living locally in his own apartment, he had moved to another state. The parents were still together.

Chapter 10

A Chronic Case

When a young person has difficulty in leaving home, the family may struggle with the issue for many years. The repeating cycle of home-to-institution-to-home becomes chronic. Both family members and social control agents become weary and exasperated with the problem, but it continues. If the problem person is a troublemaker, some institutions refuse to readmit him, forcing the family to shop around until it finds a place that will accept him. The financially well-off family sometimes proceeds from more expensive to less expensive private hospitals and finally to state hospitals, where the custody is at public expense. When a mental hospital cycle is involved, the psychiatrists typically medicate the problem person, even when they know that the medicine won't be helpful and may actually be harmful, because they don't know what else to do.

A new therapist who attempts to intervene in such a chronic cycle and persuade everyone to make a fresh start often is not met with enthusiasm. Family and colleagues have tried to start over and failed too often. Sometimes the professionals are so exasperated with a repeating client that they will not cooperate with any new therapeutic plan.

A therapist should recognize that he is dealing not with a chronic person but with a chronic situation, involving both professionals and family members. The therapist must avoid being caught up in the cycle and naïvely perpetuating the situation. I recall a family in New York with two hospitalized problem daughters, that had been in various kinds of therapy for more than twenty years. A fresh team of young therapists was about to proceed in ways that had failed a number of times before. The father rather plaintively said that he had been in therapy for twenty-four years, that he was

221

now over sixty-five years old, and that he had only a few more years of therapy to go.

In a chronic situation a family often will begin therapy but not quite do anything asked of it. Directives somehow just do not get carried out. Sometimes the family begins with an agreement to contain the problem within the family, but when there is trouble they rehospitalize the problem person, and everything must begin again. Sometimes there seem to be gains, yet they disintegrate, and no issue is ever really resolved. Sometimes the therapist is not sure whether progress is being made because crises keep occurring and thus there is excitement; yet the problem person does not achieve self-support or intimate relations outside the family.

Part of the task in the chronic situation is to change the professional and family routines. All of the participants are in a chronic routine, which is why the problem person is called "chronic." It is important to find a basic issue to change the situation so that the routine can no longer be repeated. For example, I recall a young woman who was regularly hospitalized by her parents whenever she became upset and acted strangely. Because she complained to her parents that the hospital staff mistreated her, when she returned home they felt guilty about having hospitalized her. The parents would placate her until they became exasperated and then rehospitalize her. The situation was changed when I persuaded the parents not to take her to the hospital the next time she got upset. It is always helpful to make the problem person responsible for the consequences of his or her actions. In a family interview the parents told her that if she thought she should be in the hospital she could get on the bus and go there. The daughter angrily declined and went to her grandmother's house instead, which started a new family sequence.

Whether the young person who has been a chronic problem is living at home or only intermittently staying with the parents, it is important to have the parents reach agreement on what to do whatever may happen. If the offspring gets a job and is fired, will the parents provide financial support until the next job? If no attempt is made to look for a job, will they go on providing funds to live on or set a date when their support will end? If the young person threatens to enter the hospital again, the parents need to agree on just what they will do. They might agree to make visits at the hospital or not to do so, to receive the young person home to live afterwards or not to do so. Whatever their plan, they must clearly tell the young person what it is so that he or she will know exactly what is to happen in each eventuality. What the parents decide to do or not to do is less important than the fact that they agree with each other and hold firm in whatever they plan, no matter how provoking or piteous the attempts of the young person to divide them or get them to change their minds.

One way to approach a chronic situation is to find a clear issue on which the therapy can stand or fall. If therapy fails on that issue, it may be abandoned rather than continued in the vague hope that, somehow, something may be accomplished. If the problem is apathy, a clear plan can be made, with a date set for action to be taken. All the therapy is focused on that date. If the action is a physical move out of the home, then a date is set for the move, all preparations are made, and the family is organized around that issue.

The case to be described here focused on a specific issue in a dramatic way. One of the chronic problems in the case was violence, therefore the therapy focused on the issues of weapons and violent acts. The family had been involved in community social control long enough to be considered chronic. There was a record of their being rejected for family therapy because the son was seen as too primitive and the family was considered inappropriate. The father was a working-class man in his fifties, and the mother was about the same age. There were two older brothers out of the home, and a nineteen-year-old daughter who lived at home and worked. A nine-year-old brother came to all the therapeutic sessions because he went wherever the parents went. The problem young man in the family was twenty-six years old, a handsome fellow with a mustache and a pleasant smile. He had been a problem in the family and community for eight years, beginning with his first institutionalization at the age of eighteen . He had been in and out of mental hospitals a number of times. His diagnoses were schizophrenia, paranoid type, and chronic paranoid schizophrenia, which indicate that he was not well-liked in the hospitals. They also called him a passive-aggressive personality and labeled him as borderline mentally retarded. This son had been totally deaf since birth and could not speak. He lacked the verbal ability to function in the hearing world, and his sign language was not good enough for him to participate successfully in the deaf community. He was also epileptic. He had been dismissed from both school and vocational institutions for misbehavior. In recent years he had received a welfare check. He would not work. He often took illegal drugs which put him in the hands of the police.

The therapist in the case was Sam Scott, who knew sign language. In the sessions he had to sign to the young man while talking with the family, and translate what the young man said. The parents did not know sign language, and the young man could not read lips adequately for communication. Family conversation was therefore crude, limited to pointing and to simple ideas. The therapy was done in a training context, with live supervision.

When the family was referred, a crisis session was expected. The young man was said to have just escaped from the state mental hospital. Actually he had merely left the hospital and taken a bus home. When the therapist called the mother, she said casually that he had come in and changed his clothes and gone out somewhere. An immediate appointment was made for a first interview with the whole family, but the older sons living outside the home and the nineteen-year old daughter did not come. The parents brought the problem son and the nine-year-old. The therapist first inquired about how the parents and son communicated with each other.

SCOTT: (To father.) Can he understand you if you talk?
FATHER: I don't know.
SCOTT: O.K. All right.
FATHER: Unless he pays attention to my lips.
SCOTT: (To Steve, the problem son.) Can you understand what he is saying? Can you understand him? (Son indicates that he reads lips.) Well, we'll see, O.K.? (He is doubtful that the young man can read lips well enough to understand.)

(The therapist turns to the issue of hospitalization.)

SCOTT: I know the object of the hospital is to get the person out.
FATHER: Yes, but why let him go before time?
SCOTT: I don't know what "before time" is.
FATHER: Well, now he was in there just last week.
SCOTT: (Translating into sign language for son while speaking aloud.) He was in the hospital last week.
FATHER: Now because he decided that he couldn't take the discipline there, or regimentation . . .
SCOTT: (Translating.) Didn't obey.
FATHER: He decided to come home and he left. Now how can you turn someone loose in that condition? He doesn't even know what he is doing.

(Later in the first interview.)

FATHER: When he is in the hospital, he doesn't have the freedom that he has at home.
SCOTT: (Translates.) Doesn't have the freedom that he has at home.
SCOTT: Now how do you feel about it?
MOTHER: About Steve being home?
SCOTT: About Steve being home, yes.
MOTHER: I don't mind him being home if he would just . . .
SCOTT: (Translates.) She doesn't mind you being home.
MOTHER: If he would just learn to control himself.
SCOTT: If you learn to control yourself. (Interpreting Steve's sign lan-

guage.) "After a while I want to get an apartment for myself." *(To mother.)* What other feelings do you have, Momma?[1]

MOTHER: Well, as long as he behaves himself, I don't mind, he is just one of the family.

SCOTT: *(To Steve.)* She says that you are part of the family and as long as you obey that there will not be any problem. *(Translating.)* "No," he says, "there will not be any problem."

MOTHER: I heard that before.

SCOTT: She says that she heard that many times before. *(Translating Steve's sign language.)* "After a while, first a check." I don't know about a check.

MOTHER: His check, always his check.

SCOTT: I don't know about a check.

MOTHER: Do you know why Steve came home? Not for me or not for him *(father)*.

SCOTT: She says, Do you know why he came home from the hospital? *(Steve signs and the therapist translates.)* "You don't like the hospital."

MOTHER: For his check.

SCOTT: For your check. There is no check.

MOTHER: Right.

SCOTT: *(To Steve.)* No check. No check. No more. *(To mother.)* But you feel that if he went to work and obeyed the rules in the house it would be O.K. for him to live in the house until he got a room or an apartment.

MOTHER: Yes.

SCOTT: *(To father.)* How do you feel about that?

MOTHER: It's not gonna work out.

SCOTT: *(Translating to Steve.)* She says it won't work. She don't believe you. She don't believe you.

FATHER: You know this is the first peace we had, when he was away, in seven years.

SCOTT: *(Translating.)* This is the first time in seven years that you did not make trouble for the family. First time now.

FATHER: *Every time* he is away. In seven years time I have yet to take a vacation.

SCOTT: *(Signing to Steve.)* Seven years, no vacation.

FATHER: You can't trust him home.

SCOTT: Doesn't trust you at home.

FATHER: He'll get hopped up, have your house robbed.

---

1. The therpist's inquiry about feelings was based on previous training and is not encouraged in this approach.

SCOTT: *(Translating.)* Pills. *(The young man responds with a sign indicating his head. The therapist translates.)* He says he gets headaches from pills.

FATHER: *(Expressing exasperation and doubt.)* Mm-hmm.

(The therapist arranged an interview alone with the parents to discuss their difficulties in dealing with their son.)

SCOTT: You got so many calls over your lifetime in terms of Steve. And it's like a cycle. You know, something goes wrong and he winds up in the hospital, and he either goes home or you try to get him a room and he is good. Then something goes wrong and he goes in the hospital. How many times has he been in the hospital?

MOTHER: The city hospital? About six times.

SCOTT: Six times.

MOTHER: And two times out at the state hospital.

SCOTT: Now the two times that you got the room before, one time he had a seizure did you tell me?

MOTHER: Mm-hmm.

SCOTT: And what happened the second time?

FATHER: Well then he got drugged up.

SCOTT: And where did he go from there?

MOTHER: Home.

SCOTT: He came home? And then you sent him to the hospital?

MOTHER: Right.

FATHER: He wasn't sent that time, he was taken there by the police.

SCOTT: Uh-huh.

FATHER: On Third Street, the next place he had.

MOTHER: Uh-huh.

SCOTT: He had three places, or two?

MOTHER: Two.

SCOTT: Two altogether.

FATHER: That one there he attempted an assault on the landlady. And he almost got killed there because her husband, brother, and a friend of theirs, they went up there and they must have worked him over.

SCOTT: Uh-huh.

MOTHER: I feel this way: Steven does want a place of his own for the simple reason that he wants to do what he wants to do.

SCOTT: Right. *(The therapist assumes that it is natural for a twenty-six-year-old to do what he wants, but mother means he will misbehave.)*

MOTHER: And we won't know about it. But he will get in trouble again. He cannot live by himself.

SCOTT: O.K. So that what we are saying is that this is a cycle and he is gonna get in trouble. And what we'd like to do is break the cycle somewhere. Now how can we break the cycle?

One of the ways to break a cycle is to block off one part of it. When the cycle includes a mental hospital, it is possible to change the sequence by asking that a prison be used instead. Not only are there more civil liberties for the person in prison, but the parents' situation changes too. The parents have more influence over hospital psychiatrists than they do over jail personnel and thus are more likely to lose control of their offspring if he goes to prison. Since the parents want to have influence over what happens to their child, they don't want him to go to prison. Once the parents accept prison as an alternative, mental illness disappears, and the problem is defined as a disciplinary one. In this case, the prison issue was raised in the first interview, and the parents accepted it. After that the questions of mental illness and hospitalization did not come up again in therapy.

SCOTT: *(Talking to the parents while translating to Steve.)* Suppose he does not act in a good way. What will you do if he doesn't act in the right way?

FATHER: Well then he will have to go.

SCOTT: *(Translating to Steve.)* He says you will have to leave. I would say prison if you hit someone. *(To mother.)* Would you sign a paper, if he hit you, to go to prison?

MOTHER: Yes, again, yes, yes.

SCOTT: *(To Steve in sign language.)* If you beat her, she will sign a paper, and you will go to prison. Do you want to go to prison?

STEVE: No. *(Indicated by shaking head.)*

SCOTT: Same thing with the pills. Same thing with the pills. The same thing. *(To father.)* Would you sign the paper if he breaks the rules?

FATHER: Definitely.

SCOTT: If you break the rules, you will go to prison. What? Sign, sign. *(Translating.)* You give up. You give up pills. All right, all right. Can you obey the rules in the family? Can you obey your father?

When leaving home goes badly, the cycle includes the son leaving the house when everyone is angry and upset. If the son could move out in an amiable way, the cycle would change. One way to change how he leaves home is to change the way he stays at home, by arranging rules for him to follow. In the first family interview, the therapist asked the family to make a list of rules for the son. At the second interview, the family came with a list. The nineteen-year-old daughter offered a suggestion.

SCOTT: *(Translating.)* Bernice says here, and Mother and Father agree, not to go in your sister's bedroom when she says "Stay out." *(Translating signs.)* "He says he knocks."

BERNICE: He never knocks, never knocks.

SCOTT: Tell him.

BERNICE: *(To Steve.)* You don't knock *(gesturing a knock and shaking her head)*, no, you don't.

When the therapist asks the parents to make rules, he does not necessarily expect the son to follow them or the parents to enforce them. What he is after at this stage is something concrete for family members to focus on. If the parents agree on the rules for the son, it will be for the first time in their lives, and he will be freed by that agreement. If the parents do not agree, the dissension can come out in the open and be dealt with. The pretense that everyone but the problem son is agreeable will no longer hold. Whether the parents agree about the son or not, he can move out of the house in a new way.

Making rules brings out the more positive side of the son's behavior. It is important that the therapist emphasize the son's competence, because the parents will not agree to the son's moving out unless they believe that he is able to take care of himself. Therefore the family agreement that he is incompetent must be changed. In this interview it becomes apparent that the son is responsible enough to borrow money from the parents and repay it as well as to pay room and board at home. It should also be emphasized that the therapist does not rush the idea of the young man moving out, even though that is becoming the focus of the therapy. In this discussion of rules, the therapist raises the question of what the young man wants and finds that the parents are not eager for him to have an apartment.

MOTHER: He wants an apartment for himself.

SCOTT: All right, that's fine, he should get out alone. He wants that. But he couldn't stay at the other place, he came back home.

FATHER: Look at it this way, suppose he wants an apartment to do what he pleases. What are you gonna do about it? Because I don't think he has the will to say "no."

SCOTT: Mm-hmm. Let's take one step at a time. Let's see what happens with the rules in the family. I have no objection to your finding an apartment for him, that's fine. But I think we should do it slowly.

FATHER: I don't like it.

SCOTT: Oh, what's the matter?

FATHER: I don't think he can take care of himself.

SCOTT: All right, for the time being, then he will stay home and learn to take the rules now, and we'll see what happens as we go along. What about borrowing money?

MOTHER: Well he usually would give it back to me when he got his check.

SCOTT: Well, O.K., then you don't mind that.

MOTHER: No, if I know he's giving it back.

SCOTT: He's always given it back before.

MOTHER: Mm-hmm.

SCOTT: So it's O.K. to borrow money. How about doing his laundry?

MOTHER: I do it.

SCOTT: Can he do it himself at home?

FATHER: No.

SCOTT: What do you mean, no? You want to prepare the guy to live outside, right? Isn't that what you want him to do?

MOTHER: He knows how to use a laundromat. He can use a laundromat.

SCOTT: Can he use your washing machine?

MOTHER: I don't know if he could use mine, he can use theirs. I guess he could use mine.

SCOTT: All right, all right, if you stay home, can you wash your own clothing? Can you do that? Can you iron? *(Translating.)* And you pay two weeks . . . *(To mother.)* He pays you half his welfare check for two weeks' room and board. Is that what he does?

MOTHER: Mm-hmm.

SCOTT: He does do that.

MOTHER: Fifteen dollars.

SCOTT: *(To father.)* Why do you laugh?

FATHER: I don't see none. *(He apparently has never heard this.)*

MOTHER: The fifteen dollars? He gives it to me. I do the work in the home. He gives it to me.

SCOTT: *(Surprised.)* Wait, wait, Mom says that she gets fifteen dollars every two weeks from you when you get the check, and Father says he never sees it. *(To father.)* How do you feel about that?

FATHER: Well listen, if he didn't . . .

SCOTT: No, but you said that you didn't know that.

FATHER: Well . . .

MOTHER: No, I always tell you that. You don't believe me?

FATHER: Well a lot of things happen in the house that you don't tell me.

MOTHER: I do things to keep peace.

FATHER: Peace or no peace, if he gave it to you *(shrugs)*, if he didn't . . .

MOTHER: Yes, he does and I tell you that.

FATHER: Naw.

SCOTT: Who's trying to keep peace in the family?

MOTHER: I do.

SCOTT: How about Pop?

MOTHER: Well different things used to go on and I didn't bother to tell him. Where Steve was concerned.

SCOTT: Like what?

MOTHER: Like when he would threaten me or her (referring to daughter).

SCOTT: Yeah, but why didn't you tell him?

MOTHER: Well he, he has a hot temper.

SCOTT: He has a hot temper and he gets angry.

MOTHER: Right.

SCOTT: If Steve does something wrong.

When a family is in a distressing cycle, the family members move very swiftly to maintain the stability of the family, to keep things as they are. Here the therapist has brought out the fact that the supposedly incompetent and irresponsible son is paying room and board. The mother has kept this from the father, and he begins to get angry at his wife for concealing this positive side of his son. Within seconds the mother, with the help of the therapist, has redefined the situation as one where she benevolently conceals bad things about the son to protect the son from the father's violence. There are other family secrets, as one might expect when a member is diagnosed as paranoid. For example, in a later interview the father keeps a secret from the son by concealing a bottle of pills. The son's deafness makes concealment possible even though the pills are mentioned in the son's presence.

FATHER: Just between you and I now, the police got to him on the boulevard, and they searched him, and the only thing they found on him was this.

SCOTT: How do you know the police stopped him?

FATHER: The boys told me. They were coming home from school, and they even said that he was hopped up. One of the boys was a neighbor, and he said that I know him, I'll take him home.

SCOTT: Mm-hmm.

FATHER: So the police found this capsule on him.

SCOTT: Well if the police searched him, then I can tell him what happened. Right? (Meaning that he could translate into signs since Steve is sitting there beside mother.)

FATHER: Well later, then you can decide whether or not, but I don't want him to know that I have this in my possession.

(Later in the interview.)

FATHER: They get high, not high, they get stoned with them. Just like a drunk.

SCOTT: Well, that puts you down, it makes you very sleepy.

FATHER: Oh, he was stoned, you know, when you see a drunk that's out?

SCOTT: Yeah, that's sleepy, O.K. I think it's all right to tell him that you have the pills, I think it's all right.

FATHER: No.

SCOTT: Why not?

FATHER: Because I want to keep after him until I get him out.

SCOTT: What do you mean you want to keep after him?

FATHER: Gonna keep searching him. He hides them. I know where he hides them.

Another secret became evident when mother, in the first interview, said that the son's welfare checks had not arrived. Then she revealed that they had arrived and she was hiding them because she could not legally give them to him. Later, when the legal situation changed and she could give him a check, she kept it hidden.

MOTHER: I have checks at home, I can't give them to him. Because he was in a state hospital. I'm not allowed to give them.

SCOTT: Oh, he is still getting checks?

MOTHER: Yes, but I can't give them to him, not as yet, not until they notify me.

SCOTT: Oh, I see. All right, she said that when you get your first check—out. You get an apartment.

(In a later interview.)

MOTHER: Now he didn't know one check came for him. He don't know about it. We're holding it back from him, until he gets his room. As soon as he gets his room, it will be cashed, and he will have it all. I think that's the best thing. Let him go to the mailbox every day and look for it, because it already came and he don't know it. I think that's best.

SCOTT: *(To Steve in signs.)* How much money do you have now? *(Steve signs.)* You're broke.

Every day the son watched for the mailman while his mother kept secret the fact that the check had already arrived. One of the reasons the mother keeps secrets is because she is protected in ways she would rather not be, as described in an interview between the therapist and the parents alone. She says she was "put through hell one summer."

FATHER: Steve was under drugs, plus the drinks, and he thought he was Tarzan. And he went after the bartender. Well, the bartender turned around and hauled off and squashed him. Fractured his jaw. He must have had that a couple of days before . . .

MOTHER: Mm-hmm.

SCOTT: (To mother.) You said that "they" . . .

MOTHER: Yeah, Steven . . .

SCOTT: Oh, Steven and your husband put you through hell that summer?

MOTHER: Well, my son Dick was home, he was single then. And Steven started that fight with you (to husband).

FATHER: No, it started downstairs, I was sleeping.

MOTHER: Well it started with me—oh, Dick walked in, and as Dick walked in, he saw Steven threaten me. So he hit Steven. Then Dick went upstairs, and between the two of them (father and Dick) Steven got beat up because he was fighting with them. They took him to the hospital.

SCOTT: Well, was Steven beating you up in the first place?

MOTHER: He started in the kitchen as soon as my son was coming in. Then after Steven's leg was in a cast, he had a wire in the, you know, in the mouth, and I had to take him to the hospital to get that checked and to the doctor to get his jaw checked.

SCOTT: But you said that they put you through hell.

MOTHER: Yeah, well that was hell for me.

SCOTT: Tell me.

MOTHER: Each time I took him to the doctor for his jaw, he thought he was gonna take it out. Because he couldn't eat, I had to put everything through the blender. And he would make the doctor angry and then he would come out, limping, with the crutches, he would throw the crutches around, wouldn't get in the car.

SCOTT: How did your husband make you go through hell?

MOTHER: Well after all, I went through hell that summer.

SCOTT: What you are saying is that you need a little help from your husband.

MOTHER: Well, what they should have done, I told them . . .

SCOTT: Go ahead, tell him now.

MOTHER: I did tell him.

SCOTT: Tell him again for me.

MOTHER: When he is like that, just try to quiet him down. He is rammy. on drugs. He gets very rammy.

SCOTT: Tell him.

MOTHER: I did tell him. Oh he knows, I always used to tell him, remember?

SCOTT: Tell him again.

MOTHER: I went through hell that summer.

When the son behaves himself, tension will develop between the parents; then the son will misbehave making the parents feel better about each other as they attack the son. This cycle appeared in the first weeks of therapy. The son behaved; marital tension developed; the son misbehaved. The parents then attacked the son in a way that brought them together. The parents reported that the son had been behaving all right. The therapist, reviewing the rules, found out that the son had broken a minor rule by smoking in his bedroom.

SCOTT: You didn't tell him *(the husband)* about smoking.

MOTHER: This week?

FATHER: No.

MOTHER: No.

SCOTT: Why?

MOTHER: Sometimes he gives me the silent treatment so you can't confide in him.

SCOTT: Well let's talk about it now. Huh? You two talk about it please. Because we have to talk about it sometime.

MOTHER: Mm-hmm.

SCOTT: He must know that if he smokes in the room that you are gonna do something. Now what are you gonna do?

FATHER: I'll put him out.

SCOTT: You'll put him out? Where?

FATHER: Outside.

SCOTT: For how long?

FATHER: That's it.

SCOTT: For good?

FATHER: Good.

SCOTT: That's kind of tough right now. That's kind of harsh.

FATHER: Because I don't want any more trouble in the house. I got it up to here. I'm fed up with it . . .

SCOTT: Do you both agree that that is what should be done?

FATHER: Well, what else can I do?

SCOTT: I don't know, ask your wife. How do you feel about that?

MOTHER: *(Angry.)* You mean if he breaks a rule, you want to just throw him out?

FATHER: If it's . . .

MOTHER: Get a place of his own? Is that what you mean?

FATHER: He is gonna have to go sometime.

SCOTT: So you two—you both have to agree.

FATHER: Well, so far since he's been home, he hasn't given us any trouble.

At this point marital difficulties were starting to appear. The next week the son was brought home after a drug escapade and the marital difficulties disappeared.

SCOTT: So the boys brought him home.

FATHER: Yeah, they found him on the street.

SCOTT: On the street? *(Translates son, who indicates innocence.)* "Myself, I had coffee." *(To son.)* I want to get more from Father about what happened and then we will talk with you, you can explain some of the things that happened. *(To father.)* They brought him home, the boys said they found him on the street. Was he fallen down or what?

FATHER: Oh yeah, he was out cold and they had to drag him home.

SCOTT: All right.

FATHER: And then I had to carry him on my shoulders upstairs. Now this has been going on for the past seven or eight years.

SCOTT: It's a tremendous, it's a big responsibility, and I know it, but what I am trying to do is . . .

FATHER: If he wants to kill himself, let him do it, you cry once and that's it.

SCOTT: Do you feel that way?

MOTHER: Sometimes I do, believe me, each time he got in trouble, and I had cops over to the house, and seeing him handcuffed this last time.

SCOTT: You must feel terrible.

MOTHER: You know how I feel?

SCOTT: How?

MOTHER: It got to the point where I even told my sister that I would rather go to the cemetary with a fresh bouquet of flowers knowing that he is there and no harm can come to him. Believe me.

SCOTT: Is that how you feel?

MOTHER: I really do feel that way.

SCOTT: Do you feel that way too?

FATHER: Positively.

MOTHER: I know no harm can come to him and he can't harm nobody. Because this is never gonna stop. You know, right?

SCOTT: You tell him.

(Therapist leaves room and goes behind one-way mirror with supervisor.)

FATHER: *(To son.)* If you die, everybody be peaceful! Everybody be happy. Yeah, you die, Mommy and me be happy. No, no, die, put you in grave. You, yeah.

MOTHER: You're gonna get in trouble again in an apartment.

If the parents would consistently condemn and expel the son, he might have a fair chance of disengaging from them. Instead they first attack him and wish to be rid of him, and then try to pull him back when he goes away. The therapist should assume that no matter how often or how viciously the parents attack the son, there is a perpetual underlying benevolence. This benevolence comes out later in the interview when the therapist returns to the room.

FATHER: I don't want nothing to do with him. I don't care what happens to him, I'll do my best to get him out, after he's out, he's on his own.

SCOTT: How do you feel about what your husband just said?

MOTHER: Well, that is what I want too, I want him to get his own place.

SCOTT: Well, what he just said?

MOTHER: I already told that to Steve.

FATHER: Her feelings are different than mine. She is a little—she is the mother.

SCOTT: O.K., well it's—I think that we can explore a little of it, you say that she is . . .

FATHER: She might bend a little more than me.

SCOTT: Mm-hmm.

FATHER: But I think that I've done all I could, I've bent over backwards. I was even hesitating when we first started coming here about letting him get his own place because I thought that maybe he would change.

SCOTT: How do you feel about what your husband just said now, about how he doesn't care what happens to him, he just wants him out of the house, period.

MOTHER: Oh well, I want him out, but I care what happens to him.

SCOTT: What do you care?

MOTHER: Well, I'd worry too, I'd worry about him no matter—

SCOTT: *(To father.)* That's gonna make a problem for you if she worries.

MOTHER: No, I don't make it a problem with him.

SCOTT: Why not?

MOTHER: Well, because I'm made the way I am, and he's made the way he is. We don't think or act alike. See a lot of my feelings I keep inside. I'm not the type to cry or yell or anything. That's the way I am.

SCOTT: Do you think that he knows how you feel?

MOTHER: I think he does.

FATHER: I do.

SCOTT: Sure he does, look at his face.

MOTHER: Well, I'll tell you, when he was in the hospital, *he* would go to visit him, *not me.* I wouldn't go. When he came home, on weekend passes, he was home. But I never went with him, back.

SCOTT: You know this whole thing about keeping your feelings inside of you.

MOTHER: Yeah, well that's the way I am, I've always been like this. Even when I was single, so nobody could change me.

SCOTT: I don't want to change you, I think you are delightful the way you are, you know.

FATHER: That's the way she is.

SCOTT: Delightful? Uh-huh? Is that what you are saying?

In order to break the cycle, the son had to behave himself long enough for the marital issues to become the focus of the therapy. Motivating the son to behave himself was a problem. Since the son's major interest in life was money, money was used to elicit good behavior. The therapist made a bet with the young man that he could not stay off drugs. The seventh interview was devoted to making that bet. The parents observed therapist and son negotiating the bet. The therapist marked the days on a blackboard. The father was asked to hold the stakes. As the therapist summarized it to Steve, "If you get in trouble, you lose five dollars. If you don't have trouble with drugs, you win five dollars. Have five dollars? Put it there."

The son won the bet by not getting into trouble with drugs for the two-week period. At that point the bet was repeated with the time doubled. Again the son won, so there was a trouble-free period of six weeks. As he behaved, tension developed between the parents. However, instead of having a quarrel that the therapist could focus on, a special form of separation took place. The father went away on a hunting trip, something he had not done for seven years. While he was away, the mother and son had a disturbing episode which could have made father decide not to vacation again.

This episode occurred in the ninth week of therapy, which is about the time one usually has trouble with a young person in this therapeutic approach. It is the troubled onset of the second stage referred to earlier. The young man threatened violence when the mother, and son, and daughter were having dinner. The mother told the son he should go out more. He indicated that she should be quiet, but she continued to tell him that he should go out. The son became angry, picked up a knife, and threatened her. At that point the sister intervened and yelled at him about threatening the mother. He went to the closet, took out a bat, and threatened the sister with it. No physical assault was made, but the mother and sister were upset by this episode of threatened violence. The mother called the therapist, who set up an interview that included the father, since he was just returning from his trip. The daughter, though requested, did not come.

The important task in such a situation, particularly with a chronic case, is to make a dramatic issue of the problem. Merely to talk about the problem behavior may have no effect on its repetition. In this family there was a special situation: the son never conceded that he ever did anything wrong. He said he did not take drugs, never made trouble, and besides he was moving to a place of his own one of these days anyhow. If the above episode had been merely discussed, he would probably have denied it, as he had denied other troublemaking periods, and dismissed it.

The ninth interview was planned; the first step was to place a kitchen knife and a baseball bat on the floor of the interview room. As the family entered the room, the mother, the problem son, and the nine-year-old walked around the knife and bat and looked at them as if they knew why they were there. The father had not been told about the episode and so did not see any significance to the items on the floor. As he came in he said cheerfully, "A party?" The therapist said, "Yes, a party," and they sat down together.

SCOTT: *(To mother.)* Take your coat off.

MOTHER: No, let me get warmed up.

SCOTT: O.K.

MOTHER: I didn't bother changing.

SCOTT: You look fine. *(He gestures to the knife and bat on the floor and begins to talk in sign language as well as words.)* Listen, I put a bat and knife on the floor, but I don't want you *(to father)* to discuss it, I don't want you *(to mother)* to discuss it, and I don't want you *(to nine-year-old son)* to discuss it. I want to talk to Steve about that. What is the sign for this? *(He holds up a baseball bat. The son signs an answer.)* It's a bat. And what is the sign for this? *(He picks up the knife, and the son signs an answer.)* Knife. Why do you think I put it there? Why? Why did I put it there? What? *(Steve signs, apparently saying that they happen to be there.)* No, I put it there. I put the knife. Why? What do you think? No, I put it. Why? *(Steve signs.)* It's for children? No. Why did I put it there? The reason? No. I brought them, they are mine. I brought them and I put them there. Why? What do you think? What? *(The son smiles and signs.)* Hit? With this? Who? Hit it on the head of somebody? Hit? Who? Yeah, I brought them. *(The son signs, indicating a ball.)* No ball. No ball. The bat and the knife. Why? *(The son signs and the therapist translates.)* "When I was a little boy, baseball." *(Therapist holds up knife.)* And this? How about this. Why? You don't know?

The therapist continues this type of interrogation for over twenty minutes. The son changes from a casual, joking stance to an increasingly angry one. The task of the therapist is to persist until the son reacts and acknowledges that he knows that the knife and bat are there because he threatened his mother and sister with them. The parents and younger son are required to sit and merely watch. Mother evidently knows what the interrogation is about. Father is simply bewildered by it. After about twenty minutes the son still claims innocence, but he is getting angry.

SCOTT: What? *(Son signs.)* I'm crazy? O.K., all right, all right. That's one reason. Another thought, why? No, I'm not crazy. Think a little bit. Think a little bit.

(The therapist stood up at this point and left the room to consult with the supervisor. The mother immediately turned and spoke to the father.)

MOTHER: You know why he has got those on the floor. Don't you?
FATHER: I got an idea.
MOTHER: Those are things that he uses, right? He used it last week, that's why I told him *(the therapist)*.
FATHER: Used what?
MOTHER: Well, he got real mad with me because I told him he should go out more.
FATHER: What did he use?
MOTHER: Well, he took a knife, he didn't use it.
FATHER: While I was away?
MOTHER: And then he threatened Bernice *(the daughter)* with the bat—it ain't a bat, the stick you used to have in the closet.
YOUNGER SON: Club.
MOTHER: So when Mr. Scott called, I told him, and that's why he brought them.

(The therapist, who has observed the conversation from behind the mirror, enters again and sits down.)

SCOTT: *(To father.)* What do you think? Do you know why I brought them?
FATHER: She just told me.
SCOTT: You discuss it with Steve then.
FATHER: *(To Steve.)* What happened last week when I went hunting? What happened? Yeah? *(Son signs antlers on his head to indicate that father went hunting.)* No, no, with Mommy.
SCOTT: *(Translating.)* He's saying that Mommy never went hunting.
FATHER: Yeah, when I was away, what happened at home?

SCOTT: *(Translating Steve.)* "Nothing happened, I went out with my boyfriend."

FATHER: *(To mother.)* He went out with his boyfriend?

MOTHER: He didn't go out at all. He only goes out Friday night, Saturday night.

SCOTT: *(To father.)* Go ahead.

FATHER: So what happened? *(When Steve shrugs, he turns to mother.)* What *did* happen? What caused it?

MOTHER: We were eating.

FATHER: Yeah.

MOTHER: And I told him that he should go out.

FATHER: Mm-hmm.

MOTHER: And he got mad and said that he had no place to go, and I told him that Mr. Scott told him that he was to go out, even a couple hours a day, and he got real mad and turned around and got one of the little knives.

FATHER: Yeah.

MOTHER: And I told him to put it back. Then Bernice started hollering at him, you know, to stop. So he went in the closet and got that thing like a bat and he told her to shut up or he was gonna hit her.

FATHER: Mm-hmm.

MOTHER: So she just told him to be quiet.

SCOTT: *(Responding to mother's casual tone.)* You know, when you told me on the phone, I became very excited. I was afraid when you called me. When I talked to you on the phone.

MOTHER: Mm-hmm.

SCOTT: *(Translating in signs for son as he talks.)* You said that Steve made you afraid with the knife and then Steve made your daughter afraid with the bat. It scares me. It don't scare you.

MOTHER: It's not the first time.

SCOTT: It don't scare you?

MOTHER: Well I think I'm getting used to it. If anything is gonna happen, it's gonna happen.

Although a question might be raised about who caused the trouble between mother and son at the dinner table, that is not the issue. The point is that the son must take responsibility for what he did. The family cycle is partly maintained by the son's indifference and feigned innocence in any situation. Even after it is revealed that he threatened his mother with the knife and his sister with the club, he gestures as if the acts were unimportant. After he misbehaves, he either pretends that nothing has happened or blames the misbehavior on someone else, and then dismisses it as past his-

tory. The father's reaction to the threat of violence indicates one of its functions: it keeps the father at home to protect his wife.

FATHER: See, I can't leave the house.

SCOTT: Yes you can.

FATHER: The solution is that he has to go out.

SCOTT: But on good terms. That's the difference. You can't be hating him when he goes out. He can't be hating you when he goes out.

MOTHER: No, because he thinks a lot of you. Believe me, he does. That's why I didn't tell you when you came home.

FATHER: *(Father turns to Steve and points to bat and knife on floor.)* What did you do that for?

Steve suddenly gets up, picking up baseball bat from the floor. He stands holding the bat over the therapist and at the same time opens the door. His stance toward the therapist is clearly threatening, and he makes angry noises apparently indicating that the therapist should leave the room. Father finally takes the bat from his hand and sits him down, shutting the door.

Therapy is more effective if the problem can be actively brought into the room rather than merely talked about. If a child sets fires, it is helpful to have him set one in the room. If he bangs his head on the floor, it is appropriate for him to do so during the interview rather than merely talking about it. This young man threatens violence, so it is best to have that brought into the therapy. It is most important that the therapist, after he recovers from the fear he had in this situation, continue to be firm with the young man. He must persuade the parents not to give in to threats of violence by not giving in himself.

(Steve makes noises and gestures that he will split the therapist's head open.)

MOTHER: See, you found out what he is really like now. He don't like that.

SCOTT: *(To father.)* But you can handle him.

FATHER: I can handle him.

MOTHER: He don't mean with your fist.

FATHER: I don't want to, but if I have to . . .

MOTHER: Don't do what he does. In other words, if he gets a club, you don't teach him to do that either. He's got a mean temper.

(Steve still concentrating on the therapist, gestures that he doesn't want the money he won in the bet.)

SCOTT: Ten dollars. No, no, no, you won the bet, you won, you won.

FATHER: I got the money. *(Meaning he is holding the stakes.)*

SCOTT: You win.

MOTHER: He's mad at you, he don't want your five dollars.

SCOTT: He gets the ten dollars, it's there.

FATHER: *(After a long pause.)* So we enter another phase.

SCOTT: That's right, another phase.

MOTHER: I'm glad that this happened in front of you.

SCOTT: *(Translating in signs.)* Happy this happened. I say O.K., but I don't like it. I don't like it that you walk over and pick up that bat. I don't like it. *(Translating.)* "I don't bother you. I don't bother you. No more, he's not gonna come. This is the last time." Do you want to stop? That's good, but I'm gonna tell Mother that I don't like it that you make people frightened. I don't like it. What? *(Translating.)* "Don't bother you? I don't understand. Big mouth?" *(To mother.)* Is that what it is?

MOTHER: *(To son.)* Big mouth? Me? Because I tell him?

SCOTT: *(Translating.)* He's talking about the television set. Is that what it was over? Part of it?

MOTHER: No, that was Monday night when it was raining.

SCOTT: What happened?

MOTHER: He wanted to watch what he wanted to watch and Dickie *(the nine-year-old brother present at the interview)* is not allowed to watch what he wants.

SCOTT: *(To mother.)* But I'll tell you something. When you walk away from him with a knife and a baseball bat, it gives him reason to be angry the next time in the same way. You can't put up with that, you can't. It must be terrible for you.

MOTHER: Well, let's put it that he's got more strength than me.

SCOTT: Then you have to relate to him *(father)* then.

MOTHER: Yeah, well I knew you were coming and you were gonna explain everything to him. But see, why I didn't tell him is that I wanted him to know that you *(therapist)* knew. I don't want him *(father)* to think that I am hiding something.

(Later in the interview.)

SCOTT: *(To Steve.)* Not with this. *(Indicating weapons.)* When you got angry with her, you got angry with her with this. That's bad. That's bad. You can't use that. *(To father.)* You have to discuss that with him.

FATHER: I will.

SCOTT: Now, go ahead.

FATHER: See, our intentions are to try to keep him home till after the holidays. We found him a place *(an apartment to live in.)*

SCOTT: Did you tell him?

FATHER: No.

SCOTT: Tell him. You know that is part of it, we can't keep on keeping secrets. You've got to tell him what's going on.

FATHER: Well, after we leave here tonight, you're gonna see a place.

If the goal is to disengage the young man from his parents, a move out of the home must be with the parents' permission, and it is best to put the parents in charge of the son's move. The parents should decide where he is to live, and the son should be required to come home regularly once he has moved out. Although this appears to be making the son more dependent on his parents, it actually has the opposite effect. If the parents are in charge of the son's move, they will let him go. Once he is out with their approval, he has a chance to develop an independent life.

SCOTT: O.K., you got a room and that is fine. That's fine, but Steve is still gonna come home. He's gonna visit you, and you're gonna have this same kind of problem. O.K. And we have to work with that first. Steve said that something was not working with the TV, and you and Dickie wanted to watch TV, and you changed the channels back and forth, both of you, you and Dickie, right? Now *(to mother)* you say that it wasn't over that, but that is part of it, because it adds to it. Steve sees it as nagging. But mothers have a right to nag. Sure. And he has the right to criticize, but not this way *(points to knife and bat)*, and you have to make it clear to him that this is not allowed to happen in your house. You must tell him what will happen if that is used.

FATHER: Well, when we get this room here, that will all be ironed out.

SCOTT: No, that's not enough. That is not enough. Get the room, fine, he wants to be by himself, and that's fine, that's good. But he's still gonna come home. And it's all right for Steve to get angry with Mom and criticize and say some things, but it's not right to use these *(the knife and bat)*. That's wrong and you have to make it clear for him, that there is a difference, a difference, difference. Fight, sign with hands, mouth, but not this. Now you have to discuss that with him and I think you should do that right now.

FATHER: *(To son.)* In the house, you don't use that, you talk, don't use that, all right?

SCOTT: Or what happens?

FATHER: Oh, he knows.

SCOTT: Does he?

FATHER: Then I beat him up.

SCOTT: Tell him, tell him.

FATHER: You use that and I get mad, and I don't want to get mad.

SCOTT: You get mad and what happens, you've got to tell him what happens. You have to be very explicit.

FATHER: Well he knows.

SCOTT: Tell him, tell him.

FATHER: See, when you get mad, don't use this, because if you use them, then you and me, we're gonna fight, and I don't want that.

SCOTT: But you will, tell him you will.

FATHER: But I will, all right. You be good, you can talk.

(Steve is nodding agreement.)

SCOTT: You can argue.

FATHER: You can argue, but this—no. I no use it, me. I argue, but not that. Baby use that. You baby?

The therapist removed the knife and bat from the center of the room, and the interview continued. The next week the son moved out to a place of his own. He visited home regularly. The parents survived his absence and treated him with more respect when he got into trouble. For example, not long after he moved out, the young man became involved with drugs, and the parents let him solve the problem himself.

(A later therapeutic interview.)

FATHER: This hospital called and they said he was under drugs. "He is?" I said. "Oh yeah," the woman said, "I think he's under drugs." And they wanted me to go down and pick him up.

SCOTT: And you said . . .?

FATHER: "The way he got there, let him get back."

SCOTT: Fine. *(To mother.)* How do you feel about that?

MOTHER: I wasn't home.

SCOTT: Well, let's just suppose you were home. Let's just create the whole thing, and you got the phone call.

MOTHER: I would tell them to send him back to his room, he has a room, he doesn't live here anymore.

That was the last time the young man got into trouble with drugs. The therapist continued to see the family occasionally to make sure that both son and parents survived the disengagement. In a three-year follow-up, the young man was still living outside the home and had not been rehospitalized.

Chapter 11

Special Issues:
Resolved and Unresolved

A straightforward, simple therapeutic approach is recommended for the families of mad young people for practical reasons. Complex tactics can be risked by master therapists, but the average therapist will do best with simple ones. The interpersonal skill with which these families maintain stability must be respected. When the therapist provokes a beginning change in such families, he will be tested. Any weakness, hypocrisy, or vulnerability in his administrative situation, competence, or character will be probed in unexpected ways, and he is likely to be left puzzled about what happened to him. The therapist with a straightforward approach will be able to maintain his orientation and defend and pursue his procedures.

More complex techniques, such as the use of paradox, will be discussed here as variations to be used with caution. I will also discuss different issues in the therapy and how to approach them to give the therapist an advantage. The procedures and stages in this therapy approach are constructed to deal with people who are not only interpersonally skilled but are willing to go to extremes.

PARADOXICAL INTERVENTIONS

Families in which a member is capable of bizarre and extremely deviant communication have greater skill and experience with paradoxical communication than other people. The family is accustomed to conflicting levels of message. When a young person sends his mother a commercial Mother's Day card which says, "You've always been like a mother to me," his skill in communication must be respected.[1] Although more skillful with paradox than the average therapist, the family is vulnerable to simple, straightforward persuasion as recommended here. Paradoxical interventions are extremely effective in a wide variety of therapeutic problems; thus skill in the use of paradox should be part of any therapist's training. Even with families of addicts or depressives, the average therapist might use paradox. The use of paradox with the mad is a special case, not because the mad are fragile but rather because they are willing to use a range of behavior beyond that of other people.

The use of paradox in therapy will not be reviewed here, but a few comments relevant to mad young people can be mentioned. There is almost always an extreme reaction to a paradoxical intervention, whether a therapist imposes the paradox himself or asks family members to impose paradoxes on each other.[2] When a therapist establishes a helping relationship and within that framework encourages the person or family to stay the same or become worse, he usually receives an extreme reaction and must be prepared to deal with it. The reaction can be more extreme when the therapist asks family members to be paradoxical toward each other. A spouse cannot continue with a symptom as a way of dealing with the other spouse if that spouse encourages that behavior, and rapidly changing relationships and unpredictable responses within a family system can be expected. I have suggested that therapists use paradox only with caution and follow a consistent set of stages.[3]

Using paradox with the mad has a long history and usually works best when the therapist is especially skillful and has control over the reaction of the client. John Rosen, for example, would ask an improving client to exhibit his symptomatic behavior—he would ask a hallucinating patient to hallucinate.[4] He reported that as the patient improved, he would insist that the patient hear voices behind the lamp as he once did. The patient would refuse and would cease to hallucinate.

One can also encourage a symptomatic theme rather than the symptom itself. For example, Milton H. Erickson once dealt with a patient who wore a sheet and insisted that he was Jesus Christ. Dr. Erickson said to him, "I understand that you have had experience as a carpenter." The young man had to agree and soon found himself doing constructive work as a carpenter.[5]

1. J. Haley, "The Family of the Schizophrenic: A Model System," *J. Nerv. Ment. Dis.*, 129:357–374, 1959.

2. J. Haley, *Strategies of Psychotherapy*, Grune & Stratton, New York, 1963.

3. J. Haley, *Problem-Solving Therapy*, Jossey-Bass, San Francisco, 1978.

4. John N. Rosen, *Direct Analysis*, Grune & Stratton, New York, 1952.

5. J. Haley, *Uncommon Therapy: The Psychiatric Techniques of Milton H. Erickson*, Norton, New York, 1973.

Paradox can be used in one-to-one dealings with a problem young person, or for any particular relationship within the family, or for systematic behavior in the whole family. One can specify, for example, that the young person sacrifice himself by making trouble whenever the parents have marital difficulty. The same behavioral sequence can be punctuated differently by asking the parents to threaten separation when the young person improves. Then the young person is to fail so that they stay together to help him. Sometimes such behavior can be rehearsed in the room. The therapist must give a benevolent reason for asking such behavior of the family. He must put it in terms of family members helping each other or understanding their problems better. He must also be prepared for unexpected reactions.

The Milanese Paradoxes

A group led by Mara Selvini in Milan has specialized in the use of paradox with mad families.[6] The group has published a book on their work which describes their innovative and ingenious techniques. It might be argued that their theory section, which does not cover organizational theory, does not provide an adequate framework for their therapeutic procedures, which seem to be designed to induce organizational change. Yet the therapy is unusual and well-described. The authors examine the family situation with great care before choosing a particular intervention. Often they write down the intervention so that the family must read it and therefore cannot lose it by ambiguity or forgetting. One example is a twenty-year-old daughter who dominated her family with delusional ideas and psychotic behavior as part of a malfunctioning family hierarchy. The therapists decided that she was miming a tyrannical father in contrast to her own weak and ineffectual one. Therefore she could be made the paternal authority in the family. As a step in the therapy they asked her to take charge of the family, and asked the family to request her permission for everything. The therapists pointed out that although they did not agree with her ideas, they respected her honest conviction and her sacrifice of her youth and femininity for that conviction. They also said that they could not tell her how to take charge, since she was already in charge (a paradoxical definition of the hierarchy since they had put her in charge). The family responded to this paradoxical intervention with improvement, and the therapists continued to encourage the behavior they wished to change.

6. M. S. Palazzoli, G. Cecchin, G. Prata, and L. Boscolo, *Paradox and Counterparadox*, Jason Aronson, New York, 1978.

Therapists should study the work of the Milanese group and carefully examine its social context before attempting to replicate their approach. Some of the main points can be summarized:

1. The families they choose are a select group rather than the random collection one faces in mental health clinics or mental hospitals. Only a few of the families they describe have the problem of young people leaving home, thus they are not focused on the disengagement of a young person and his family.
2. The families usually come some distance at some sacrifice to be accepted by the program. Therefore the therapy directives carry the weight of family investment.
3. Usually the family has been asked to cut itself off from other therapists and sources of therapeutic support. Thus it is not in a position to decline what is offered by turning to other involved therapists.
4. The family presents the problem and receives a long interview and a careful consultation among several authorities. The directive that issues from that consultation carries power. The experts have carefully examined the situation and come to one conclusion.
5. The family will not see the therapists again for a month, and the therapists will not respond to crises or emergencies with an interview. Therefore the family cannot get back at the therapists with an immediate response to the directive. This is in contrast to a family seen daily or weekly, with the therapist always available and on call (and thus more vulnerable).

The average therapist, working in a situation where he must deal with social control agents, colleagues with power over his case, administrators of his clinic or hospital whom the family members can appeal to over his head, a regular therapy schedule, undesirable medication, and families only tentatively involved and uncommitted, should approach such paradoxical interventions with caution. A paradoxical intervention is only as powerful as the therapist's ability to deal with the response: paradoxical therapy is not a single intervention, it is a sequence of interventions and responses.

An admirable factor in the Milanese group's approach is the careful consideration they give to the family situation. They assume that the mad behavior is functional and changeable; they assume that they can change it if they select the correct intervention; and they plan the timing of the directive and the way it is to be given as much as they plan the intervention itself.

An Example of a Paradoxical Intervention

In the following example, a paradoxical intervention was used—as is often the case—after a variety of straightforward attempts at change had been frustrated. A twenty-year-old young man had been in therapy, including family therapy, at a number of places. The family entered therapy with Dr. Gary Lande in a live supervision setting and was seen for a number of interviews. The primary problem was the apathy of the young man, who had recently been discharged from a mental hospital. Although he was a healthy, athletic-looking youth, he would not go to work or school. There were two younger children doing reasonably well. The mother was a quiet, distant woman. The father was a plump, helpless man who was unable to demand anything of the son and who forgave him for any failure. Father had a family business which he had inherited and disliked, and he wanted the son to work in it. The son refused by going there and falling asleep.

The family had set a date for the son to look for work, with consequences if he did not, but when the son refused to go look for a job, the father collapsed and was unable to carry out the consequences. All straightforward plans by parents and therapist failed because of the inabliity of the father to be firm with his son in any way. The son had been required to do some desultory work around the house, but essentially he did nothing all day. After a variety of approaches were tried, it was decided to use a paradoxical technique. The first stage of that procedure was to accept the father's benevolence and to ask him if he was willing to help his son. He said that he was. The therapist then asked him to agree to do something that would guarantee that the son would get a job. This "something" would be good for the father. However, the father would not know what this "something" was until he agreed to do it. He was given a week to think it over. The father was doubtful about agreeing to a "pig in a poke" but finally did so because of the guarantee that his son would go to work. This type of directive is more often followed if there is a delay in giving it and a promise extracted in advance. The emphasis on guaranteed success also encourages people to follow it to prove the therapist wrong, since they have tried everything and believe nothing will solve the problem.

The therapist got the father to agree to do whatever the therapist said if the son did not get a job that week. The following week the parents came in with the son and reported that he had not looked for a job.

LANDE: That's an extraordinary thing.

FATHER: What is extraordinary?

LANDE: For a young, healthy— (To son.) Stand up for a second. (The son does. He is an atheletic-looking young man.) —Young healthy football

player *(he played football in high school)* for two weeks not to be able to—
not to even look for a job is an extraordinary kind of feat.

FATHER: It's not like he spent two weeks not looking for a job. He tried
last week.

LANDE: How long did he spend not looking?

MOTHER: A week.

FATHER: A week.

LANDE: A week not looking?

FATHER: Yeah.

LANDE: That's an investment.

FATHER: Right. *(To son.)* Did you get discouraged that first week you
went out?

SON: No.

FATHER: No?

SON: No. *(The son never helps the father out by going along with his
excuses. He simply declines to look for a job.)*

LANDE: That's good, Eric. Watch what your father is going to do now.

FATHER: Make an excuse for him?

LANDE: *(Laughing with mother.)* He's too weak, and he's too small, and
he's too . . .

SON: He's trying to understand me, he's trying to understand me.

LANDE: He's trying to understand. He's a nice guy.

SON: *(Laughs.)* Well . . .

LANDE: You don't want to think the one possible thought.

FATHER: What?

MOTHER: What?

SON: Oh no, no, no, no, that's true. I'm lazy.

MOTHER: Yes.

SON: That's true.

LANDE: But that's what he's trying not to say, that you might be lazy.
He'll say you're too this and you're too that. And you've had this very
complex psychiatric history.

FATHER: Right.

LANDE: But God forbid he should say you're lazy.

*It is apparent that the family does not need "insight" into the ways they
behave. They have had quite a number of therapists who provided that. Here
they easily anticipate the therapist's suggestion that father will make
excuses for son and will never say he is lazy. Later in the interview the
directive is given.*

LANDE: As part of our agreement for last week, which is what you've
been waiting for.

FATHER: Yeah.

LANDE: Which was something you would have to do for yourself if Eric didn't start working, that's between you and I. You remember our agreement?

FATHER: Yeah.

LANDE: Yeah. Which is now what we're going to talk about.

FATHER: Right.

LANDE: O.K. When was the last time you had a medical examination?

The conversation continues about father's physical health. He is overweight and smokes two or three packs of cigarettes a day. At his last examination the doctor told him to lose weight and smoke less.

LANDE: As part of our agreement for last week, if Eric wasn't working, you would have to do something which would be doable but hard. O.K.? What I want you to do is to do something about getting yourself back in shape.

FATHER: All right.

LANDE: I'm going to reconfirm what your doctor said at your last exam that you are more overweight than you should be for your age and health.

FATHER: Right.

LANDE: And that there's no reason to be. And that you're also smoking more than you should.

FATHER: Right.

LANDE: I'm a medical doctor also, and I think there's no reason for it.

FATHER: Right.

LANDE: So what I want on our agreement is this. That you're going to start tomorrow on a program that I'm going to begin to outline for you, about getting yourself in much better physical shape. Start taking care of your body better. Partly by losing weight, and partly by taking care of your lungs and stopping your getting lung problems by beginning to do something about your smoking. O.K.? And this will be a program that will continue every day until Eric works. At that point it will be the end of our agreement.

SON: That would mean if I didn't work—*(pause)*—the more I didn't work, the better shape he'd get. *(Scratching his head.)* Well, that's—O.K. is that . . . ?

LANDE: This is between your father and me. How many pounds overweight are you?

FATHER: I go now about two hundred and thirty.

LANDE: And how much should you weigh?

FATHER: One eighty-five, one ninety. I'm a good forty pounds overweight, forty-five pounds.

That was the introduction of the paradoxical intervention. It should be noted that the mad son immediately recognized the significance of it. He said, "The more I didn't work, the better shape he'd get."

It was assumed that the son's not going to work was a way of helping his father and "keeping him in shape." The father could avoid dealing with issues in his life and his marriage by focusing on his failing son. Assuming the son avoided work for the father's sake, asking him not to work for the father's sake was a paradoxical directive.

With this intervention the therapist can succeed no matter which of several things happens. If the son does not go to work, father will get in shape by losing weight and stopping smoking and so will benefit and be more capable of executive behavior in the family. If the son goes to work under pressure from the father who wishes to eat and smoke, the son will benefit. If the father tries but fails to stay on a diet and not smoke, his claim to be dedicated to helping his son will be punctured, since he will not carry out this simple task to help him. The unfortunate closeness between father and son will be destroyed, and the son will be helped to disengage from the parents. The therapist continues to ensure that the task will be carried out.

LANDE: What he's going to do—and that's why I'm talking to you *(the wife)*—he's going to make various reasons why he can't do this. Because he doesn't put himself first. O.K.? But he's a gentleman and a man who keeps his word, and he has an agreement with me. Now I'm consulting with you because—do you like to see your husband, I mean, in a couple of years when he's smoking so much . . .

MOTHER: Everybody's worried.

LANDE: So you're worried about him.

MOTHER: Yes.

LANDE: So you wouldn't mind participating in helping him get a little healthier?

MOTHER: No, I wouldn't mind.

By giving the mother a task as part of the plan, the therapist further encourages the father to carry out the directive. The more family members involved in a task, the more likely it is to be carried out. Mother is put in charge of the husband's diet. Later the therapist turns to the smoking issue.

LANDE: You're smoking between two and three packs of cigarettes a day?

FATHER: Yeah.

MOTHER: Mm-hmm.

FATHER: Three packs. There's only one way I can stop smoking, and that's cold turkey. I can't stop—there's no such thing as cutting down.

Either I stop, or—if I say like ten cigarettes or five cigarettes a day, that doesn't work for me.

LANDE: What happens?

FATHER: I walk around thinking about a cigarette all day.

After the discussion, the therapist sets the task in relation to cigarettes.

LANDE: You're a man who describes yourself well and is always honest about it. So as part of our agreement, and this will be the last part—I don't have a third hidden—as of midnight tonight, no more cigarettes. Until your son goes to work. Then it's up to you whatever you want to do about it.

FATHER: He *(the problem son)* knows that if I'm not smoking and I'm on a diet, I'm gonna be a goddamn bear. He knows that, he knows that. I'm going to be walking around with a short fuse. *(To son.)* You understand that? You better get a job! *(Everyone laughs.)* Or stay out of my way.

With this instruction the paradoxical intervention is complete. The son, who is helping his father by failing, is asked to fail to help his father improve his health. He has been in charge of his father's health; and he is put in charge of it. The father is predictably angry at his son for not working—each time he wants a cigarette, he thinks of his son depriving him—while at the same time he is forced to concede that his son's not working is good for him in that he should lose weight and stop smoking. The mother, who wants the son to go to work, is pleased that the father is losing weight and not smoking, which will end if the son goes to work.

The outcome was that the father stayed on a diet the following week and smoked only a few cigarettes at desperate moments. The son did not go to work. The following week the son got himself a job as a dishwasher in a restaurant. The father went off his diet and began to smoke.

This outcome achieved the goal of getting the apathetic young man to go to work. In that sense a paradoxical intervention was successful. When using paradox with such families, however, one must keep in mind their skills and look at the long-term results. So often, one later wonders if one was outmaneuvered. In this case the son got a job and held it for months; but it was a job below his abilities. He was a failure, in the sense of not having a job that was appropriate for the middle-class status of the family. Therefore he was defined not as normal or successful by the family but as a handicapped person working at a job below his abilities. The fact that the son had a job did take the pressure off the family, however, since they were coming to therapy largely because of their need to have the son out of the house and working. With the son working, the family began to lose interest in the therapy. It was difficult to keep them involved, and a few weeks later they said that they had accomplished their goal and terminated.

In a follow-up the next year, it was learned that the family was taking the son to a vitamin therapy program because he was still disturbed. The outcome of the therapy was not satisfactory in the long run, despite the short-run success with a paradoxical intervention.

BLAMING PARENTS

Since it is emphasized here that families of severely disturbed young people are interpersonally adept, one might ask, "If they're so smart, why are they in such trouble?" One can respect the skill of such families and still acknowledge that in general they have fared badly because of therapeutic mistreatment. The antagonism toward such parents by therapists has been remarkable. Somehow therapists have decided that the "patient" was their responsibility and that the family was simply an unfortunate handicap. In the past it was not unusual for a therapist to do therapy only with the problem young person and to tell the parents to stay out of it and just pay the bill. Blaming parents and attempting a "parentectomy" produced pointless and unnecessary misery and despair. With such an approach the therapy usually failed with the young person, sometimes in tragic ways.[7] This meant that parents who went to an expert for help were often blamed and rejected, and after considerable expense were still suffering with their problem child, who had not improved. Often the parents went for help for a misbehaving young person and ended up with an irreversible neurological problem because of the antipsychotic drugs used by the expert, who had no training in what to do except to medicate. Tardive dyskinesia, the tremors of the hands and compulsive movements of the tongue, has become the sign of psychiatric treatment by medication.

In addition, parents were often confused by different experts who advised different procedures and offered differing diagnoses and prognoses, so that no one seemed to know what he was doing. I recall a family with an eighteen-year-old daughter who became depressed and upset after entering college. She had been a brilliant student in high school and had a variety of scholarships. The parents, who were academic intellectuals with experience in psychodynamic therapy themselves, followed medical advice and put the girl in a psychiatric hospital. Observing her there, they decided she was getting worse and courageously removed her against medical advice and amid staff threats about the danger of suicide. They were advised to take her to a particular psychiatrist and did so. Unfortunately he practiced far from the city where the parents lived and where the daughter had been going to college. They therefore placed the girl in her grandpar-

7. For the tragic story of a family mistreated by orthodox procedures, see James A. Wechsler, *In a Darkness*, Ace Books, New York, 1972.

ents' house, where she would be only an hour's travel from her psychiatrist. There the girl could not go to school or work and had no social life, and she sat in the house doing nothing. Twice a week she went to the psychiatrist and talked about how depressed she was. On weekends she would visit her parents and sit in their house doing nothing. As she became more depressed, medication was increased, and new types of medication were used experimentally. She became more upset and depressed. Her psychiatrist considered hospitalizing her, decided against it, and then advised the parents to consult another psychiatrist about hospitalization. An appointment was made with a consultant, and before the visit, the girl improved. The parents consulted despite the improvement, and the second psychiatrist advised them to hospitalize her in his private psychiatric hospital. The first psychiatrist was uncertain but didn't want to go against the consultant he had recommended. The parents did not know what to do, since the girl was now better and had previously worsened when hospitalized. The parents were also intelligent enough to hesitate about going doctor-shopping and adding more conflicting advice to what they had already received.

The social situation of the girl was depressing but was considered secondary or irrevelant by the parents and by the psychiatrists. The theory was that the girl was depressed because of internal conflicts. Only the grandparents said that an eighteen-year-old girl could be expected to be depressed if she sat around all week doing nothing and had no plans for doing anything. Yet she could not return to college because she would not be able to commute to her psychiatrist and so would risk giving up therapy. Besides, the parents hesitated to require anything of their daughter because more than one of the psychiatrists they had consulted told them that they had been too strict and rigid with her and that she was depressed because of inner conflicts about meeting their past demands. The parents thought they had been permissive; they could not recall being rigid and expecting too much of the girl, but since she was depressed, and since the experts said that the parents' strictness was the cause, they gave up suggesting that she do anything. Essentially they left her without guidance at the age of eighteen. Feeling guilty about their daughter's problems, the parents were pleased to pass her on to the grandparents in the hope that they could do better. Yet from the girl's point of view, if she improved with the grandparents she would be indicting her parents and saying that her mother's mother was more successful with her than her mother had been. The girl did not improve. The conflict among the experts was reflected in conflict between the parents, as well as between the parents and grandparents, about what to do with her.

The therapist, the consultants, the girl, the parents, and the grandparents were all in a context where depression was appropriate, and none of them could do anything to change anything. A number of intelligent people were trapped by the way the problem was defined. In such a situation the interpersonal skill of the family members is used to prevent change rather than to produce it. The therapist who views the context and sees both the predicament and some practical ways to solve it should not assume that sensible advice will be welcomed and followed. Determining what to do is often easier than actually getting it done.

JOINING A FAMILY

If one wishes a family to do certain things, it is necessary to persuade them. A first step in that persuasion is to speak a language they will understand. One cannot speak Chinese to a family that only speaks English and expect cooperation in a joint venture. Similarly, if a family thinks of the problem as a "sick" son, they can only be puzzled about why they have been asked to come to an interview with him unless the therapist frames the endeavor in a way that makes sense to them. (Many families resist agreeing to "family therapy" since that might mean the exposure of all their misfortunes. Yet they do not object to coming to therapeutic interviews to help their son get back on his feet. It is best not to try to sell a family on "family therapy" but rather to persuade them to come together for specific goals.)

Every family is unique and each one speaks its own language. The more adept the therapist is at that language, the more cooperation he will receive. He must listen to the ways they express the problem and their situation and then offer a solution in that same language.

What follows is an example of a therapist using as a framework the language of a family. The therapist, Dan Merlis, began therapy in a live supervision training program in Baltimore with a twenty-six-year-old man just discharged from a Veterans Administration hospital. The young man had been diagnosed as manic-depressive and had not responded to a variety of medications, including lithium. He had been in and out of mental hospitals for six years. His episodes might have begun with drug experiences, although that was not clear. (In a state hospital he enjoyed taking illegal LSD because he preferred hallucinations to looking at the other patients.)

When he entered therapy his father, mother, and elder brother expressed hopelessness about him. The elder brother worked and lived at home. Father worked at a middle-class job, and mother had worked until six years ago. The parents hoped to retire to Florida in a few years, they said in a later interview, and expected both sons to move with them.

At the first interview the young man said that his goal was to be an Indian so that he could be supported by the government. He had had enough of white people and felt that being an Indian would be better. He was receiving a disability check for a small amount. It was not enough to live on, but he planned to live at home and get additional money from his parents. He assumed that his parents would support him forever. He did not want to move to a place of his own, even though he had previously lived away from home in an apartment for over a year. He also declined to go to work or even look for a job. He had once completed a course in accounting but had not gotten a job. The parents said that he slept all day and if he went out at night it was to hang around bars with what the mother considered unfortunate women. The son said that he wouldn't mind finding an older woman who would support him. He was a nice-looking young man, physically well-built although he was getting a little fat. In his black leather jacket the young man gave every appearance of being a bum who would not work and did not mind admitting it. For the last year he had done nothing. He was on medication, and his parents thought of him as "sick."

In the first interview the therapist and parents set the date of February 3 for the son to move out to an apartment of his own. The parents agreed to supplement his disability income with money until April 1. By then he was expected to go to work. The response of the young man three interviews later was as follows:

MERLIS: What have you done about getting yourself ready?

JOHN: Not much, just, uh—I want to stay at home, but they won't let me. That's about all. I don't feel I should have to leave.

MERLIS: What have you done about looking for work?

JOHN: Nothing. I don't want to go to work.

MOTHER: Now we're back to that old routine of going out in the evening. You know, as soon as the sun goes down, you know, John is great. But he stays in bed all day. He gets up and he comes down for breakfast at one o'clock. Then back up to bed, and after he finishes eating, you know, he's sleeping on the table like this *(head on arms)*. Then he goes upstairs and stays until dinner just lying down. Then when it starts getting dark and a girl calls, he's ready to go. And then he's out every evening.

JOHN: I'm just going to collect Social Security.

MOTHER: We're back to that whole situation where we were about two years ago. Back before he, you know, got his other apartment. I mean, to me its very depressing seeing someone lying in bed every day—you know, all day, it's like being in a hospital or something.

When the son previously had an apartment of his own, the mother went there daily to clean it, shopped for his groceries, and often cooked for him. The mother had little of importance in her life except the care of this son.

JOHN: All I wanted to do in the hospital is just lay around.

MOTHER: Yeah, but that's—home is not the hospital, and you're not there.

MERLIS: I agree with you that your job as parents at this point is to see that he gets off to a good start.

Later in the interview the son again brings up objections to moving out.

JOHN: Why can't I just live at home?

MOTHER: Because I don't like stepping over bodies all day, John.

JOHN: I say you all just don't want me there. Why can't I just stay home? My brother gets to stay there.

MERLIS: Look, the problem you bring up is an important one. The way things seem to be organized; how he's using his time.

MOTHER: He's not using his time except for the evenings.

JOHN: When do I get off these pills?

FATHER: Just recently his social life has picked up.

MOTHER: And we're thankful for that; I mean, he should have a nice girl.

FATHER: He goes out with his friends, and he met this gal, a nice little girl.

The son continues his objections, usually emphasizing that "I'm men-tally disabled." The therapist talks to the parents about their plans, to retire to Florida. After retirement they won't be able to give the son the money that they give him now, so he must begin to support himself. The therapist talks to the parents about their disappointment in John and about the hopes they had for him when he was young.

MOTHER: We thought that there was nothing in the world John couldn't accomplish, because he had accomplished so much throughout high school. I thought he would have been a scientist or a doctor, or something like that.

FATHER: I thought he would aspire to science too.

They describe the awards he won for writing and for nature study when only in junior high.

FATHER: He knew every seashell, he could tell you every dinosaur that ever lived when he was seven years old. And we'd go down to the museum and see the bones.

It also turns out that at the age of nine he had been a sufficiently noted butterfly collector to be written up in the newspaper. He won awards at state and county fairs for his collections of butterflies, moths, rocks, and plants.

The supposedly inadequate son who wants to be a bum turns out to have had a quite remarkable history of accomplishment. One should always assume that young people who fail at this age of leaving home are not failures by nature. They only appear to be failures. In most cases, they are out of the ordinary in intelligence and sometimes in accomplishments.

This young man was not only an outstanding science student in high school, he was also an athlete. In fact, he was enough of an athlete to have won four first places in one day in a track-and-field event. The amount of self-discipline required for such a feat is extraordinary, particularly in a young man who now appears to be without self-discipline of any kind and who cannot even get up in the morning.

The therapist begins the task of motivating parents and son to attempt once again to have the son achieve something in life. The accounting business was not a field for which he had any enthusiasm, which is perhaps why he dropped it. His interests were nature and athletics. The therapist's problem is how to make the parents motivate the son to achieve something again in one of those areas. Since the mother seems as depressed as the son and uncertain about what to do in her life, the therapist must motivate the mother to do something. She has declined to look for work, return to college, or follow any interest of her own. It was therefore decided to have her investigate the possibilities in the nature field for her son. She is to find out what jobs are available and then take the son to look for work. The overweight father is to work out with the son in the local gym, thus dealing with the son's athletic side.

The therapist needs to motivate a hopeless family to act. He faces a son who has abdicated. The son says, "I want to stay at home and live on these checks. Because I think really that I am mentally disabled now because of my views and philosophies that I have towards life. Everyone's concerned about whether I'll get the job, and get the money, and pay the rent. You know, live in a place and make some sort of life for yourself, you know, but I really don't want to do that. I'd rather just keep on going the way I've been going right now."

The firmly depressed position of the young man is almost equaled by the unwillingness of the parents to try anything to get him doing something again. They can only think of moving him out of the house so that he will sit in his own apartment instead of sitting at home. When the therapist brings up the question of a job in the nature field, the son puts the idea down.

MERLIS: You're a guy that's interested in nature and the outdoors and these kinds of things. What about the idea of working in parks and forests, things like that?

JOHN: Yeah, that would be good, but they don't need you. I've tried it already.

The therapist begins to talk to the young man and his parents in a language they can understand, one that has become familiar to them over the years. First of all, he drops the terms "ill" and "manic-depressive," which both family and experts have used, and says instead, "Well, you're in a slump. A lot of guys have had to pull out of slumps before. A lot of good athletes." The son replies, "Yeah, really they do."

The nice thing about the analogy of a "slump" is that it is normal, it is temporary, and one must be competent to have one since a slump means a descent from something higher. It is also an analogy familiar to the family of an athlete.

The therapist begins to talk about games and their rules, and the son responds predictably.

JOHN: Did you ever feel that way? Where you just don't feel like playing the game anymore?

MERLIS: I think it's natural to feel that you want to change some of the rules. One of the rules that you have shown everyone, demonstrated and signified, was that you could measure up. That you have enough value that you can measure up.

JOHN: I've taken a lot of knocks.

MERLIS: And that's one of the rules you wouldn't want to change—that you can measure up.

JOHN: Yeah, I can measure up.

MERLIS: And that you're a brave guy. That you've got a lot of courage.

JOHN: Yeah, I do. Yeah, but it's to no avail it seems like, nobody seems to care.

MERLIS: Well, we're meeting here because we do care, because we've seen you go into a slump.

JOHN: I think everyone's worried about me, is what it is.

MERLIS: In the past I know that your folks have seen you come out of slumps, too.

JOHN: Yeah.

MERLIS: Any athlete who really wants to measure up finds a way out. And that for an athlete to get out of a slump he generally needs a good coach. He needs somebody to help him organize. A good baseball player who goes into a slump needs a coach.

JOHN: A coach.

MERLIS: A football player who just isn't hitting hard enough needs a good coach to tell him, to help him organize.

JOHN: You seem to be a good coach yourself.

MERLIS: I am. Your folks have coached you for a long, long time. From the first days of walking, getting up on your feet, holding on to things. They helped you get on your two feet when you were—how old?

MOTHER: When he walked? Oh, before he was a year.

MERLIS: Before he was a year old. And all along the way, every step that he took, when he needed a little help, a little coaching, he could turn to the two of you.

JOHN: I think I just need a long time out.

MERLIS: It's a very fortunate thing now that when he needs help, when he needs some coaching, when he needs to find some way to measure up and to really come out on top in the competition, that he can do it.

MOTHER: Yeah.

MERLIS: There are ways that you can really help him now. To help him get a job that he is really going to like. That's going to be meaningful for him. And he has so many interests, in nature and the outdoors. The simple things, the good clean things in life. And certainly there are places around the area between parks and zoos and other possibilities which you haven't even looked into.

MOTHER: Right.

MERLIS: Things he could do, something of value in which he could feel that he's measuring up.

(Later in the interview.)

MERLIS: I think you get into those kinds of moods, and you don't feel like budging, you really need a little assistance here to get back on track.

JOHN: I'm off the track, I know that, 'cause I must be off the track if I've been in a nuthouse.

MERLIS: *(To the parents.)* There are ways you can do that, and you have done it over and over again over the years. You have done it. You've had to deal with his moods repeatedly. And then you had the satisfaction of sitting back and watching him go out to the competition and really come out on top. And you have medals and trophies which signify that.

JOHN: Yeah.

MERLIS: Which signify that. Forever.

JOHN: When I pole-vaulted, I used to stay about an hour, an hour after everybody went home, after the whole rest of the team was beat and cleared off the field, I stayed about another hour and practiced.

(Later in the interview.)

MERLIS: One of the problems I was curious about when I watched the Olympics—they train someone for the decathlon, and that involves a number of very separate skills.

JOHN: Yeah.

MERLIS: It occurred to me what kind of a logistical problem it would be to have—to always be on top as a trainer and as a coach—seeing somebody master the hammer throw, for example, and yet note that they're a little slow on the javelin this week. And how do you help them—it must be very complex—how a coach just knows intuitively that when somebody is doing something well, he's on track with something, that he's got to get his athlete moving in *other* directions, you know, to really come out in the decathlon, which is a multiple event. And clearly there are things he's on top of right now.

JOHN: Have you seen the moths, the big ones that fly at night in the summertime, have you seen one of those?

MERLIS: No, I haven't.

JOHN: Oh, boy, they're the most beautiful things.

MOTHER: Well, why don't you bring one in to show him?

MERLIS: Yes, bring one in.

JOHN: With nature there's nothing I don't know, I mean I'm like those Indians. But I mean, I'm not trying to brag or anything, but moths fly at certain times in the summer. You can catch big green ones, big yellow ones, and all kinds of different ones at different times. And there's a certain moth that's black, and it's smaller, but it's very rare. In fact it's the truth that I'm the only person in the whole history of the state, past or present, that ever caught one. Now they've got it in the Smithsonian Institute.

(Later in the interview.)

MERLIS: What I was saying before is this, that you're in a sort of multiple event competition, and in a number of these events there's really no question that you're going to come out on top.

JOHN: Yeah, I'm good at everything.

MERLIS: I'm asking your parents now to really get in there and pitch for you, and help you in all the ways they know how, to come out on top with these other events. And I can't believe that put up against the other competition for some of these good jobs that you cannot come out on top.

JOHN: Yeah, that's what I think too.

MERLIS: It may be that you'll have to spend some time organizing and getting information about such jobs.

The therapist assigns to the mother the task of gathering information from the employment office and government pamphlets about the availability of jobs in the nature field. It is assumed that if the mother takes up this new interest, the son will begin to do better. When mother and father are doing well, he will begin to succeed. The therapist's use of this kind of analogy is a powerfully persuasive vehicle for getting parents and son started again and doing something. But such an analogy and the power of persuasion are not sufficient. The therapist must also require the parents to insist that the young man do a series of acts, beginning with getting up early in the morning and following a schedule of activities, until he begins to do them on his own.

Three weeks after this interview the parents called the therapist over the weekend to report that the son was upset and anxious. They thought he needed to be hospitalized. The therapist disagreed. At the next interview, when the mother reported on the week, it was apparent that both the therapist's firmness and his analogy to athletics had taken hold on the parents and the son.

MERLIS: A bit of rough weather, hmm?

MOTHER: Yes, it was. He started the crying. I had it a couple of mornings straight in a row. And he was begging me to put him in a hospital. I said, "John, I think they'd land on us (*meaning the therapist*) if we went, but if you want to go, I'll take you." I called my husband at work, and it took three calls to locate him. Then John didn't want to go. So my husband did come home and I said, "John you're not sick, but we'll go." So Henry (*the husband*) called Dr. Fox (*Michael Fox, M.D., the medical consultant on the case*) and he talked to us both on the telephone. He said it sounds like John could be reaching a turning point. That his strong reaction showed he understands we're doing what we should be, and subconsciously—he doesn't realize it—but we really mean business this time. So we convinced John he really wasn't sick. And we even called the psychiatrist (*at the state hospital*) to tell her the situation. And she said, "I don't want him back here." And so I told John. I'm honest with him, you know. I told him the phone calls were made and all. She said, "Don't let him come back here," so I told him, "They don't want you. They won't let you come back. Because you're not sick."

One of the important factors in this turning point was that the professional community held together: the therapist, the medical consultant, and the psychiatrist at the state hospital all declined to hospitalize. The mother described the difficult week and the son's nervousness:

MOTHER: I said this morning, "You know, John, when you went to pole-vault, you must have been awfully tight." He said, "No." I said, "Well, you know why, don't you. Because you were prepared for everything you went through." I said, "Now these walks, everything we're doing, you're preparing to meet life. And you're prepared." He said, "I can't work." I said, "Not today, I agree, but you know we're going to keep trying."

MERLIS: Things are changing, and as he gets over this depression he's going to be a bundle of nerves for a while.

MOTHER: Yeah, well he didn't throw up today. He's eating today. You know he hasn't been eating. I mean he really had a remarkable loss of weight. But I think the most important thing—he said, "Why do we have to come here *(for the therapy)*?" I said, "I like it. Because they don't believe in mental illness. They just won't stand still for it." I said, "Their job is to get everybody out of the hospital and stay out. That's why I have the confidence. You're not sick, you're not mental. You're nervous and you have anxieties, but I have them too and I can have empathy with you. I can identify with you. Because it's darn painful. Like this also means I have to drive through traffic *(which frightens the mother)*. But through all this therapy with John, it is just now beginning to dawn on me fully what you all are trying to accomplish. My husband is my mother, and I've got to start breaking away a little. He's too much my life, you know.

MERLIS: You've had a lot of work with John this week, how has your husband helped you?

MOTHER: Well, he got John up every morning.

The therapist compliments the mother and father on how well they dealt with their son's problem and even asks the mother if she would mind advising other mothers who have similar problems with sons.

One of the theories about the cause of depression in young people is that their parents have expected too much of them. Although the evidence to support this contention is slight, it has led to criticism of parents. Therapists have told parents that they are at fault for their offspring's depression because they set too high a standard and expected too much. Parents typically respond to this interpretation by feeling guilty and by not requiring anything of the offspring for fear that they will ask too much and increase the depression. The consequence can be an offspring who sits and vegetates.

The therapist in this case took the opposite approach. Rather than put the parents down for expecting too much, he built up the son's accomplishments so that they met any parental expectations. He defined an interest in a job in the nature field as of major importance in today's world, where the environment and ecology are a major focus of conservation. The son's interest was not a trivial one in comparison with other professions but a major contribution to the field of science and the conservation of human resources. By presenting the son's interests in this way, the therapist could continue to have the parents press the son to get out each day and take action to be self-supporting rather than vegetate. In this way he achieved the therapeutic task, which is not merely to motivate the son to come to life again but to motivate the father and mother to take those steps which could ultimately cost them their son, since if he succeeded in life they would be left with only each other.

Motivating the Mother of Twins

Parents can deal effectively with their mad offspring if they are not blamed for the problem and if they can be persuaded to take action. In the following example, mother was asked to push her twin sons, diagnosed as paranoid schizophrenics, out into the cold. She had the idea that a sick child should not be asked to do anything.

The family lived in a Philadelphia suburb. The twenty-two-year-old twin sons were apathetic and sat at home doing nothing. They had done little or nothing for three years, especially in the last few months. Twin A had been hospitalized and diagnosed as paranoid schizophrenic. He came home from the hospital and was the presenting problem as therapy began with therapist John Barnett. Twin B returned home after therapy started, and he too collapsed. They seemed to compete with each other to be mentally ill (as the genetic twin studies seem to have shown). Neither would go out of the house. Twin A said that "Blackjack," perhaps an imaginary person, and other secret enemies were after him. Twin B said that enemies were using radiation beams to get him, and his life would be endangered on the street. As a consequence they both sat at home all day watching television while mother and father worked. One younger daughter was in college and another was in high school, both doing well.

The therapy focused on getting the twins out of the house to be self-supporting. The therapist persuaded the parents to set a date for them to be out of the house looking for work every day. The date set was one month away, on February 1. The sons protested that their lives were being endangered. As the weeks went by and the deadline approached, Twin A became increasingly nervous and anxious; Twin B talked to the television more vigorously and also arranged to visit a psychiatrist. He too received a diagnosis of paranoid schizophrenia. The therapist had agreed to the visit to the psychiatrist at the mother's request, assuming that it was a consultation rather than treatment. The psychiatrist, however, medicated Twin B and recommended that he be hospitalized. He also refused to answer the family therapist's telephone calls, which were made in an attempt to set up a professional collaboration to deal with this complex problem.

The medication situation of the twins became unusual. Twin A had been the primary patient, and a medical consultant was gradually eliminating his hospital-imposed medication. When Twin B went to the psychiatrist, he was given the unusual combination of Melaril with Cogentin for the side effects. Twin B stopped taking the Melaril but continued to take the Cogentin. Since Twin B seemed to feel better, if not a little high, Twin A began to take his twin's Cogentin too. So both young men were taking a medication for the side effects of another medication which they were not taking, and both were pleased with the results.

When the February 1 deadline was two weeks off, the mother began to express her doubts about it. In this family the mother was the "soft" parent and the father the "hard" one with the sons. Father said that they must go through with the plan, and mother said, "If it would work, I think it would be great, but how can it work? Really, the thought of having them hanging around the house out in the cold weather just upsets me." The father said, "Why, I can drop them off at the bowling alley, or at the bus terminal. They can sit there all day until finally they decide maybe it would be just as much fun to get a job and work in a nice warm office someplace, you know." The twins then protested that they would "freeze their ass off," and Twin A said, "You're not dropping me off anywhere, I'm moving out." This is the offspring's routine threat when the parents become firm. Father asked how he would pay rent, and the son replied, "I don't know."

The father was asked to reassure his wife that the sons would be O.K.; he tried to do so, but she protested that it was cold (while Twin A protested that he was mentally ill). Mother brought up the fact that Twin A had applied for vocational rehabilitation and should have his testing. She said she wanted to postpone the deadline for a "couple more weeks, till he finds out about it." The therapist said, "O.K., we made an agreement a few weeks ago, and I find that when you make an agreement and you set a deadline, it tends to work in a way to get something accomplished. When you start to change that deadline and postpone it a little bit more, it sets up the expectation that it can again be changed and postponed. I find that it works a lot better to stick with the original deadline." There was a discussion of whether any delay should apply to both twins, since only one had applied for rehabilitation. The family behaved in a typical way. Father shouted and called the sons essentially bums. Mother disagreed and wished to procrastinate rather than demand anything of them. The twins said that putting them out in the cold was an outrageous and unfair plan. When father said, "It's not like we're sending them to jail," Twin A interrupted and said that kicking them out of the house "in the coldest month of the year is worse than jail. Prisoners don't get treated that bad." The parents, both of whom went out in the cold to work every day, agreed to discuss the issue further the following week. Mother said that she wished to consult the private psychiatrist that Twin B had visited and get his opinion.

The following week the therapist saw the parents alone, and the mother reported on the conversation with the psychiatrist.

MOTHER: I did talk with Dr. Wise this morning. First I asked for a diagnosis. "Schizophrenia, paranoid." Sounds terrible. I asked, "Can he work?" "Not really, unless he gets the ideal job in a stockroom somewhere." That his concentration is not what it should be. His dealing with people, he doesn't feel that he can cope with that. He said that he sees him as doing better than a month ago. But he's sliding backwards and forwards. I said, "We're bugging him to death to get a job." He said, "Well, if he gets the ideal job, it's O.K. If he gets something he can handle. I asked if it was a cycle thing. He said, "It could be, yes." Anyhow, he's not a well person, is he?

The psychiatrist presents a view of the son that is essentially hopeless: he is sick and can be expected to work only in some special situation. The implication is that he will always be this way. Any improvement is only part of a cycle; he will get worse again. The view is one which totally handicaps both therapist and parents and leads to helpless apathy in everyone. The therapist makes the situation explicit to the parents.

BARNETT: We're in a difficult position because Dr. Wise is telling you one thing and we're really telling you another. You're caught in a position where you have to decide who to believe and who to follow. Our approach is a new approach in some ways, but it's also a well-accepted approach now, in current treatment of these kinds of problems.

The therapist points out that the issue is not one of sickness or health, madness or malingering, because the therapy must be the same whatever the diagnosis. To consider the youth ill and to medicate him in a hospital will lead only to his coming home as apathetic as he was before. If the parents treat him as an invalid, he will sit at home and do nothing, becoming increasingly demoralized. Whatever the cause of his helpless apathy, he must be pushed into normal behavior. As the therpaist puts it, "What is really important, regardless, is that they both get back into the mainstream of society and start trying to function as normally as possible."
The mother says that Twin B talks to himself: "He does definitely have verbalizations with something."

BARNETT: Has he been doing more of that lately?
MOTHER: They're more acceptable, they aren't wild, crazy things like the FBI, the CIA, or the radiation beams. They're really kind of, you know. . .

FATHER: Within the realm of possibility.

MOTHER: Right.

FATHER: I think he purposely does it now. His brother is the same way, he used to do the same thing, and then he started keeping his mouth shut. But I think he still—he does, he hears the voices.

BARNETT: Why do you think they've cut this stuff down?

FATHER: 'Cause we tell them we don't like it, they know we don' t like it.

MOTHER: Yeah, "If you want to stay in this room and watch TV, shut up. I want to enjoy this game, or program."

BARNETT: The way I see it is, the more expectations you place on them, and the more emphatically you put these expectations upon them, it seems the more they straighten up and start to act normal. And that's the course that I'm trying to follow right now—it's for the two of you to expect them to act in a certain way, and for them to live up to your expectations.

Mother says that she gets angry at them, but then gets upset because "I'm so angry with a sick person." Father says, "Yeah, you don't know whether to feel guilty or pitiful of them, or just give them a good kick in the ass, you know."

The therapist points out that as they have expected more, the sons have improved. "I've seen the improvement. I can see it today and I could see it last week."

Mother says that if Twin A doesn't get to go through the vocational rehabilitation testing, he'll regress. She wants to give him a chance. She says that he didn't even want to come to the session, but she insisted. When the therapist compliments her for getting the son to do what she wants, she says, "I can do it once, I can do it twice. Then I weaken and give up. My husband can do it once or twice, and he gets upset."

In the discussion of treating the twins as separate individuals, mother says, "Actually they were separated last year most of the time, even over the summer." Father says, "Yeah, one was an alcoholic and the other a manic-depressive." Mother adds that they were potheads. The therapist points out that they have been labeled schizophrenics, manic-depressives, potheads, and alcoholics, and probably don't know how to behave. Mother adds that now they aren't acting like any of the above; they're just sitting around like vegetables.

Out of the discussion comes a compromise. The parents agree to put the sons out of the house the day after Twin A is tested. They will put them out from 9 A.M. to 5 P.M. for three days and then have a therapy session to discuss the next step. As in so many situations, a refusal to do something can be dealt with by a compromise. The therapist says that he wants the parents to present this plan to the twins when he brings them back into the room. He adds that he wants to do something different.

BARNETT: I want you to see if you can do this. I'm not sure you can. I want you *(the mother)* to be the tough guy, O.K.? When they come in here, I want you to be the tough guy, and I want you *(the father)* to be the nice guy.
FATHER: That's going to be awfully hard.
MOTHER: *(Laughs.)* O.K.

The sons are brought in and the mother lays down the law with surprising firmness, given the doubts she expressed earlier in the interview. In one hour she has shifted to a determined position. She tells them that they will be out of the house on the sixth, seventh, and eighth of the month, and that in the meantime both of them are to look for jobs. The one who wants to be tested will receive testing, but he will get a job while he's going through the tests. She then asks the sons to repeat to her what she has said. They do so. The father, despite encouragement from the therapist, is unable to be soft with the sons. He is hard as the mother, which makes both parents firm in their expectation that the sons will behave normally.

Length and Regularity of Therapy

With difficult families, the therapist must be predictable enough to be relied on by the family, but not so predictable that he can be easily anticipated, thus he can bring about change. One must be predictable and consistent in one's commitment to solving the family problem but unpredictable and inconsistent in moment-to-moment maneuvers.

It was once customary to see a family with the regularity of a clock, a schedule that often led to failure. One interviewed the family at a certain time, with certain family members there, on a certain day, week after week and month after month. The family learned how to use this clockwork approach to stabilize, even though they quickly learned to make the right noises according to the therapist's theory. Meeting at regular intervals in a fixed way for an indefinite period and asking, "How did things go this week?" led to repetition and stability rather than change.

Although I recommend that the opening interviews be standard, from that point on the therapist may vary what he does on any particular day. He may see the whole family, the mother or father alone, the two together, only the siblings, or whatever combination is most relevant at that moment. The family that is set to be interviewed in a certain combination is unbalanced by unexpected arrangements. When family members are surprised, quite different information is provided and new alliances are made.

The therapist is intruding on a tightly structured organization, one that repeats its sequences. To change and break up those sequences, it is helpful to change the ways the therapist intrudes. Interviewing the family two days in a row may be better than waiting a week; changing the time and the day may likewise be helpful. Of course, such changes are sometimes difficult because of everyone's schedules, but administrative schedules are secondary to changing the family.

When dealing with young people who are severe problems, the therapist should always be available at the time of discharge from custody. That kind of time commitment need not continue after the first week or two of therapy, however. Regular and scheduled appointments are usually sufficient. When trouble erupts after a few weeks at home, and rehospitalization is threatened, the therapist should again be available at any time to help the family past this stage.

The general approach of this therapy is intense involvement and rapid disengagement whenever possible. As change takes place, the therapist can begin to see the family less often, perhaps only once or twice a month. This does not mean that the family is being abandoned, it means that the changes can continue without such frequent meetings. In fact, changes sometimes seem to occur more efficiently without the therapist's intervening to set the pace. If the relationship with the therapist is such that the family will call when it is in trouble, the infrequency of meetings helps therapist and family to disengage. However, if the family calls the therapist when there is trouble, the therapist may become part of the family cycle. Family problems cannot be resolved without him: he becomes built into the system. One way to avoid this is to arrange appointments when the family is doing well. These meetings are not part of a self-corrective cycle in relation to trouble. It may also be helpful for the therapist to delay seeing the family in trouble. He risks the possibility that the crisis will cause a rehospitalization, but he gains the possibility that the family will solve the difficulty without him, and he will see them after they have worked out a solution. He is then an interested bystander rather than part of the family problem or solution.

The goals of the therapy are to help the young person live in a normal way and to stabilize the parents after the young person has disengaged from the family triangle. Typically there is a transition from the focus on the problem young person early in the therapy to a concern with the problems between the parents later on. Often this transition occurs easily, but at times it is difficult. The parents need to be assured that the therapist can deal with their problems, or they will continue to focus on the offspring.

The time for the therapist to shift is usually when there is an improvement in the problem child. As difficulty arises between the parents, the therapist can explicitly say it is necessary to deal with the issues between them, or these issues can be focused on without a formal shift in contract.

This work has not recommended that a therapist encourage analogic or metaphoric communication by these families. Yet at this time of transition from a focus on the problem offspring to a focus on marital issues it is sometimes helpful for the therapist to encourage analogic communication. For example, if at this stage the mother says that the son threatens to leave the family if rules are enforced, the therapist should hear her as also saying that the father might be threatening to leave the family if she insists that he do what she says. That is, the *item* in the class of messages is "son threatens," but the *class* of message is "people in this family threaten to leave." Similarly, if father says that daughter never finishes anything, he could be heard as also referring to mother's behavior. If the therapist does not point out the meaning of what the family members are saying but only responds in a way that encourages similar communication, the parents can loosen up their ways of communicating about their relations with each other. Sometimes it is helpful for the therapist to let the family member know, without saying so explicitly, that he or she understands they are referring to more than just the problem child. For example, if mother says the son is stubborn and refuses to do what she says, the therapist might respond that "sometimes males respond to females that way." The therapist thereby emphasizes the class of the message—males—and so father is included as an item in that class as well as son. The mother will hear that the therapist understands what she is saying and, if the therapist is courteous and does not make the issue explicit, she will give more information about her problem with her husband while talking about her son. As another example, the father can talk about a daughter's attitude toward men in general in a way that includes mother's ways of dealing with father (that he objects to). The item in the class is daughter, but at the more general level the mother can be referred to as well. Although this kind of analogic communication is not recommended early in the therapy, at this later stage it helps make the transition from the child problem to the other family issues.

When the therapist deals with the marital issues of the parents of a mad offspring, he should keep in mind that the goal of the therapy is not necessarily to make a happier marriage for the parents. A new contract concerning the marital relationship may be arranged, but when the offspring was the presenting problem an unsatisfactory marriage with the young person self-supporting is a satisfactory outcome. Often the therapist becomes involved in marital therapy which sometimes threatens to become interminable. The therapist must ensure that the young person will not be brought back into the marriage when the parents become unstable. The therapist can replace the young person in the family triangle, and the family will remain stable as long as the marital therapy continues. Only after the therapist leaves can he be sure that the parents will not bring the problem young person back into the triangle. Therefore the therapist has the responsibility to do follow-ups, checking on the family over the months to be sure that the young person has remained outside the triangle after the therapy has terminated.

There are also problems with the young person which require special decisions. One occurs when the problem young person recovers and behaves normally but continues to live with the parents. Going to work or school, leading a normal life, the young person seems to have achieved the goals of the therapy. Yet he or she still lives at home. It may be that the young person has still not disengaged from the triangle with the parents. When the time for physically moving out of the home comes, the family may destabilize as it did before when the young person developed the problem.

The therapist might recess therapy until the time of moving out. If the therapist does not see the family, however, in a few months an upset may lead to the reinstitutionalization of the young person without the therapist's knowledge. Then therapy must begin again.

An alternative is to carry the therapy through and encourage the young person to move out of the home. There are problems with forcing this move, however. At times disengagement has taken place even though the young person is still living at home, and the move out would merely be an inconvenience. This is particularly true when college or job training is going on and funds for separate living are low. In addition, many subcultures do not consider it correct for an offspring to move out of the house at a young age. In many subcultures women do not move out of the family home until they are married, and it would be quite unusual for an unmarried eighteen- or twenty-year-old girl to move to a place of her own. Therefore such a move would create an abnormal situation.

There is no simple answer to this dilemma; each case must be dealt with individually. A male in his late twenties may be encouraged to move; likewise a female with a history of multiple hospitalizations and conflicts with her parents. Sometimes one cannot determine if the reluctance of the young person and family to separate physically is due to resistance to leaving home or is reasonable in that particular situation. Perhaps the rule should be: when in doubt, encourage a move out.

The other problem is the frequency of individual interviews with the young person. In this approach it is generally better not to see the young person individually much more often than the parents, except when the parents clearly expect that to be done. As therapy ends, the parents are dealing less with the young person and more with each other. At this point the young person must be able to establish a life independent of the family. This involves working, making friends, courting the opposite (or the same) sex, and living within the rules of society. Sometimes the young person has sacrificed so many years struggling with the family that when he leaves home, he is socially unskilled. It is tempting to offer therapy to help the young person into his new life. But several points should be kept in mind. First, one must acknowledge that these young people are interpersonally skillful. The fact that they used that skill to fail does not mean they will not use it to succeed when that is appropriate. I have been impressed with how socially withdrawn young people suddenly knew how to socialize when they were free to do so. I have also seen apparently dumb and dull young people become quite the opposite in a short period of time. Yet granted these skills, young people who have been in and out of institutions for years also have deficits. They are behind their peers in many ways. For example, they are beginning serious courtship years later than the people they are courting. In job situations too they are more inexperienced than their fellow workers. The shyness and doubt typical of young people are often exaggerated in these problem people because their history damages them in the eyes of others, whether potential mates or employers.

The community has aftercare facilities for such young people, to help them get started again. These are halfway houses, group homes, job training programs, and ex-mental patient self-help groups. The problem is how to use these facilities without confining the young person within an abnormal culture of the handicapped. In some states, even to obtain job training the person must be legally defined as disabled and thus officially stigmatized. (It is unwise for a therapist to sign a statement that a person is disabled when there is nothing physically wrong. That only announces one's failure as a therapist and encourages the problem person to pursue the career of handicapped person.)

What one must do is encourage young people to live in normal situations and do normal work whenever possible. Job training is the most helpful aftercare program since it can lead to self-support.

At this stage young people often need the encouragement of a therapist who is willing to extend himself to get them settled and working in the community. By this time, however, the therapist may be exhausted with the case, especially if it has been a chronic one that has called for considerable effort to disengage young person and parents. Here it is sometimes helpful to introduce a new therapist who can approach the final stages of the therapy with more energy and enthusiasm. The original therapist has a responsibility to see that both parents and young person are helped through this difficult time. But if he is tiring and thus responding in sterotyped ways to new situations, the needs of the young person are sometimes best met by a new therapist.

When considering whether to interview the young person individually as he or she is entering the community and disengaging from the family, it is best to think in terms of whether the young person's difficulties are something a therapist can resolve. Granted that encouragement and reassurance are helpful to such a young person, regular therapeutic interviews to help the person "grow" may be unwise. Merely to listen and encourage the young person to talk about difficulties and uncertainties may or may not be helpful. A basic fact is that each therapeutic interview defines the young person as still incapable of making it on his own. The safe procedure is to see the young person at the final stages of the therapy only if a problem is formulated clearly enough for the therapist to help resolve it. This applies to behavioral problems on the job, in school, or in social life. As the specific problems are eliminated, the therapy ends.

THE POSTURE OF THE THERAPIST

In closing this work, it may be helpful to clarify the difference between a therapist and other professional people. A social worker, psychiatrist, or psychologist need not be a therapist. Those professions include many endeavors which are unrelated to doing therapy. What therapists have in common is independent of a particular profession. Professional schools should long ago have been set up to train therapists, independent of other academic endeavors, in the development of skills for changing problem people.

The skills needed by a competent therapist are too numerous to list here, but certain generalizations can be made. A therapist must find a way to follow the rules of his clinical profession and also be a therapist, and at times the two are incompatible. Similarly, to be both human and a professional expert is a difficult task for some therapists. Because the situations a therapist encounters are so various, he needs a wide range of behavior. Sometimes he must take charge; at other times he must be helpless so that others will take charge. He must be serious but at times introduce humor; he must be flirtatious at one moment and distant at another. One of the therapist's tasks is to be intensely involved in a situation at one moment and to sit on the periphery of it the next. Sometimes the therapist must be repetitive, insisting over and over on the same behavior; at other times he must be changeable and not offer the same directive twice.

Among the many problems one encounters in teaching therapy, two are of particular importance. One is to teach a therapist what is basic in a situation and what is peripheral. I have emphasized that issue in this book by discussing the transition in what has been considered "basic" over the last twenty-five years. It was once thought of primary importance to explore the meaning of the young person's mad thoughts on the assumption that they caused the mad behavior. Later, mad thoughts were considered to be a product of a communicative situation among intimates. The basic issue was not the thoughts themselves, but their cause—the behavior within the system that provoked them. A focus on communicative behavior in the family and institution became primary, and therapists had to learn to restrain their curiosity about the wonderful world of mad ideas. This book argues that another shift has taken place, and that what is now considered basic is the kind of organization that is inducing the communicative behavior, which in turn causes the mad thoughts. Understanding the systematic behavior that creates a malfunctioning hierarchy and planning ways to shift that hierarchy are the basic therapeutic tasks; other matters are peripheral.

In addition to the problem of teaching what is basic and what is peripheral, there is an even more crucial problem in teaching therapy. One can teach what one knows to a good student. But the basic task is to teach a student how to innovate, how to create the new ideas and approaches that one does not know. As one learns to distinguish what is basic from what is peripheral, the world changes, and new issues become the basic ones. How to train students to adapt to changes and invent new ways of dealing with problems is the task of teaching, and also the task of therapy.

Index